# BEHIND THE
# PRESIDENTIAL
## CURTAIN

**Inside Out** of real
**Paul Kagame**
from his former bodyguard

NOBLE MARARA

Copyright © 2017 Noble Marara

All rights reserved.

ISBN-13: 978-1974552412
ISBN-10: 1974552411

# DEDICATION

This book is dedicated to all Rwandans who were killed as result of nonsense political and ethnic conflicts that occurred in Rwanda in various time since Rwanda was established as a country.

# CONTENTS

**1 Chap I: Where all begun 1**

   *1.1*    *The first Peek* 1

   *1.2*    *The truth about the death of General Rwigyema* 6

   *1.3*    *My escape to France* 18

**2 Chap II: Kagame assaults and Killing field 27**

   *2.1*    *The teenager house maid assault* 27

   *2.2*    *President Kagame and his house staff's abuses* 30

   *2.3*    *Kagame a mad man* 39

   *2.4*    *The Conspiracy of Massacre of our Commanders.* 45

   *2.5*    *Kagame's unreported killings* 60

   *2.6*    *Who Killed Kagame's personal Doctor, Dr Gasakure?* 67

   *2.7*    *Asiel Kabera was a humanistic man* 70

   *2.8*    *Brig. Gen Dan Gapfizi died a similar way he used to killafande Late Adam Waswa* 73

**3 Chap III: Kagame simply a dictator 79**

   *3.1*    *Similarities between former president Idi Amini and Kagame* 79

   *3.2*    *President Kagame told citizens of Rwanda to tolerate and remain silent* 84

   *3.3*    *According to Paul Kagame all Hutus are convicts of genocide* 87

   *3.4*    *Paul Kagame, Edouard Bamporiki encouraging Hutus to apologise, even those who never committed a crime* 92

   *3.5*    *The genesis of the grenade attacks on our land* 98

   *3.6*    *Rape: The 'friendly fire' of the Rwanda Civil war in 1994* 103

   *3.7*    *Reasons why President Kagame will cling power forever* 107

   *3.8*    *2017 Kagame to become a Ceremonial President* 115

**4 Chap IV: Kagame's Deceptions, betrayal and paranoia in the**

name of Power. 119

- 4.1 We paid our Dues 119
- 4.2 Kagame self-harming by incarcerating his brothers and comrades 124
- 4.3 President Kagame threatens to imprison to save his name 129
- 4.4 Inyumba Aloysia's betrayal 132
- 4.5 Kagame slapped in the face twice in lifetime 135
- 4.6 (RSSB) Rwanda Social Security Board coffers dry up and Kagame Locks Kantengwa 138
- 4.7 The infamous Agaciro Fund 142
- 4.8 Kagame's obsessions with cars and driving 147
- 4.9 The poisoning of Paul Kagame 152

5 Chap V: The First family Honours, power and selfishness. 158

- 5.1 President Paul Kagame to receive the NRA medal of honour after 26yeras. 158
- 5.2 President Kagame rising from being a failure in school to addressing Oxford University 163
- 5.3 Once a good mother now a killer 169
- 5.4 The selfish president of the tiny landlocked nation of Africa 173
- 5.5 Why our King remains in Exile part 1: 177

6 Chap VI: Kagame Proxy war in Democratic Republic of Congo and His troubled relations with Neighbouring Countries 192

- 6.1 A hungry President, the truth behind Congo War 192
- 6.2 Kagame's next tactic in order to govern DRC 196
- 6.3 A summon to my good old comrades: M23 Saga 201
- 6.4 Kagame planning to terrorise Burundi 207
- 6.5 Kagame misses the opportunity to Kill Nkurunziza 212
- 6.6 The suspected Rwandan Killing hand in Burundi 213
- 6.7 Kagame an honest man 216
- 6.8 Kagame and Museveni troubled relationship 220

- 6.9 *Kagame Concocting Regional Battle* 228
- 6.10 *MONUSCO/SADC will wipe Rwanda out one day.* 232
- 6.11 *The Great Lakes Region muddle on Again* 236

# 7 Chap VII: Kagame love hate relationship with West 248

- 7.1 *The panel Vs Greening and Kagame* 248
- 7.2 *Anxious wait of the UK government decision on Aid provision to Rwanda (2012)* 256

# 8 Chap VIII: oppositions party power struggle, disunity and Weakness 263

- 8.1 *Political parties in Rwanda* 263
- 8.2 *The Genesis of Marara's fallout with Rudasingwa* 269
- 8.3 *Is Rudasingwa's arrogance destroying RNC? (Before RNC divorce)* 272
- 8.4 *General Kayumba save RNC or risks Dr Rudasingwa tearing it apart (Before RNC divorce)* 279
- 8.5 *Rwanda National Congress (opposition party) disunity was predicted.* 280
- 8.6 *Continuously Mourning for Col Karegeya boosts enemy morale* 282
- 8.7 *A message to our leaders* 286

# 9 Chap IX: My tribute to comrades and my commander 292

- 9.1 *A tribute to Sgt Blackman* 292
- 9.2 *A tribute to Afande Col. Karegeya a principled man* 301
- 9.3 *To my Dear commander, Tom Byabagamba.* 305
- 9.4 *Young Muhirwa saga* 310

# ACKNOWLEDGMENTS

I thank my children without whom this book would not have been accomplished. I also thank all editorial team of Inyenyeri News and Inyenyeri Radio for all your support and assistance in writing this book.

Lastly I want to thank Inyenyeri News Management and Global Campaign for Rwandans Huma Rights for supporting this book publications so that it can be able to reach as many people as possible.

# Introduction

I had always loved writing; I'd kept Presidential Curtains as weekly publication, written short stories and had ideas for books. I'd never thought about writing a consolidated story but there came a point where I wanted to share it to try to release myself from the past and its haunting memories.

I should explain that I grew up in exile and life shaped me into an ever-wanting man like Oliver Twist. In Charles Dickens, full-length novel **"Oliver Twist"** the major theme is the classic theme of **Good versus** Evil. Indeed, the fall out between President Kagame with me and his former comrades who even sacrificed their own lives to bring him to power have been victims of exposing Kagame's evil.

Despite many difficulties I have managed to excel in school and well qualified from University in the UK and working as Psychiatric Mental Health Professional. In my confused mind, I had become the deaf dumb and blind in the captivity of the RPF and Kagame that had captivated me for many years.

In this book, I therefore share my experience as body guard of President Paul Kagame since 1992 until 2001. In this book, I also describe what I witnessed in Kagame's personality, relationship with his troops, decision making, leadership style and his uncontrolled temper.

I further analyse some Kagame's actions using my professional skills and experience as result of working for him. In fact it's when I left the military and I became mental health professional specialist that I found Kagame's state of mind wanting, such as **anger**, **sadness**, or *jealousy*. I therefore used my mental health expertise to analyse his state of mind. There are important historical events that I describe as I witnessed them on the side of those who were making relevant decisions at the RPF headquarters. All that information is provided in a compilation of articles and speeches since 2012.

As I write this Book I feel a sense of relief that I was getting my experiences down on paper. Indeed, this book is intended for the world to know more about President Paul Kagame, when it came to writing about difficult and painful events and my experience and Kagame I had to consider what I really wanted to share with Rwandans and the international community because Kagame's dark side has never been made public and it can only be known by someone like myself who has been very close to him for more than 10 years.

This book will help others as well as myself and to inform present and future Rwandan Politicians or professionals, academics and anyone wanting to gain an insight into politics. Indeed, this book will help many people encountering with madness or politicians who not only behave like sycophants but also politically bankrupt. Writing this book is empowering me and it is important for me to tell my truth, my experience with a dictator and for my voice to be heard. Writing makes me stronger and helps me to feel more resilient and know who I really am.

London 5th August 2017

## Acronyms

BCDI: Bank of Commerce Development and Investment

BRD: Bank Rwandaise de Development or Rwanda Development Bank

CND: Legislative Assembly, National Development Council

DRC: Democratic Republic of Congo

EWASA: Energy Water and Sanitation Authority

FAR: Forces Armées Rwandaise

FDLR: Forces Democratique de Liberation du Rwanda or Rwanda Democratic Liberation Forces

FDU: Forces Democratic Unifiées or Unified Democratic Forces

FEDEMU: Federal Democratic Movement of Uganda

FNL: Front National de Liberation or National Liberation Front

FOBA: Force Obote Back Again

FRONASA: Front for National Salvation

MRND: National Republican Movement for Democracy and Development

MTO: Military Transport Officer

NEC: National Executive Committee

NRA: National Resistance Army

PPU: President Protection Unity

PTSD: Posttraumatic stress disorder

RNC: Rwanda National Congress

RPA: Rwandan Patriotic Army

RPF: Rwandan Patriotic Front

RSSB: Rwanda Social Security Board

SADEC: Southern African Development Community

UPC: Uganda People's Congress

# 1 Chap I: Where all begun

## 1.1 The first Peek

When the Rwandan Patriotic Army (RPA) evaded Rwanda in the late 1990's, it relied on Uganda's government and its National Resistance Army as their main source of supplies and logistic support. We relied on the Ugandan army on weaponry, ammunition and even withdraw routes whenever needed.

Apart from the government support, Uganda like all our neighboring countries, harboured countless Rwanda refuges and sympathising citizens than cared to support our cause.

Most of these Rwandans were very wealthy and gave most of their hard-earned wealth to the Rwandese Patriotic Front Cadres worked around the clock to convince everyone how Rwanda Patriotic Front (RPF) was going to make a historical change.

These sponsors gave as much as they could afford, but unfortunately few of them now are eligible to work or even live in the country they fought for. Many of the then RPA supporters who helped RPF to get into power have since been persecuted by Gen Paul Kagame.

I remember a few years before the RPA evasion in 1990, people in around our villages in Uganda where I lived sold most of their livestock (cattle, goats, and chickens) in order to finance the attack on General Juvenal Habyalimana's dictatorial rule.

Myself as a foreigner in Uganda, as I grew up it was beyond my understanding that we will ever have the right to settle and become free. When President Museveni finally helped Gen Fred Rwigema and his forces to return to the home most of us never set foot in, it was everyone's responsibility to use any available effort for the just cause. Fred Rwigema was the deputy Minister of Defense, after the National Resistance Army in Uganda captured state power in 1986.

After the four years struggle which saw the loss of our beloved leaders, the genocide that took millions of lives and the unwinding regional wars we were left with the infamous unreflective His Excellency, Commander in Chief, entrepreneur president, Major Gen Paul Kagame winner of every mockery award.

Kagame's unreflective behaviours and financial hunger has led him to hunt individuals that helped him become who he is today. People like Trilbert Rujugiro, Sam Nkusi, Edgar Rwangabwoba, Valens Kajeguhakwa, Kalinda of sweet bread, Kajangwe, Kalisa BCDI, Donat Kananura, Gregory Karuretwa, Pascal Nouveau-riche, Haroun Kalimba who gave away their wealth, personal participation in the bush and many more.

Most of these individuals have personally been humiliated, detained and robbed by the person who was supposed to protect them Gen Kagame.

Paul Kagame has portrayed himself as a God in our society for the people to be afraid of him. Unfortunately, he can kill or imprison whoever he feels uncomfortable with because he does not take advice or challenges.

Kagame labelled his colleagues killers or unaccountable people just to get rid of them. He is the man who can do something that gobsmacks everyone around him and blindly believe that nobody is sensitive or recognises what he has done.

In the year 1997 while I was still under Kagame's close protection unit, Mrs. Jeannette Kagame for some reasons realised that Paul Kagame her husband was spending most of his time at Mr. Kajangwe's home, this was unusual because Paul Kagame is not a man who likes socialising.

I remember a day while on Kagame's convoy at senior officer's mess at around 9:00 pm, I was instructed by Maj Willy Rwagasana to take four soldiers with me and save Mrs Kajangwe from the intruders who were allegedly trying to enter her house. As we drove off, Willy called on the hand-held radio to tell me to drive fast and find out what was in Kajangwe's garden.

We drove obviously quickly with alarms, horns, and full beam lights as was our norms of VIP protections and intervention. It was embarrassing because nothing was there when we arrived at Kajangwe's home I called on the radio to inform Willy who fed the information to Paul Kagame that there was no one at the residence of Mrs Kajangwe.

At the time Mr. Kajangwe was in America and he was scared to come back to Rwanda because he knew that his wife was having an affair with Paul Kagame, and obviously he had run for his dear life.

Willy told me to come back to the officer's mess but surprisingly when we arrived, the phone call from Mrs Kajangwe rang again and this time she was crying and stated that someone was forcing the door in. We were told to go back this time and arrest those who were on the door. It was a bit silly because when we arrived again no one was there, I reported to Willy that no one was there Willy asked us to stay there and that meant that Paul Kagame's convoy stayed with only one car excluding his own.

At around 1:00 am Paul Kagame arrived at Kajangwe's residence where he stayed until 5:00 am in the morning. It was obvious that Mrs Kajangwe did not hold any position in the government and so the conversation was a bit emotional or something else.

It was not until Jeannette exchanged words with Mrs Kajangwe that Paul's visits were reduced. Days after, Kagame had to visit Gregory Karuretwa home to have a good counsel with Mrs Karuretwa a motherly figure to Kagame. This is the lady who had arranged Kagame's marriage with Jeannette years before and she is actually his God mother.

It was after this visit that Mrs Kajangwe was closely escorted by one of our vehicle to the airport and made sure she boarded the plane to America to find her husband. Kagame to meet Jeannette, this lady was always the peace maker of Kagame's

Mrs Karuretwa looked after Kagame while still a teenager in Kampala. Mr. Karuretwa was a wealthy man who sponsored the war and played a fatherly role to the young Kagame who later mistreated and impoverished him.

Likewise, Mr. Kajangwe sponsored the war like many others for our return to Rwanda and used his own money. He later became his personal friend due to the fact that Jeannette grew up with both Mr. and Mrs Kajangwe back in Burundi.

Mr. Kajangwe was personally betrayed by the man he thought to be a friend Paul Kagame. However, Kajangwe and family are not alone, the list of people Kagame has betrayed is endless, from comrades to friends and actually his own family.

Paul Kagame has betrayed so many people that he cannot remember himself; research shows that in order to know where we are heading we need to reflect on where we've been, this is a generic term for those intellectual and effective activities in which individuals engage to explore their experiences in order to lead to a new understanding and appreciation.

After many years that I spent besides President Paul Kagame, I realised that, there are many crucial leadership skills that Paul Kagame lacks and they include reflection as well as communication skills. Reflective skills would have helped Kagame remember where he came from and avoided the betrayal incurred to his colleagues and friends.

Communication is the exchange and flow of information and ideas from one person to another. It involves a sender transmitting an idea, information, or feeling to a receiver. Communication occurs only if the receiver understands the exact information or idea that the sender intended to transmit. These problems have damaged Paul Kagame's performance and made him isolated after losing the important people that he desperately needs for our country's best interest.

As we all know how decisions are made today in Rwanda we can sense where the country is heading. Looking at the rise of Kagame, we can only see the victims some from freedom fighters that died during the war on the battle field or those killed by Kagame's intelligence network after questioning his competence.

This brings questions especially after losing all of the fourteen main sponsors, who sponsored the RPF war. Kagame's family had nothing financial to offer apart from the old Tata lorry (Mabeko) which he had robbed from the one Mukasa of Mpigi town while he was head of Basima house after accusing him of being Nkwanga's supporter and killing him.

Kagame's betrayal continues as we speak prisons and other safe houses are full of men and women being accused of false allegations. That is our

Kagame the leader who is praised by the ignorant and encouraging people to scrap off the presidential term limits just because he used the aid wisely by building the roads, presidential jets, ballistic and scud missiles strong weapons, and the sky scrapper that belongs to himself when normal citizens cannot afford the basics.

## 1.2 The truth about the death of General Rwigyema

It has been more than 23 years since Gen Fred Rwigema died in his mother-land leading before leading an exodus of Rwandan children who had been incarcerated in exile for over 30 years.

Fred Gisa Rwigema (10 April 1957 – 2 October 1990), born Emmanuel Gisa was a founding member and leader of the Rwandan Patriotic Front. Rwigema was born in Gitarama, in the south of Rwanda. Considered a Tutsi, in 1960 he and his family fled to Uganda and settled in a refugee camp in Nshungeezi, Ankole and later Kahungye in Tooro following the so-called Hutu Revolution of 1959 and the ouster of King Kigeri V.

After finishing high school still in his teenage years, it is said that he went to Tanzania and joined the Front for National Salvation (FRONASA), a rebel group headed by Yoweri Museveni the current President of Uganda, his brother Salim Saleh (Caleb Akandwanaho) was a close confidant and friend to Fred. It is due to his turbulent life as a child refugee, the love for his country and hate for injustice that led him to liberate African countries including his own.

It was at this point that he began calling himself Fred Rwigema. Later that year, he travelled to Mozambique and joined the FRELIMO rebels who were fighting for the liberation of Mozambique from Portugal's colonial power. In 1979, he joined the Uganda National Liberation Army (UNLA), which together with the Tanzanian Armed Forces captured Kampala in April 1979 and ousted dictator Idi Amin.

Upon the liberation of Uganda and Idi Amin he was a member of the elite group that launched the National Resistance Army (NRA) with its leader Museveni, which fought a guerrilla war against the government of Milton Obote. After the NRA captured state power in 1986, Rwigema became the deputy Minister of Defense.

He was a regular on the front lines in northern Uganda during the new government's offensive against remnants of the ousted regime disregarding his ministerial post. It is in these offensives that he was regarded as a god of war (Mungu wa vita, Swahili language) by his highly motivated troops in the operational zones of Uganda.

He is still remembered as a father, husband, commander, brother, comrade to all soldiers he served with, and most of all a national hero to Uganda not only to his love of Express Villa Football Team but also a friend to many in that country.

Afande Fred was the best commander of all time in all of the countries he served. Afande Fred who was a Major General as a young man who always put his nation and people first. I am captivated to demonstrate how General Rwigema went the extra mile during his plan to return his people to their mother-land.

In preparation to his return to Rwanda, General Rwigema sought a unifying solution to all Rwandans not only his only for his own Tutsi ethnic group. It is demonstrated by the effort Rwigema used by including all Rwandans that had been harassed and exiled by the then dictatorial regimes. General

Rwigema contacted among all Colonel Alexis Kanyarengwe and actually he became the chairman of the RPF while Gen Rwigema concentrated on armed wing which he maintained best soldiers. Col Kanyarengwe knew the regime's in-and-out and according to Rwigema he would bargain better with the government that they were about to invade.

We all believed that he would live forever because of the love we had for him. I was only twelve years old when I first heard of General Rwigema in Uganda because we grew up with the stigma of being non-citizens. When Fred emerged as a high-ranking official in Uganda, he became a hero to all of us, the youth, and the only hope to the Promised Land which we had been denied by the dictators of the time.

He selflessly pulled everyone together in a very limited time, not only in Uganda but the whole diaspora and he did all this in combination with other commitments which involved maintaining security of Uganda, his own young family (God bless them) plus building his Rwandan Army inside a host Army (Uganda).

He did all this with great sensitivity and concern for the departure of his forces that would not shake the Ugandan forces. His aim was to return the Rwandese back home but also to make sure that Uganda stays strong and un-shaken due to the withdrawal of the Rwandese forces.

Afande Fred Rwigema the man who arranged, planned and managed to put in action what was a dream to all of us from childhood, was meaninglessly lost within a day of his return to the land he had left as an infant.

## *Who Killed Gen Fred?*

The answer to this question is ambiguous up to the present day and the vacuum still persists in the hearts of many Rwandans and Ugandans alike. A lot has been said but still not convincing to people like me, and many others. Yes, I was not a soldier at the time when Afande Fred Rwigema died however, having spent most of my early age alongside my fellow brothers who were in the Forces back in Ugandan and then joined the army in Rwanda a little while after, I strongly believe that General Fred Rwigema's death should have been explained differently or much clearer.

Before I outline my concerns, let's look at what the government said about Fred Rwigema's death:

## *Stray bullet theory:*

There are several theories about the abrupt death of the General, the most commonly adopted by President Paul Kagame's government being the stray bullet scenario:

"It is widely spread on all media outlets including the recent YouTube clip claiming that General Fred Rwigema was shot by a stray bullet from the enemy APC (armored personnel carrier) or military Jeep."

In this theory, we see one of the bodyguards of General Fred Rwigema, Happy Ruvusha who holds the rank of Colonel at this present time explaining the death of his beloved commander.

However, what is very disturbing is the fact that Happy Ruvusha claims to have buried Fred with the company of only 3 other soldiers. He mentions one Matungo and Nkubito who are all senior officers at that time but the fact is that all these three individuals were non-commissioned officer at the time, and this leaves one to wonder:

- Why a military General would be buried by only 4 of his (NCO) non-commissioned officer bodyguards.

- Upon the death of Fred Rwigema, the RPA had senior officers who were actively in combat until late of whom some still survive to the present day. Here one would mention Lt Col Adam Waswa, Maj Chris Bunyenyezi, Maj Dr Bayingana, Maj Steven Ndugute, Maj Sam Kaka, Maj Kabura, Capt Dodo Twahirwa, Capt Bagire, Capt Ngoga, Capt Charles Muhire, Capt Kayitare who was Fred's Aide at some point, Capt Kizza, Capt Bitamazire, Capt Gashugi, Capt Musitu, Capt Sam Byaruhanga, Capt Alphonse Furuma, Capt Mico and many more combat hardened commanders. Major Paul Kagame was not among the officers and men who started the war, as he had decided to go for a course in the US while his comrades prepared to wage a liberation war.

- It is in the military norms that soldiers of the same ranks if not closer ranks bury their fallen comrade, therefore why leave him to be secretly buried by just his bodyguards.

- Matungo, Nkubito and Happy Ruvusha were all NCOs at the time of their boss's death, none of them would drive, and it is common knowledge that Fred's Driver was Sgt Blackman who died in Kigali years later. However Happy Ruvusha makes no mention of this individual.

- It makes no sense how people like Capt Kayitare, Emmanuel Kanamugire, Okwiri Rabwoni, Sgt Mtamani who used to drive Late Fred at times, Alex Rubamba Shumba and many more much senior soldiers might have missed out on their friend and boss's burial however secretive it could have been

- He mentioned that they had been driving his body in the vehicle after his death, having not decided where to get him buried. How honorable would that be to drive the top commander's body around in a truck instead of getting him to rest in the rear of the combat zone when it is documented that Kagitumba was made a tactical sickbay and headquarters upon the initial RPA attack on 1st October 1990.

- Why would Fred's body be not taken back to Mbuya military morgue in Uganda as a norm to all fallen combatants in all operations no matter where, given the fact that Fred had not officially resigned from Uganda?

- What would have been the motive of burying General Fred Rwigema in secrecy? It doesn't make sense to me nor any sane minded country loving comrade or citizen.

- Could Happy Ruvusha be covering something he knows well? This leaves me wonder. On the other hand, I remember Happy Ruvusha very well, a person I worked alongside as Paul Kagame's bodyguards. I remember he mourned General Fred Rwigema all the time and he seemed never contented of the loss of his boss due to the relationship Fred had with all his troops including Happy himself who was his Kadogo charged with his tent and meals.

-

## *The Bunyenyezi/ Bayingana theory:*

The second version that caused trouble to the families of the RPA top commanders was the Major Peter Bayingana and Major Bunyenyezi theory. It is alleged that the two top commanders executed their boss over a power struggle. This theory further alleges that after his execution they were also killed by other soldiers in retaliation or that General Salim Saleh came in himself and executed them.

This version drew much trouble not only to the families of the trio but also to Ugandan leadership especially Gen Saleh who was a close confidant since their high school times and a comrade of all battles they had both fought across Africa.

This version draws many more questions; since it was documented in the former government forces (FAR) Forces Armée Rwandaises in their monthly publication la victoire that Major Bunyenyezi and Bayingana were ambushed and killed in the Ryabega ambush and took the Artillery Pieces they were taking to reinforce Maj Sam Kaka who had sieged the enemy in Nyagatare. These Artillery pieces included a 14.5mm 4-barrel anti-aircraft gun and a 105mm Katyusha multi-rocket launcher. This incident does match with the confirmation that the duo was killed about 3 weeks after the initial attack. Their death would be heard later and be celebrated in Bikindi Simon's heroic songs praising the bravely of the FAR.

## *Lt Kato Theory:*

The investigations done by myself with the help of the fellow former RPA veteran women and men who were in the forces at the time, indicates that there is another version which has been kept a secret for so long. It is alleged that in the late 1980's General Fred Rwigyema told Major Paul

Kagame, the then Intelligence Officer who later ended up becoming the President of Rwanda after the death of almost every sensible officer in the RPA struggle, to select young men and women who would attend different leadership courses in preparation of the Rwanda offensive.

In the first graduation of the cadet officers selected by Major Kagame was Lt Kato who was sent to attend a special snipping course in South Korea and later Libya acquiring very good sniping and Commando skills.

In the second Cadet intake to pass out just days before the invasion was 2nd Lts James Kabarebe, Kayonga Charles, Alex Kagame, Vincent Gatama, Tom Mphaka, Rose Kabuye and others. Paul Kagame knew James Kabarebe as he had been in Museveni's bush war but had deserted due to not being able to cope with the situation. He would later come back to NRA after Museveni captured the country in 1986, which time he stayed until the attack of Rwanda.

It is alleged that slightly before the attack on Rwanda General Fred Rwigyema had been selected to attend a military course in America by President Museveni of which he declined the offer due to his preparation but suggested to send Paul Kagame to the course due to his lack necessary strategy.

Before his departure, it is alleged that Kagame introduced Kato and James Kabarebe to Fred Rwigyema, he stated that James Kabarebe was a Political Science graduate from Makerere University and was going to make an excellent advisor on international relations issues, he also explained to him the importance of benefiting from Kato's skills.

Rwigyema trusted Kagame from their childhood like any honest person would. A source from the RPA veterans goes on to explain that General Rwigyema owned a sniper gun he handed to Kato and joined the soldiers on his entourage. It was also the time when Kagame indicated the need for James Kabarebe to replace Emmanuel Kanamugire as the ADC to General Fred Rwigyema however Rwigyema objected and Kabarebe was left with no post.

Kagame left to America for training and afterwards the RPF/RPA attacked, it is alleged, that it was with the sniper gun that Rwigyema had handed to Kato which was used to shoot General Fred Rwigyema. It is alleged that Kato was seen coming from the hill and everyone was fighting to hide the death rather than finding the killer.

This Veteran explains that Kato was made close to Paul Kagame after his return from America and was subsequently deployed to join Kaitare's Mobile Unit. It was James Kabarebe who informed Kato that he was being transferred and on his way and hence shot by Silas Udahemuka who is Kagame's cousin blaming his death on an enemy ambush.

It is alleged that his execution was to hide the information regarding General Fred Rwigema death as the war was heading to an end during peace talks. Kato was a brother to Major Mupenzi who was injected with a poison just after we captured Kigali, Mupenzi was a very reliable man and a twin brother to Kato, and he had attended the same cadet course with Kato. He was killed to hide information like his brother.

After Kagame arrived from his unfinished course he was appointed by Museveni to take over from Afande Adam Wasswa who later died of an undefined death.

It is further alleged that after the execution of General Fred Rwigema by Lt

Kato on Kagame's orders, Kagame rushed in to deceive Museveni into believing that it was Bayingana and Bunyenyezi who had killed him therefore deceiving Museveni in revenging his friend.

It is therefore alleged that Museveni then ordered his brother and best friend to General Fred Rwigema, Gen Salim Saleh, to personally execute the two with immediate effect.

It is said that contradictions appeared in the high command of the RPF as to the advisability of launching the attack when peaceful prospects were clearly becoming plausible. General Rwigema was ready to accept Habyarimana's welcoming hand if he ever did, while other members of the RPF Command favored a military solution and hence the extermination of their top leader.

*This theory like the preceding ones raises disturbing questions:*

- Given the number of General Fred Rwigema well trained combat hardened bodyguard, why would they spare Lt Kato the Sniper, after he shot their boss?

- What reason would Kato have had in executing a commander who was much loved by his own troops?

- How simple would it have been for General Saleh to cross into Rwanda, execute the two officers and walk back to Uganda untouched?

- Why is it that the bodies of Bunyenyezi and Bayingana have never been buried or recovered? Could it be because they were actually taken by their killers in the Ryabega ambush?

- Why has President Kagame never carried out a thorough investigation in the deaths of these commanders to clear our suspicion? Could he be hiding something by relying on the evidence of Happy Ruvusha who held the rank of Corporal at the time of Gen Rwigema's death?

- Why is Gen Rwigema's death and history fading away in thin air as we speak now while President Kagame assuming the heroism that he never deserved.

- If Paul Kagame was hero enough as he self-portrays, why did he decide to attend a course as the whole group was planning such an important move?

It should be remembered that the original RPA hero's day was first and foremost to commemorate the death of General Rwigema and other fallen heroes and hence the 1st of October of each year. Why has President Kagame changed this date to different dates?

Why is General Fred Rwigema membered and respected in Uganda than Rwanda the country of his birth and subsequently his death? Either way the question remains as to who really killed our hero Gen Fred Rwigema!!

## 1.3 My escape to France

Like many RPA innocent service men and women who suffered similar rewards, by the end of the year 2000, I was incarcerated in Camp GP (Presidential Guard) in Kimihurura. This was President Habyalimana's protection Barracks that Kagame had inherited with all its notoriety, well known for its torture chambers that then laid in the hands of the infamous Capt/now Lt col Silas Udahemuka the so-called Intelligence Officer (I/O) camp GP.

I had lived in that Barracks since we took over power in 1994 but had not been in a position to spend a night in a notorious detention cell for any wrong doing let alone being maliciously accused.

My detention was either silly or malicious due to the way it was handled. I was the Military transport officer (MTO) of the presidential protection unit (camp GP), the President had travelled abroad and I was not briefed on when he was expected back to the country only until he had landed at the then Gregory Kayibanda International Airport.

This was contrary to the norms of the VIP protection rules whereby I should have been notified at least a few hours before he touched down so that I held all the presidential drivers and vehicles on standby.

I with the presidential motorcade arrived at the airport five minutes late and luckily enough the president was still speaking to the journalists and so it was not recognised by himself and the protocol. This was evident that either my senior commanders lacked information about the president's return or they lacked the professionalism or skills in VIP protection or even were malicious and just wanted me to get into trouble which would have cost me my life.

I was very sensitive about the situation right from the time we had reached the airport. On arrival at the president's office I was sent to the famous Camp GP cell where I was asked to sign a statement which was already written without my consent or knowledge. In the statement, I was being accused of three main allegations:

- Talking to unknown people who are trying to overthrow the government,

- Planning to kill his excellence by not maintaining time, and

- Supporting and sympathising with the king's forces,

All this came as a dream to me, and it was so embarrassing that none of my fellow comrades would be broad enough to denounce these baseless allegations, but on the other hand I have come to understand them since none wouldn't risk their skin for my sake however how innocent I seemed to have been to them.

What I learnt from that system was that, when the so-called intelligence department investigated any allegation, they only expected to attain the negatives out of any case but not the positives. They had already started discussing what my punishment should be, while one of them had already gossiped about the suggestion.

It was obvious that I find way to escape before I faced my fate under this merciless so-called intelligence department. During my time, I came to realise that the un-known people were the Canadian friend of mine who they thought that I was feeding information of what we experienced during the war.

During that time, it came to my understanding that when any one of us had a (mzungu) white friend especially those who worked for non-government organisations (NGO), they would be under intelligence scrutiny and surveillance.

After my escape to a nearby country, news reached the French embassy and secret service about my presence. The French seemed hungry for any news and testimony about president Kagame. They promised me a *"safe heaven"* in exchange for the so called top secrets about Kagame. I mentioned to them that I wasn't safe around the East Africa due to Kagame's intelligence network and the fact that I have deserted his close protection unit.

The French were so eager to offer me a travel permit and air ticket to fly to Paris and they promised to offer me the much-desired asylum in their country or anywhere far from my motherland. On arrival in France, the game changed the rules;

First of all, they instructed me that I should not mention to anyone that I flew to their country on their travel documents, on looking back now, this is due to the fact that I would already have been qualified as a refugee in their land according to the Geneva convention 1951 just by landing on the French land with a French travelling document.

That I should not communicate to anyone that I was already in France, they threatened that they would be in conflict with the Rwandan government in case the Rwandan government found out.

The only communication I was allowed was when I was persuaded or ordered to call individuals that they wanted information from or spy from my comrades back home.

What surprised me the most was that the French government knew and revealed to me that Kagame's rebels had shot down President Habyalimana's aircraft a few years back and they were still angered about the incident.

Like Kagame himself at that time most of us viewed Habyarimana's death as a necessity not a death to moan about but to celebrate. Habyarimana's was the president of the government that we had fought with arms for about 4 years then most of us young and inexperienced, his government had kept us refuges for a few decades most of us born in exile, and he was our number one enemy.

It was common sense that if Habyarimana's troops had a chance of killing our leaders Alexis Kanyarengwe or Kagame then, they would have celebrated. They had managed to kill Gen Fred Rwigema, Maj Chris Bunyenyezi and Maj Dr Peter Bayingana and hence brought to us the misery of Maj Kagame to start with.

On airing out my individual views, the French seemed rather disturbed, I had mentioned to them how we lost all the above mentioned senior officers and more officers and men under the supreme command of the French officers both at the battle fields and at the Habyalimana's army headquarters in Kigali during the whole war.

This reminds me the fact that the French had been involved in the actual training of the Interahamwe militias and arming them let alone the Ex-FAR that they fought alongside in all battles right from day one in 1990.

It is evident that they flew in the French commandos with the task of not rescuing the ethnic Tutsi who were targeted for extermination at the time but also protected the government that carried out the massacres creating a shield all the way to the Congo.

They created zone turquoise which shielded and slowed our advance to Gikongoro and Kibuye (western region) while the militia carried out the cleansing of the Tutsis of Bisesero and other areas under the French occupancy.

I was later handed over to a French judge Mr Jean-Louis Bruguière continued with the questionings. He was most interested in the downing of president Habyarimana's plane and when I repeated the same feelings I had for the incident he got more furious, he was actually spitting feathers.

I have now grown not to condone violence or terrorism, but if the insurgents we fought all the years before I left Kigali had to be lucky to ambush our motorcade and killed President Kagame for sure it would have been a victory to them, and fact is that everyone involved with his regime would be saddened by the loss. Same applies to the downing of president Habyarimana's plane while dictator Kagame has remained unapologetic.

There was an indication that the politicians and families of the French pilots who were shot down with the former Rwandan dictator Habyarimana demanded that Kagame Generals are indicted and the judge did a moment after.

Bruguière said to me that I will not get asylum in their country, that I will leave for another country but only if I cooperate and work with the French police in order to gain more contacts in order to finalise their investigations. They needed more connections to the primary soldiers who knew more than I did.

But what caused distress to me was asking me to go back to the Congo and to join the rebel groups fighting the government that I had just fled after fighting for all my teenage life. This added insults to the already injuries they had inflicted on me by treating me on the contrary to what we had agreed upon before we left Africa. They had promised me a ***safer place*** to live, far from Kagame and now they wanted me to engage him military in the bushes of the Congo.

They stated that because I had the background of the RPA, that I should be able in position to know vital information like our military strength, ammunition, command structures and capabilities. I declined to discuss all this information with them, since I thought it was very sensitive information that I wasn't ready to discuss with individuals that now wanted to send me to the Congo jungle.

Commander Pierre Payebien of the French Foreign Intelligence Service called me arrogant like my boss President Paul Kagame for not respecting their leaders. I told him that I was a deserter who was looking for asylum and not in a position to discuss such issues. Their language was discriminating. I remember one officer asking if I was a Hutu or Tutsi. I was fuming deep inside me and kept wondering why he didn't mention Twa being the other part of the Rwandan population.

Looking back on the two governments (France and Rwanda), they both need each other by all means they need mutual collaboration in hiding each other's crimes. France has dug out to evidence of crimes committed by Kagame including the downing of his predecessor's aircraft killing of innocent Hutus in the Congo. Kagame on the other hand has uncovered crimes committed by the French which includes training arming of the Interahamwe and supervision of the killings of Tutsis by the French troops.

Kagame realised that he was going to lose the whole of the European support, the Francophone world if he didn't maintain his status with France. This has ended up with Kagame giving up on the value he had always preached his countrymen.

It was a surprise to hear Kagame saying while at his visit in France that he has had to move on and forget the past. However, it was evidence that the forgetting of the past seemed single sided or if I may say it was only an individual Mr. Paul Kagame let alone his entire country. I was therefore left to wonder if the Rwandan people were ready to move on and forget what role the French has had in the killing of thousands of innocent Tutsis.

What is evident though is that France has failed to move on. At the time Sarkozy was the president, his former French foreign minister Mr. Alain Juppe has boycotted meeting with president Kagame and being the foreign mister meant that the whole cabinet didn't welcome our president to their country which again voided the status of Kagame's visit personal visit rather than the planned visit.

France has remained adamant in recognising their role in the genocide let alone apologising. France again being a developed country, Mr. Nicolas Sarkozy could not force his cabinet in receiving Mr. Kagame against their will as it is the case in Rwanda and other developing countries.

I urge the people of Rwanda to come together and not to be separated by the individuals like it has been before.

Mr. Kagame's friendship with Sarkozy's and the rest of the European community has raised loads of suspicion. It is evident again that France will not just turn the page and forgets about Kagame's role in the killing of innocent Hutus in the Congo and the pilots of Habyarimana's jet.

We have had enough of this nonsense most of us understand when we talk of reconciliation we need to talk of conflict and the causes of it. Most Rwandan know that in order to move on as a country, and have a well-founded reconciliation, we have to build a stronger and proper justice system, embrace honesty, truth but most of all democracy.

We all know that we do not have democracy and that is why we have innocent Prisoners and killings of those thought to oppose the government. My fellow citizens let's not jeopardise our reconciliation process by allowing these politicians to confuse us, the case behind what happened in Rwanda will be sorted by you and me.

# 2 Chap II: Kagame assaults and Killing field

## 2.1 The teenager house maid assault

I might admit how after a long time I keep recollecting on a few incidents that I witnessed as a young man charged with the security of President Kagame.

It is today that I remembered and realised what a sadist and a bully then boss president Kagame was, throughout all this time it has stuck in my head the surprise action he used to take and lead us to.

I can never forget one afternoon in 1998 when Kagame asked then Lt Willy Rwagasana to dial Maj. Ndushabandi's telephone who was then the head of Kanombe Military Hospital. When the phone rang, Kagame grabbed it off Lt Rwagasana, to me it looked like he was eager to speak to Dr Ndushabandi.

To his surprise the phone on the other side was answered by a female voice who asked to be told who wanted to speak to Dr. Ndushabandi who was having a siesta.

Kagame said to the girl who we later happened to find out that it was a sixteen-year-old maid of Dr. Ndushabandi to put Ndushabandi on the phone.

The poor girl did not know that she was speaking to the top man of Central Africa the then Vice-president of Rwanda and Minister of Defense Major General Paul Kagame by informing the person on the phone that she was not going to put her boss Dr. Ndushabandi on the phone before she knew who was on the phone.

At that moment Kagame hung up the phone and started charging at his bodyguards demanding to know who knew where Dr Ndushabandi lived. He looked disturbed, angered, very upset and appeared frustrated. We drove straight to Ndushabandi's home in Kanombe a distance that is less than eight miles. On our arrival we forced ourselves in, Kagame charging in front of us inside the house while asking who had answered the telephone.

The young maid responded by saying that she was the one. Immediately Kagame jumped and started beating the poor girl up, punching, kicking, pushing and demanding her to wake Ndushabandi up.

When Ndushabandi heard the chaos, and woke up Kagame asked him why he employed such an undisciplined girl. At that time Dr. Ndushabandi was explaining himself shaking and anxious, saluting repeatedly and apologetic that he did not know that the girl was indiscipline.

We later found out that this girl was sixteen years old maid from Gitarama, she had come to Kigali looking for a job in order to support herself and her family. Kagame ordered for her immediate dismissal from her job and the poor doctor had to abide by his boss's crazy orders.

I wonder where this poor girl is at present. And left to wonder why Ndushabandi a doctor and a Major in the armed forces would not take the right decision to save his own employee. I stayed all along wondering what the two men thought of their actions to the poor girl and much more the storming of a senior army officer and commandant of the army hospital by his minister and vice-president of a state.

The poor girl left crying as we were all watching including my colleagues but all of us including Ndushabandi were evidently helpless to her since all were in the hands of the top man Kagame. Before we left Ndushabandi and Kagame had a brief chat in another room for few minutes thus delivering the message he had intended before the girl's intervention.

It was normal to us to see crazy Gen. Kagame beat up, abuse and assault his soldiers of all ranks including generals, but this time it was disturbing to see him with his age assaulting a teenager while on her duties. I am still sure the teenage girl had been briefed by her boss to humbly ask whoever was on the phone before passing it on to him of which she had obediently done. Kagame is an angry man and due to being a powerful man he has found it difficult to control his anger, research indicates that anger is a strong emotion of displeasure caused by some type of grievance that is either real or perceived to be real by a person.

The cognitive behaviour theory attributes anger to several factors such as past experiences, behaviour learned from others, genetic predispositions, and a lack of problem-solving ability. Anger is an internal reaction that is perceived to have an external cause. Angry people almost always blame their reactions on some person or some event, but rarely do they realize that the reason they are angry is because of their irrational perception of the world.

Angry people have a certain perception and expectation of the world that they live in and when that reality does not meet their expectation of it, then they become angry.

## 2.2  President Kagame and his house staff's abuses

In 1994, our soldiers went out from Byumba to Musha, when I talk of our soldiers I mean the high command alongside President Kagame, we found a child of three years old her parents had been killed. Though she was three she had been sent to explain more about herself. She was unable to provide her own name to the soldiers, so she was given the name of Kavutse. She came to Musha with Kagame and all of the entourage he requires. She grew up in the hands of Lt. Rosa Rujeni, Kagame Auntie who was a Lieutenant at the time and is now a Major whereby the heroes from the front lines never even obtained a sergeant, Rosa was responsible for cooking food for Kagame and housekeeping.

After sometime Kavutse came to think she was growing up in her own family, Kagame family turned up from Uganda where they had lived and Kagame would visit them when other soldiers were not allowed to visit their wives during the war. This girl stayed in the family for a few days and she was getting used to Kagame's children. She believed that she was a member of Kagame's family. But because Kagame did not understand how this child felt at the time he decided to send this girl to the orphanage home. This was seen as a normal thing at the time and myself, I did not question much about it because I knew the girl did not belong with the family legally.

However, after some time and reflecting on what this child felt like living there, I think she was betrayed. That is your Kagame. He doesn't want anyone to feel like he does, enjoying the best of life and not wanting anyone else to have the same opportunities. He thinks that he and his family are the only people to be served by the people and the government. He did not stop there. Patricia, who was his personal secretary, had gone to the same school with Kagame throughout their lives. She was the only woman to answer the phone calls, especially ones from abroad before they can be passed on to HE. After that time Patricia, from 1994-2000, was having a relationship that had to be hidden because of Kagame did not want her to be in a relationship with anyone. You wonder why? This woman was not married to Kagame, she was only a personal secretary who was to answer the phone calls and deal with the finances in the house. This woman fell in love with Lt Ronald Mugabo.

He was the person who prepared Kagame's clothes, Ironing and washing. He was a sergeant and promoted to a lieutenant after some time. He was the first escort of Kagame who had walked alongside him even when he was a captain in Uganda. Lt Ronald Mugabo was a young man who I came to find out that I was related to in his last days of his life. Lt Ronald Mugabo was found to be in love with Patricia after 1999 and was poisoned and killed because, obviously, Kagame did not like this.

*He did not stop there;*

Harriet, was responsible for taking care of Kagame's children including washing clothes, tidying the house and preparing meals with cooks. She was a very trusted girl because she was passed on to Kagames family by Major General Kale Kayihura who was a very close friend of Kagame who become a tycoon as well as a general. Harriet was a very friendly girl and loved the soldiers very much. At times, she used to bring us milk outside where we were always waiting for Kagame to come out of the house. We would never know when Kagame would come out to leave so we were always on standby even for 24 hours at a time.

She took care of us, not only Kagame s family but because she thought so much about the soldiers. She fell in love with one of my colleagues Pte Tito Gahigana. Pte Tito Gahigana was in a silent love with Harriet as well because obviously when it was found that one of the staff was in love with a soldier either that soldier would be imprisoned or expelled and sent to another unit and no one wanted to leave the presidential guard. It is very surprising because we never liked living alongside Kagame because we did not enjoy working with him but we thought it was our responsibility to protect the president as the nation wanted it.

When Pte Tito Gahigana got Harriet pregnant it turned out to be a very bad situation because Kagame and the children they had lived with Harriet for many years and the children did not want Harriet to leave and Harriet was not willing to abort the child. So, Kagame's wife decided that Harriet could stay there until she gave birth because of the job. Finally, because Harriet used to live in Kagame's home, she was sent out to live in the local community and she would come to work in the morning. She gave birth and then she was asked to bring the child to Kagame's wife and explain who the father was. Harriet revealed that the father was Pte Tito Gahigana and he had to escape to Uganda but Harriet kept in touch with him. Harriet was fired from caring for Kagame's children when it was discovered that she was in touch with him.

Pte Tito Gahigana was tracked down in Uganda in order to apprehend him and bring him back to Rwanda because anyone who works for President Kagame is unable to leave their post due to the information they hold. Pte Tito Gahigana continues to be in hiding and his whereabouts are not known even until now.

*Rwandan president General Paul Kagame's dictatorship dwarfs General Idi Amin Dada's rule*

Most authoritarian leaders come across as caring and loving individuals who are keen to defend the defenseless. Behind this 'sheep's' skin there is normally a 'wolf' waiting for the right opportunity to pounce. No dictator in modern history can match President Paul Kagame of Rwanda in playing the roles of; victim, defender, saviour, nationalist, great statesman, global leader, liar, villain and aggressor, simultaneously. He has perfected the art of PR (public relations) to a level that even the experts in deciphering illusions are left helpless to his disingenuousness. Some seasoned politicians, academicians, philanthropist, clergy, youth, people of good will and Rwandan nationalist have fallen prey to Kagame's insidious misinformation.

Those who remember General Idi Amin Dada, of Uganda, will recall how he managed to entrap some of the most educated Ugandans and other unsuspecting individuals in his early years to his deceit. He came across as a nationalist, expelled Indians in the national interest, stood up to the west, made Uganda a member of Islamic League of Nations, championed his flagship 'keep your city clean operation' (equivalent of Umuganda in Rwanda), declared economic war and invaded neighbours. He infamously joked that he would make Tanzanian President Mwalimu Julius Nyerere (RIP) his lover at the height of his plans to invade Karagwe, in North West Tanzania. This has similarities to Paul Kagame's threats of 'hitting' President Kikwete at an appropriate time. Amin bought Embassy buildings in most big cities around the world to house Uganda's missions abroad. He also bought planes for the then Uganda Airlines, the national carrier, and boosted of a strong and well-equipped army. One cannot forget his building of a 'terror organisation' in what was called State Research Bureau. To some Ugandans and Africans, he was a hero while to many others he was a villain. I still wonder how history would have portrayed General Amin had he invested in PR like General Kagame of Rwanda has done.

President Paul Kagame's junta in Kigali has perfected General Amin's beguiling ways by investing heavily in public relations (PR) machinery. This has helped the Kagame junta to sustain their deceit and obscure the reality on the ground in Rwanda and its neighbouring region. It has even managed to entrap well respected academicians like those in, Tufts University and Stanford Graduate School of Business to buy into Paul Kagame's, the man, masked 'wolf'. George Bernard Shaw couldn't have been more right when he stated that, "Men are wise in proportion, not to their experience, but to their capacity for experience". These academicians and others who have fall prey to Kagame's beguiling ways are no wiser too. Just as they can't help being fooled by visual illusions, they have fallen for the 'decision' illusions of Kagame's junta PR has managed to show their mind. I strongly believe that sooner or later some of these academicians will live to regret their decisions to ignore 'numerous cries' from Rwandans, Congolese and others in Great Lakes region who are real victims of their disingenuous 'guest'. Most of you remember the case of London School of Economics academicians who were full of praise for Col Gadhafi's junta. You may also remember how dictator Suharto of Indonesia was praised while annihilation of East Timorese was taking place. President Suharto's Indonesia that was leading in the rise of the 'East Tigers' was left behind at the expense of the silent Singapore and South Korea who though authoritarian to some degree were not brutal to its people. Indonesia is still grappling with the after effect of Suharto's dictatorship and poor leadership despite the many awards that various universities in the US awarded him.

Like General Idi Amin, General Kagame has assembled the most brutal state security apparatus in Africa at the moment, Rwanda's DMI. Led by General Jack Nziza, a Mufumbira from Kisoro in Uganda, it has built a terror network that uses most of the brutal tactics of Amin's State Research Bureau, which was led by Kakwas from Congo. Where it has surpassed state, research is its abuse of international institutions like the Geneva

Convention that accords diplomatic immunity to key Embassy Staff to export its terror beyond its, Rwanda's, borders. Paul Kagame does also play the 'nationalist' card that most dictators, like General Amin, Hitler of Germany, Pinochet of Chile and Suharto of Indonesia, played to appear state minded and doing things in the interest of the state. Unlike General Amin, Kagame has amassed a lot of personal wealth at the expense of other hard-working Rwandans and he continues to grab properties of Rwandans perceived to be contesting his style of leadership. He has privatised even the national treasures like King Faisal Hospital and many other organisations to benefit his cohorts at the expense of Rwanda's citizenry. Whereas Amin did not kill relatives of victims or grab their property, Kagame's junta does kill or impoverish even those thought to sympathise, let alone having blood relation, with the victims of the wrath.

The comparison would not be complete with explaining why these two dictators managed to create the illusion of being nationalist and sometimes even masquerade as pan-Africanist. During Amin's era, there was resentment on Indians like there is resentment of immigrants currently in Europe. General Amin to divert attention for his killing of prominent Ugandans like Ben Kiwanuka, Kalimozo (the Makerere Vice Chancellor at the time) and many others, he expelled Indians in what was dubbed 'Mafuta Mingi Operation' and part of his mis-guided so called 'Economic War'. In Rwanda, as legal proceedings were starting to take shape in what had triggered the Genocide, General Kagame expelled the French in a bid to divert attention and play the nationalist card as most survivors and international observers had been beguiled into believing that the French had a role to play in planning the 1994 Tutsi Genocide. Here you can see similarities in these dictators' ways of diverting attention. In all their speeches, you will always find a line of standing up to the colonialists and trying to justify the archaic argument that it is colonialist that have led to our state of affair. I always challenge those who buy into this absurd argument with the words of Joe Hill (1915), "Don't mourn, Organise." My argument is based on the premise that our leaders like Paul Kagame and Idi Amin divert our energies for scrutinising their misdeeds to an archaic and misleading fact of history, in the process disorganising us. America was colonised too, but it is now the most powerful in the world. The Americans organised and set up institutions that are enduring and were stronger than individuals. If it was not the case maybe they would be having George Bush Senior as president, his frailty notwithstanding. After all the Algerian President Elect or Magabe of Zimbambwe are good examples of frail and 'fixture' presidents. I do of course deliberately avoid the mention of the contentious issue of Rwanda's 'TWO TERM LIMITS' of presidency enshrined in the supreme institution, Constitution of Rwanda, of the land. 'Habwirwa benshi hakumva beneyo'. Is it the colonialist flouting that Rwandan institution?

I am sure most the readers who are of a sober mind will appreciate my reason for concluding that President Paul Kagame and his junta has our 'smarted' General Idi Amin's junta in perfecting the art of preying on people's minds by using PR. One can argue that Kagame has been able to out 'smart' Amin for mainly four reasons. The information age we live in has provided a vehicle that gave Kagame an advantage. The continued support from the west, in terms of Billions of Dollars, has enabled Kagame to hire big names and firms to do his PR unlike Amin who relied on individuals like Bob Astley.

The guilt by big powers to take RPF's advice to not intervene early in the Genocide and the inaction of key actors at the time like President Bill

Clinton and Tony Blair (who as opposition leader should have pushed for Britain's intervention) have allowed the support to take a long time. The last reason is better viewed as academic. The west and major global institutions like World Bank, IMF and United Nations are under pressure to provide a case(s) of success in Millennium Development Goals (MDGs).

These same institutions messed up the original object of the Washington Convention that was aimed at poverty reduction. They now have no choice but to go into 'unholy' marriages with deluded leaders just to save their faces and jobs for the mess in MDGs as next year, the target date, fast approaches. Paul Kagame with his 'charming' offensive PR was a natural perfect candidate for this 'unholy' marriage. His 'Economic War', the Amin style is to grab land from peasants, privatise national treasures, grab properties from real or perceived opposition and 'sell Genocide' in the name of economic success, or miracle. What Economic 'success' with national wealth in the hands of very few Kagame's cohorts and little purchasing power locally, as result of the poor RPF policies, to stimulate demand? This reminds of United Kingdoms 'boom and bust' of Tony Blair's, Kagame's advisor, era.

I think Tony has done a good job of advising on 'spin' and authoritarianism. Remember the Iraq 'dodgy' dossier? Don't you see similarities with Kagame's current accusations of RNC and continued allegations about FDLR? As the Paul Kagame candle dwindles, we wait and see how history will judge and portray the scale of delusion inflicted by Paul Kagame the man and his PR machine when the curtains finally close. However, the balance sheet of the human losses inflicted by Kagame's junta in my opinion is far, far greater that General Amin inflicted on Ugandans.

## 2.3  Kagame a mad man

As I sat on the sofa to read the transfer window of the British football league which is booming, my phone rang but the number was hidden, normally I never answer hidden numbers but this time answered because being a father you expect unknown calls from school or play grounds.

This call was not from my children but from Rwanda. The caller was male and had the countenance of that of a priest with a calm voice and he began reminiscing of our history together in the RDA and invited me to return home to Rwanda. These memories included when we engaged in escorting His Excellency the President of Rwanda Paul Kagame, we worked together with the president since I joined the RPA in early 90's we had shared the little we had in those hard times, but ended up losing touch after the war as he was transferred to a different post within republican guard unit.

He urged me to totally denounce Rwanda National Congress (RNC) an opposition party in exile, and forget about being a member of this organization; he reminded me how President Kagame was special and how he was elected by the people of Rwanda in landslide election. During the course of our conversation he became threatening and I became uncomfortable speaking with him further. He reminded me of the times that I left behind, which involved believing some one's decision even their stupid judgments, mismanagement and poor planning. As I listened, I remembered my time as a body guard and driver to Paul Kagame, and every horror that I witnessed during my service.

Growing up in Uganda I had always wished to go back to Rwanda, my uncles were older than me and in the Ugandan forces as well as my elder brother. When we attacked Rwanda, I had all the names of RPA commanders in my head from the late Afande Fred Rwigyema, Late Adam

Waswa, Late Ndugute Kalisoliso and others.

I continued to think of what is going on today in Rwanda and reminisce about times gone by. He continued in his quest to convince me that I should denounce the RNC and have a better future in Rwanda, which obviously I could not accept. As a person who had lived alongside President Kagame for so long I still recall his character of abusing his commanding officers, his wife and anyone else around him. I responded to the caller by saying, "I was around him for so long and I find it easy to know where I belong Mr.," and I hung up.

*"I witnessed Kagame making a full of himself so many times and so I cannot dare follow him again".*

In 1994, I witnessed him slapping Gen. James Kabarebe (actual Minister of Defense) for not answering the radio, when he called Nyinyi Wajinga as if it was his call sign, James's call sign was 66 Golf but he was beaten because it was his responsibility to know that Wajinga means anyone with a radio.

In 1995, President Kagame started becoming anxious that afande Ndugute was planning to kill him, so we used to spend nights at his mother-in-law's house and occasionally at his brother-in-law's house until he dropped all his commanders and appointed new ones. This is the time I remembered how our army planted a landmine in front of Ndugute's home in Kinihira, around 93-94 which he survived. This landmine went off but afande Ndugute was in a car and fortunately no one was injured. It was not a long time before afande Karangwa had just been killed by a landmine which was planted by our own soldiers. The young soldier, who I cannot I identify because of his security, asked Masumbuko if Karangwa was not going to use the route, Masumbuko told him to hurry and said that he knew what he was doing.

At some point in 1995, I was travelling in a Land Rover Jeep which belonged to the late Fred Rwigyema; this army Jeep was getting old even though it was not being used regularly so I asked Rogers Rutikanga who was responsible for President Kagame's transport who actually ended up replacing at some point, if we could use that car instead of parking it forever. He said that he could not see the reason why we couldn't use it; I wanted to drop off one of our causalities, Captain Leandre, who lost his sight during the war so he got into the car and we drove off. He is a very nice chap who can use his other senses to figure out what is around him. With his funny stories, we started driving and talking about the world as well as life in general. As we were getting out of Camp Kigali we saw the convoy of President Kagame who was coming into Camp Kigali. He was viewing schools to see if his children would join the Camp Kigali Primary School which he did not like anyway.

He stopped and asked me if I knew who that car belonged to, I responded affirmatively and he slapped me in the face twice. He told three of his guards, Sentongo, Kizima, and Rwoganyanja to lay us down and continue beating us, Captain Leandre was left wondering why this was occurring. I and another guy named Bosco were beaten, he then asked me about that car and where it has been for all those years and I told him and then he looked at Bosco who was breathless and said that we should take him to the Hospital. I started asking myself why we were beaten but I could not get the answer until today.

In 1997, he was anxious again that there were plans to kill him, this time the alleged plan included several of the senior army officials, he later dropped several others but before dropping them we were ordered to spend the night in the middle of the road to Kinyinya for four days, we would leave at eight o'clock and come back home at six in the morning. This time he ordered the assassination of Major Birasa John who they accused of knowing of the plan to overthrowing the Government but never reported it to his superiors. He was assassinated by a section of nine soldiers sent by the now Colonel Silas Udahemuka who was a captain at the time, he is currently a member of the security detail of Kanombe airport.

The nine soldiers commanded by W011 Mugabo, who was later promoted to a full Lieutenant and is now a major, killed Major John Birasa alongside Captain Eddy Rwigyema who were traveling together with him in the same car. This is the same year when President Kagame ordered Rutatina to administer a poisonous injection to afande Ndugute which later killed him in South Africa. The post-mortem report indicated that he was in contact with a detected poisonous fluid in his lungs and was in the rest of his organs.

It's evident that President Kagame's killings are endless, as all Rwandans know, but let's just focus on what might be the cause of these characters. Like many Rwandese refugees in foreign lands, he was in his early teens when he lost his father. It was at this time that he needed his father as a role model, he was a student at old Kampala school, his father lived in a settlement with his mother and sisters unfortunately his father became seriously ill so a good Samaritan arranged his travel to Mulago hospital in Kampala.

It did not take long before President Kagame's father passed away in the hospital but and received a visit from my uncle who was a lorry (truck) driver in Kawanda research, he went back to visit him and they told my uncle that Kagame's father Rutagambwa had passed away, he sent a message to the settlement but after waiting for two days with no response he asked for the permission to bury him in a government land in Kawanda research which was a farm on Makarere University.

All my time while protecting Kagame I wished I had asked my uncle to show him where he had buried President Kagame's father. According to the scientific research losing one of your parents between the ages of 11-15 years can be traumatic that it affects all your upbringing and the decisions you make in life. This has affected Kagame, he is so emotional and he does not trust anyone, his voice is so emotional and the body language does not match his affect.

When he is talking he assumes that everyone has to accept his words, and if not, he presents aggression once he realizes that there is a sign of opposition. He cannot tolerate the media and sometimes he bangs on the table which is a sign of a personality disorder. I was able to see President Kagame shout at his mother and at some point, his wife, she spent eight hours at a friend's home when she was scared of him after having an argument. He kicked the window in when his son Brian locked himself in the room; this is the time when he attempted to beat his sister Marice for not being observant. Rwanda is ruled by a mad man.

He used to ask us to wake him up so he can watch boxing in 90's, this was normally 2:00 o'clock in the morning because most of the time it was between Mike Tyson and whoever but when we were late by only 2 minutes he nearly killed us. He was very slender compared to now; I used to question myself why would this man enjoy boxing at that size? Look at his arms and his legs.

He later came up with a very good Idea of playing tennis which I thought that suited him and he actually became a better player. My time as his body guard is not regrettable though I told myself that I was working for Rwanda and that kept me going, but I still think that he has betrayed our nation by killing politicians, false imprisonment, killing our commanders after realizing that the war is ended, because he never commanded any war, we used to move to a safe place after clearance of the commanders I mentioned earlier especially Ndugute who was the operation commander. I will always stand on the truth and I am willing to explain my role in any position that I held during my time in Rwanda.

## 2.4 The Conspiracy of Massacre of our Commanders.

The syndicate and planning of the massacre of the RPA/RPF Senior commanders and officers was ordered and supervised by Kagame and his right-hand men. Capt Sam Byaruhanga was assassinated in 1991 in Rubanda Kabale in Uganda, while he was coming a meeting from Bishop Harerimana. As he was coming from the meeting he picked up supplies from one of bishop Harerimana's house, the meeting he had attended was briefing about the conduction of operations in Rwanda.

He had been repeatedly complaining about the death of Gen Fred Rwigyema, he was among the best fighters the RPA had, he would conduct operations and always regretted Rwigyema's death, and Sam Byaruhanga did not believe that Major Paul Kagame was capable of leading the force, indeed Sam believed that Maj Kagame had a hand in Rwigyema's death. At times, whenever Sam talked about Rwigyema's death would shed tears in his eyes and did not have any respect for Kagame at all.

The operation to kill Captain Sam Byaruhanga was conducted by Banga who was an intelligence officer, he had briefed Mustafa who was Deputy to

Gadhafi Kazintwari the commanding officer of Sierra battalion. Mustafa and Banga were briefed to kill Sam Byaruhanga the whole operation was overseen by Banga and the trigger was pulled by Mustafa on their way from Rugano to Mutara. Mustafa was put in jail, however after the war was rewarded a large amount of money with houses and loans to commence business.

Lt Colonel Adam Waswa was killed by a planned car accident on his way from Uganda, at the time Major Kagame had just arrived, Adam Waswa who was on a higher rank than Major Kagame had taken over after Gen Rwigyema's death. Also, Lt Colonel Adam Waswa had been questioning the death of Gen Fred Rwigyema, this made Maj Kagame uncomfortable due to Adam's experience on the field, Kagame was determined to finish off all the experienced commanders and so he could become the top man.

Similarly, Lt Katongole was killed due to complaining about poor explanation of how Gen Fred Rwigyema had been killed, it was in December 1990 when an attempt was made to kill Lt Katongole however he managed to abscond back to Uganda in Mbirizi, unfortunately Jack Nziza followed him together with Gasana Rurayi and brought him back to the sick bay in Mburo National park and was killed there.

Lt Musisi John who was Colonel Lizinde's head of body guards was killed after being accused being close to Lizinde, was also suspected to be giving Lizinde so much information, his killing was directed by Steven Balinda.

Lt Lutalo normally worked in medical department and was very close to Major Bayingana, he normally told soldiers that Maj Bayingana never killed or planned Gen Rwigyema's death, he was killed due to pointing a finger to Major Kagame's men.

A lady called Kaitesi was picked from Kampala and brought in Rugano, she was killed by Mugisha Kanwa. She had been accused of feeding information to the then Rwandese government.

Lt Rwamanywa was tied by his colleagues when entering Rwanda thrown in the river Kagera, fortunately he never died. The locals untied him and went back to Uganda, he had been suspected to communicate with the enemy which was untrue. He was killed by Alex Ibambasi in Uganda on his way trying to get back to the front line.

Senior officer Musisi Kugaya was born in Gitarama but came to Uganda and joined the NRA later came with RPA, he continuously complained of the people being killed in cross fires, he was an OPTO in 101 battalion of Vedaste Kaitare, he was later killed in Rushaki for being accused of trying to escape.

Senior officer Mutimbo Xeno was an optician in the NRA and was close to Gen Rwigyema who played a big role in forming the RPF, he was killed after the questioning of the killing of the top commanders. He was sent on training and got killed by Nyamvumba after a dangerous torture despite begging that he had a heart condition. His appeal was not listened to until he died; Major Kagame had sent Patrick Nyamvumba among the instructors to make sure that the only optician who was also responsible for Major Kagame's eyes is dead as he recently murdered his former Physician Dr. Gasakure.

Captain Muvunanyambo who was a General Administrative Officer (GAO), he had been rescued from Ruhengeri prison together with other senior's officer of the EX-FAR, he had been elevated to the RPA member of high command (MHC), he was later killed by Gen Jack Nziza. As I have mentioned above Muvunanyambo was rescued from Ruhengeri prison when the RPA attacked the Ruhengeri town, he was imprisoned following the fall out with the then President Habyarimana government. Captain Muvunanyambo was killed after approaching Major Kagame and asked him about the killings of Hutus who were being killed in Gishuro Karama and Tabagwe, he came to Gikoba in Shonga and asked Major Kagame as to why civilians were being killed. Captain Muvunanyambo was killed by (Bucyana) who is normally known as Agaba, he served as an intelligence officer in Steven Ndugute's body guards; the death of Captain Muvunanyambo was supervised by now Gen Jack Nziza with directives from Kagame and his immediate aids.

Lt Bucyana Agaba had a brother in law who was married to Kangobe a sister to Bucyana, this brother in-law who was known as Mutambuzadembe a lorry driver, he was suspected to be supplying information to Rwanda then government. This brother in-law was killed by the RPA soldiers, and Lt Bucyana was working alongside now Gen Jack Nziza, he questioned his in laws death and attempts were made to kill him but then he run away asking for Senior officer Ndugute to save him, Ndugute spoke to Kagame that Bucyana was innocent, despite Kagame's assurance that Bucyana will be spared, he was later deployed in Bungwe with Rose Kabuye and was killed there in 17th battalion under the command of senior officer Kananura.

Another senior officer Kaitare Vedaste was killed by now Colonel Karemera aka Mudaheranwa who gambled with examinations and ended up baptizing himself Karemera. Kaitare had been Rwigyema's chief escort who was loved by all the forces, Kagame ordered his killing just because he was a good commander and loved by all forces. Dr Colonel Karemera administered a poisonous injection to Kaitare when he required medical attention for a malaria fever.

Senior officer John Gashumba was killed by a landmine in Bungwe simply because Kagame thought that he was Kaitare's close friend, and Kagame thought that he was capable of maintaining Gen Rwigyema's legacy and possibly revenge about the killing of his close to commanders.

Senior officer Ntaganda who was deputy Yanky mobile force commanded by Fred Nyamurangwa was killed after a meeting in which he confronted Major Kagame to stop killing Hutu's, he said that I came from Uganda with you but I am a Hutu and you are killing Hutu's, he said that it doesn't make sense capturing an area and killing local civilians just because they are Hutu's. Ntaganda was killed after Kagame ordered his return to headquarters and stopped from operating on frontline, was killed by Epimaque Runanira and Gasana Rurayi.

Major Musisi Nyanjunga was an OPTO 7th battalion, he had a girlfriend that was also going out with now Gen Kabarebe James, he knew that James Kabarebe was HIV positive and decided to complain to Kagame. He was killed after allegations that he had said that Kagame was building a group of uncontrolled people. He was shot at just in the outskirts of Kigali.

The RPF soldiers killed each other for many reasons after capturing Kigali, among the reason as trivial might seem to be, houses and women were among the most, one of them is Lt Kinyata who was based in 5th battalion was killed for speaking about one of the then top commanders who had used his position to take Ben Karenzi's girlfriend (fiancé).

Gen Karenzi Ordered rape and killing of our only Grace, Grace means God's favor: Lt Grace Rukasi was a senior nurse, our Nightingale, a sister and a savior to our wounded or fallen men and women on the battled field. Lt Grace Rukasi born in Kabale town to mother Kamashara who was allegedly called Gen Habyalimana's cousin. Never the less Lt Grace was born and educated in Uganda, grew up with Major and medical Doctor late Peter Bayingana who were neighbours from childhood. Doctor Major Peter Bayingana also had encouraged Grace to join the army and Grace spent most of her service treating soldiers and in hard situations.

After the arrival of Major Kagame he received information from his right-hand men that Lt Grace Rukasi was very close to the soldiers, all casualties were calling Grace, she was an empathetic nurse who could not rest until she got a solution to cure those in need, she was a dedicated nurse who was equipped with professional values, honesty, empathetic, responsible, trustworthy, and respectful. Grace had moved from being a nurse to a solution in any given situation. The casualties were many in numbers and the wounded plus traumatised forces due to the enemy fire.

Kagame believed that the closeness of Grace and the RPA forces was due to seeking information to send to Kigali rather than nursing values, Grace was taken by Epimaque Runanira, Mugisha Kanwa, Gasigwa who was based in the sick bay as an RCM. The above were briefed by Gen Karenzi Karake who told the three to rape Lt Grace and throw her in the river Kagera. This was all done as Karenzi Karake ordered, our empathetic nurse was raped by colleagues, all three took turns of raping her, then threw her in the river Kagera, miraculously she was pushed aside by the water and got stuck on the grass, she was breathless, anxious, appreciatively the locals picked her up and brought her back to the sick bay. She was looked after by other nurses, and started appealing to other commanders and begging for mercy because she knew that she was blameless. Gen Karenzi who had raped Lt Grace at some point had also reported to Kagame that Grace was communicating with Gen Habyalimana's intelligence service.

Lt Grace who was born and grew up in Uganda, only spoke poor Kinyarwanda like many of us and instead spoke fluent Runyankole but was being accused of possible family relationship to Gen Habyarimana by Kagame and his poor intelligence network. Lt Grace Rukasi was imprisoned and later kept under surveillance by the directorate of military intelligence; her monitoring was headed by the top men.

Lt Grace would move around treating wounded and ill forces under surveillance until the end of war, then was later killed by a lorry which drove into her from behind while driving on Kanombe Kigali high way, this done because Major Paul Kagame and his Gen Karenzi Karake, Jack Nziza and other top men believed that one day, Lt Grace will speak out on the treatment she received from colleagues who were supposed to support her, but instead physically, psychologically, sexually and emotionally abused her.

The lorry that was staged to kill her was driven by Sgt Nyirumuringa who was later killed as well, apparently the top officers thought that no one will ever speak out about this malicious killing.

Comrades we will always remember you hope Colonel Tom Byabagamba with sun glasses will be released one day. A Courageous, friendly and hero Captain Kamugisha Herbert alias Mucocori was born in Mpororo in Uganda, attended Kitante secondary school and later Kyambogo College, is described as a hardworking man who valued others by those who knew him well. Like many young Rwandans of his time he joined the NRA in 1980's with a view to returning home one day. In 1990 his dream came true together with colleagues RPA attacked Rwanda, during his service time he was on field most of the time, mostly on operations, he conducted special missions, he was the man who would know the sabotages and killings of opposition leaders in Rwanda to blame it to Gen Habyalimana's forces.

He would investigate on enemy positions and feed back to our commanders who would conduct the attack after designing a strategic plan based on Herbert's report.

He spent most of his time in the outskirts of Kigali with his men who were known as abatekinisiye, together with Captain Kiyago there hard work will be remembered in history.

Kamugisha was later killed due to the hate and recklessness of the Kagame right hand men. He was assassinated in Ngenda by his close colleague who was an intelligence officer of 17 battalion Peterson Gasangwa is now a major in RDF. Major Herbert Kamugisha had acquired a Pajero and a nice house in Kigali, he was ordered to hand his car to Gen Sam Kaka and his Audi car to another top commander, despite all this, he reminded the dual top commanders of how he came in Kigali on missions when none of them could face the enemy. As further punishment by these commanders, he was deployed in the villages away from Kigali, another officer Justus Muhizi was sent by the above top commanders to disorganise Kamugisha's wife who later fell in love with Justus Muhizi. He was also reported to Major Kagame as an officer who was subversive among the RPA forces.

Again, as what they had done was not enough, he was reported to Major Kagame that he was communicating the atrocities which were committed during the war to what they called their enemies. The order was released for Kamugisha to be killed immediately; he was shot while asleep in Ngenda by Peterson Gasangwa who was a 2LT at the time. He never thought that his fellow officer had been deployed to finish him, he lost his cars, house and wife plus the country he had fought for in his entire life.

At the funeral service, a brother to Captain Kamugisha who was a preacher in Uganda explained that his brother did not commit suicide as it had been reported by the army command, he instead said that his brother had already reported his worries to him, and that his commanders were planning to execute him. He however said that those who participated in killing Herbert Kamugisha will be questioned by "God". Immediately boarded the car and returned to Uganda, left everyone at the funeral gobsmacked.

Major Mugisha Richard alias Cyojo, described as a spirited intrepid officer was injected a poisonous liquid by a counterfeit Gen Rutatina in Kanombe military Hospital. Major Mugisha was being framed that he had married a Hutu wife and himself was half Hutu and half Tutsi, was accused of telling Hutu in laws of how the Kagame Government was killing Hutu's in war zones and DRC.

Major Mugisha had started to question injustice in the army, Mugisha had fragments in the head he sustained during his time on front line, even though many of our commanders who required medical attention were taken to overseas for treatment after the war. Kagame said that Mugisha should not be taken abroad, Kagame believed that Mugisha was half Hutu and married a Hutu woman and so was capable of showing or practicing his Hutuness by engaging with what he called enemies and ex-far. And so Kagame briefed Rutatina and Jack Nziza to eliminate Mugisha at any opportunity. And so was called as he was on waiting list for hospital treatment, the opportunity was created and poison was injected as part of his treatment. After his death in Kanombe the mother and his brother who was a Lieutenant in the RPA also known as Mugisha took the body to Rwamagana hospital and the post-mortem revealed a poisonous liquid in the head, the Rwamagana Hospital did not know that the person they conducted a post-mortem, had actually been killed under the directives of the top men. The brother and his mother all relocated to Uganda. The brother had been working in the Directorate of Military Intelligence, is now hiding but still being hunted like many other comrades, Major Mugisha was also accused of collaborating with Captain Serwada who had been indicted of starting a rebellion.

Captain Serwada was once described by friends as a tiger on frontline, those who knew him recalls that he could not rest until all comrades are out of enemy lines, meaning that he was always ahead in attacking the enemy and would be last online returning to the defense. He cared more for others, speaking Swahili and Luganda mainly. His Kinyarwanda was not fluent, the wrongdoing Captain Serwada was blamed of grouchy about injustice and nepotism among the RPA forces, he was accused of being a Hutu, he further questioned the logic of killing of guiltless civilians, and Captain Serwada writhed to differentiate Hutu from Tutsi because he had grown up in Baganda communities. The only thing he knew was that civilians should be protected and only fight the armed forces, Captain Serwada only thought that the war was to be conducted the same way he had evidenced and participated in the Museveni National resistance army Uganda. But Captain Serwada realised he was wrong when it was too late. He was at the time under the brigade of Col Dodo Twahirwa in Kibungo, questioned by his superiors as to why he was spending much time with Hutu civilians.

Poor Captain Serwada found out that he was going to be killed by his colleagues, from a reliable friend. He decided to run away and returned to the jungle next to Kagera national park, the area he had spent time during his guerrilla war time. Captain Serwada took his gun with ammunitions, and was looking for the way out of Rwanda through the national park full of animals with his AK 47 alone but fighting for his dear life, with a view to returning to Uganda. Unfortunately, couldn't make it as he was followed by his colleagues and hunted down by over 100 soldiers who had been given orders to shoot and kill. The soldiers had been briefed that Captain Serwada became a rebel and was with hundreds of Hutu recruits in the jungle, was found alone pleaded for mercy but Col Dodo Well-ordered Captain Serwada's execution

Major Hassan Mwungeri was born from a Hutu father and a Tutsi mother who was close to the royal family, born in Uganda grew up in Uganda like many RP/RPF soldiers.

Real force up for the wage of war 59 with Charlie mobile force in 1992, unfortunately most of their commanders were eliminated by Kagame's poor intelligence services on his arrival supported by the Uganda army.

He always maintained the ideas of uniting people, he believed that Hutu /Tutsi were just words he was proud of having both parents from those ethnic groups.

He attended army cadet course in Jinja, as an NRA officer with parents originally from Rwanda had also been part of the Rwandese community. As an army officer, on arrival in Rwanda Hassan Mwungeri was Major and immediately served as officer in charge of A company.

He would speak to soldiers about the importance of uniting our poor and ignorant citizens, always would take the words Hutu/Tutsi as a joke, and so he repeatedly called himself a Hutu and would tell peers that we are all the same, there is no difference from all of us.

Major Hassan Mwungeri was always surrounded by forces at war. One of his close friends who was a Tutsi too of whom they grew up together in Mpororo Uganda, always kept a close eye on Hassan Mwungeri because he was aware of the dangers of being Hutu in the RPA/RPF. He would ask him to maintain his voice or even avoid some of the words he normally used in his proudness, but Hassan was the commander who behaved like a philosopher, he was ahead of everyone. He believed that ignorance was the issue between the two ethnic groups; he thought that Twa's were just an innocent ethnic group and vulnerable.

During the attack of Ruhengeri on the 8th/march/1993 which was aimed to highlight the RPA potential and the capacity of RPF, indeed, the attack was also aimed to force the Habyarimana government to stay in negotiations Arusha peace initiative be respected.

Hassan Mwungeri who was good commander was transferred from 157 to Charlie mobile force, the RPA was worried that he will reveal the killings of innocent civilians.

Hassan always believed in Mandela and saw him as his role model; Hassan's attitude was Kagame's main worry because he fought wars and always objected the killings of civilians.

Gen. Ibingira who always pleaded to Kagame that Hassan Mwungeri was dangerous because he did not agree with the RPA system, and had always complained from day one about divisions and nepotism, was relieved when Kagame allowed him to deploy him to Charlie mobile force with a group soldiers who eliminated him, Major Hassan Mwungeri was killed near Basse by his own colleagues.

Dona Tukahirwa was an excellent intelligence Officer who was sharp and successful in his work, had worked alongside Kagame in the directorate of military intelligence.

He had worked as an operation Intelligence officer for senior officer Sam Byaruhanga, Dona operated in many areas of Rwanda and had shown his disappointment due to the death of late Sam Byaruhanga who had been killed following Major Kagame's orders.

The death of Kizza was as a result of the death of both men Hassan Mwungeri and Sam Byaruhanga, Kizza and Sam had always been close friends and only enjoyed wars, shared evening chats sitting around fire, singing, they never considered Kagame as an officer because he was never at war and so their experience was different.

Major Kagame was always nervous of respectable commanders, he thought that his command would be successful if he only promoted young commanders who do not know his weaknesses however would only succeed after eliminating the senior commanders who expressed opposite views.

Another officer who was killed due to the catastrophe of Captain Sam Byaruhanga's was Captain Nshoza, who was born in Mbarara Kyamugoranyi, the son of Nyiragakomo is remembered for being a fearless fighter, officer in charge B company in Charlie Mobile force died the same date of 8th/03/1993 when many officers who had opposite views when a number of officer's men and women were eliminated, had been one of Sam Byaruhanga's body guards.

Captain Nshoza was killed on Nyamagamba hill, because Kagame's intelligence service believed that he will revenge due to Captain Sam Byaruhanga's death.

Prior to Captain Donna Tukahirwa's death, he was misled to plant a landmine which caused injuries that led to the death of senior officer Gashumba Kijana following the instructions of Major Kagame.

One of the soldiers asked Captain Donna Tukahirwa that afande Gashumba was going through the same route, immediately was told to "shut up". The following minutes was injuries and death of young men on the entourage of the young commander Gashumba John.

Senior officer Gashumba who always said that he was a Twa by ethnicity, was born and grew up in Mutara Rwanda near Rwempasha, he always said that his father was a servant to Ryumugabe the grandfather of Rukayaya, Rutuyuyu Alex Baguma, and Asumani Mukongoto. He later died of poisonous injection administered by Rutatina in Rubaya sickbay, according to the reports we hold Gashumba had to be injected as he had survived the landmine and his wounds were treatable. Like many crucial officers, he was killed because of being close to officers such as Captain Sam Byaruhanga, Donna Tukahirwa, and Ndugute Kalisoliso.

Senior officer Gashumba, in 1982 he crossed the border and entered Uganda, as a young man with an intention to join the NRA, served as a private soldier in 9th battalion, rose in ranks day by day in the National Resistance Army ranks and was later recognised in Gen Fred Rwigema's lines of forces to attack Rwanda. In Rwanda, he was an experienced officer who planned and executed wars, unfortunately he criticised Kagame's system and challenged the discrimination of Hutu. He was also a close friend to Kayitare Vedaste (Intare Batinya) who was also unwilling to accept Kagame's legacy. He told Kayitare that Kagame was not the right person because he is guided by discrimination towards Hutu's and his behaviour was not suitable for leading a united nation.

## 2.5 Kagame's unreported killings

A Rwandan from Canada known as Mugesera Leo was justifiably returned to Rwanda in 2012 to face the charges of inciting the 1994 genocide with his recorded messages. But, as one reads this piece they should wonder how many other murderers or those who called for the senseless killings of innocent lives still roaming free? Why does the international community continue to turn a blind eye to the atrocities committed in Rwanda? Do the regional mineral resources gained really justify the cost of lives of thousands and thousands of innocent men, women and children

President Paul Kagame of Rwanda has repeatedly denied killing his own people, let me focus on some of the killings he ordered and some that were ordered by his spies. President Kagame has portrayed himself a God figure in Rwanda and according to him no one can judge him or question any of his decisions.

I often ask myself, why do people kill each other? Because mankind is too sensitive for their own good, we have too much emotion and difference in thought. Jealousy, hatred, revenge, money, religion, status... ALL of these are simple reasons for some people to just go ahead and pull the trigger. Not everyone has the same mindset that killing is bad, and certainly people that do kill are not afraid of the consequences themselves otherwise they wouldn't commit such an act in the first place.

The killings I will talk about today were committed by Kagame and his RPA, which appear to have gone largely unreported, and took place in north-eastern Rwanda in mid-April 1994. Others have occurred in southern and western Rwanda once the RPA took control of these areas in May and June 1994. There are also reports that the RPA, as well as RPF supporters, were responsible for numerous killings of unarmed civilians in August and September 1994 in south-eastern Rwanda. Some corpses of the victims were dumped in the Akagera River which flows along the border between Rwanda and Tanzania.

During peace talks in 1992 President Juvenal Habyarimana claimed that Rwanda was a small country and there was not enough space for the Rwandan refugees who were in neighbouring countries to return home. He encouraged the Hutus to relocate and gave them the land surrounding the Uganda/ Rwanda boarder, just to prove that Rwanda was full and that there was no space for any more people. The relocated Hutu's started farming as a way of monitoring our (RPA/RPF) movement in the area; these were areas of Kagitumba, Nyabwesongweizi and all the surroundings. It was a large community and when we captured the area there were thousands of people in those villages.

Major Karangwa, who is now the head of Kami military detention, which is well known for hosting people with serious cases, and where the torture, killings and many horrific acts are inflicted on people suspected of collaborating with any opponent of Kagame's Government. Major Karangwa was a Sergeant in 1994, he was the head of a small detach of 50 soldiers; Major Karangwa ordered the killing of the entire community of Nyabweshongweizi. The RPA arrived in Kagitumba on 12 April 1994. At first our fighters were told to be very friendly to the local population in order to create the trust so that even those who were in hiding would come out, and convince the community that the RPA was determined to protect the local people who were then summoned to a public meeting at Gishara. On 13 April unarmed men, women and children gathered at Gishara in Kagitumba where RPA soldiers were addressing the crowd when suddenly, without provocation or warning, the soldiers opened fire on the crowd and threw grenades at them. It is unclear how many people were killed.

It was President Kagame himself who briefed his senior intelligence commanders to use the tactic of being friendly to those they were planning to kill, at some point they gave out sugar and salt, cooking oil and soap to the locals that our soldiers had looted from shops just to make them come out of the hiding only to be killed in the end. Our soldiers were taught to be friendly at first then open fire without warning or provocation. All of these plans of how and where to kill were all done by Major Karangwa. Other inhabitants of Nyabwishongwezi were Rwandese nationals who had recently been expelled from Tanzania where they had been living for many years. Government soldiers had withdrawn from the area several weeks earlier. When RPA forces occupied the area in February 1994 the local population first fled but was convinced by the RPA to return.

In March, the RPA called the first public meetings during which RPF officials told people that they had nothing to fear. At one such meeting in April the RPA fired a rocket and threw grenades into the crowd. Others were shot and killed while others sustained severe injuries. The RPF denied that any killings had occurred in Kagitumba. Despite this position the people did not believe them and they continued to flee from Nyabwishongwezi. RPA fighters reportedly started a man-hunt for the Hutu, killing many using bayonets and guns.

I arrived in Nyabweshongweizi with Major Ruhetamacumu and Lt, who is now Lt Col Happy Ruvusha in April 1994 on a special mission and I looked in Karangwa's eyes as he was explaining the job he has been doing as if it was something interesting to talk about. They had dug a mass grave in which he was saying that the plan was to keep it open until it was full. He had more than 300 bodies in the grave and the hunt was on-going in the whole village. The village smelled strongly of death and I could not wait to leave that place. Finally, we left and headed to Kaborogota, the guys we left behind looked like butchers as they would kill people easily and toss them into the grave like they were trash.

Most of the killings of civilians were ordered by President Kagame himself. Kagame is a very dangerous person and most people are still unaware of what President Kagame is capable of doing. He had an unspoken motto that, 'as long as you can bury a person there is no problem in killing them but if you left them alive you would also be killed.' In each village, there were two civilians who would be made to dig the grave and then when it was time to bury the bodies over two different civilians would be brought up to complete the task. Then in the next village those two men, who had buried the bodies, would be the first to be killed and thrown in the mass grave as the village was being slaughtered.

When the 7th Battalion was deployed in the areas of Rushashi, Tare, Mbogo, and Rurindo in 1998 the director of schools at Rwankuba, the Bourgmestre of commune Rushashi as well as the agriculture officer of that commune were murdered over the same night. RPF hurriedly blamed their death on Interahamwe insurgents, yet they had been killed by its own elements.

The same year of 1998 Kagame planned to kill all the civilians who were watching the world cup tournament in a Hotel called Pensez-Y and blame their death on insurgents. Fortunately, the operations officer of 7th Battalion, Capt. Kwizera who had been assigned the task, got drunk and failed to properly coordinate the operation.

Indeed, when the soldiers, who were to disguised as Interahamwe insurgents, reached the Hotel they found many RPF soldiers mixed with the civilian crowd which was watching the world cup tournament. They contacted the commanding officer, Major Eugène Nkubito, who angrily told them to tell all the soldiers present to report to their respective positions. When some civilians noticed this movement, they suspected foul play and also left the hotel. A few moments later, the Hotel was burnt to ashes and the civilians who remained watching the TV were killed in the fire. After the operation, Radio Rwanda announced that the Interahamwe had burned that hotel and killed many people.

Despite the number of casualties, Kagame was not happy because the plan did not go the way it had been hatched. He summoned to himself Capt. Kwizera in the officers' mess, sent his own presidential jeep to collect sticks and beat Captain Kwizera. I was on Kagame's convoy had seen with my eyes, Kagame was chasing us to bring sticks; he ordered SGT Aimee Claude and LT Joseph Nkubito to beat Kwizera. The captain was given 100 strokes, demoted to the rank of private and put behind bars until he was dismissed from the army. This was done in public and many people watched the scene.

Another glaring example of President Kagame's murderous ways were the killing of western tourists in Bwindi National Park, which was prominently featured in western media. The RPF immediately blamed it on the Interahamwe and so did the western media. Yet, they had been killed by RPF soldiers disguised as Interahamwe. The decision to kill western tourists venturing in that area had been taken mainly for two reasons:

- The issue of Interahamwe would be more internationalized if they were accused of killing innocent western tourists. As a result, RPF would be given a free hand in fighting them the way it wants and wherever they are suspected to be.

- RPF suspected some of the Europeans of sympathizing with Interahamwe by disclosing to them the positions of the RPF. Moreover, the presence of foreigners near an insurgent area was hindering RPF atrocities perpetrated under the guise of counter insurgent's operations.

I was astonished when I heard the Rwandan leaders then endeavouring to explain how the Interahamwe killed the tourists. I don't think that they knew anything about the plan apart from being told what to say. When the late Andre Kisasu Ngandu, the vice-chairman of the late President Laurent Kabila was killed, the Government of Rwanda, which was fighting alongside Kabila to overthrow the Government of Mobutu, announced that Kisasu Ngandu was killed in an ambush by the Interahamwe and the ex-FAZ (ex-Force Armées Zairoises). Yet, he was killed by the RPA officers and men who are up-to-date serving in the RPF army. His assassination was planned by James Kabarebe and Jack Nziza under the orders of Paul Kagame because Ngandu was opposed to the killing of refugees.

## 2.6 Who Killed Kagame's personal Doctor, Dr Gasakure?

In Summary Dr Gasakure *(former Kagame's personal physician)* knew Kagame's diagnoses and had fallen out with the government for arresting and mistreating his friends. Gen Jack Nziza, Dan Munyuza were concerned that Dr Gasakure may seek refuge in another country to spill the beans.

There is overwhelming evidence of Rwanda's direct and indirect involvement in the violence and mysterious death of many Rwandans like that of Dr. Gasakure especially those who have been close confidants of president Kagame.

Dr Gasakure once lost unspecified documents belonging to Rwanda's presidential entourage that had accompanied President Paul Kagame to Uganda for the Christmas holidays; he was killed by police in a staged drama of escape and grabbing a gun from a police officer who had escorted him to a toilet.

Dr Gasakure was not only vulnerable like other senior officials who have been sidelined by Kagame and are no longer on the milk bottle, but was a close friend of Col. Tom Byabagamba. It is an open secret that anyone who has served alongside Kagame whenever is no longer in the visible position, he/she becomes a target of elimination either physically or politically.

Rwanda intelligence agents and DMI Special Forces are directly involved; and will disguise as police officers if there is a target of assassination or other cruel methods of extra judicial massacre. In 2015, they played another drama when they said that an executive in Musanze was trying to escape and the police officer shot him. These are brutal massacres that must be condemned by all human rights organizations in the strongest terms possible.

In light of that, the government of Rwanda should be put to task to explain who these officers killing unarmed and defenseless people in the cold blood. It has not been easy for the families of Dr Gasakure and his friend Captain Kayitare who was also killed in a mysterious circumstance, Rwandans remain silent with no answers following the death of Rwigara Asinapol, Dr Murego and others.

In February 2015, according to the Rwandan Spokes Person a man was fatally wounded after an attempt to disarm a police officer on duty ended in a bloody scuffle that left the man dead and the police officer seriously injured. According to the Police Spokesperson Chief Supt Celestin Twahirwa, the man, identified as Dr Gasakure, asked to use the toilet and on his way assaulted the officer.

"The deceased requested to go for a short call, was allowed but on getting out of the cell assaulted the officer on guard and tried to disarm him. In the ensuing scuffle, the deceased was fatally wounded while the police officer sustained serious injuries and was rushed to hospital," the spokesperson said.

The incident took place shortly after 6:30 p.m., at Remera Police Station in Kigali. The deceased was a suspect being held in Police custody as part of investigations into offences that include illegal entry on other person's property, causing damage to property, illegal confinement and issuing threats.

"Investigations into the unfortunate incident have been launched. The police regret the incident and will keep the families informed as the investigation proceeds," the spokesperson added.

What are they informing the families that they don't know? In fact, the families should know that Dr. Gasakure was murdered like other many Rwandans who have been killed, disappeared, or incarcerated without any justification. The family of Mr. Andrew Rwisereka Kagwa has never got justice since their beloved one was decapitated and his body thrown in the swamp. Where are the investigations? The recent drama of an accident of Mr. Rwigara Assinapol ended with the police saying that they have the driver of the lorry that crushed the car of Mr. Rwigara but they never said who he is, and until today the family of Rwigara cannot demand justice for their loved one.

Indeed, the European Union's definition of "terrorist acts" should dispel any lingering doubts one may have had that the violence against Rwandans within the country and beyond qualifies as terrorist acts:

"Terrorist acts" mean intentional acts which; given their nature or context, May seriously damage a country or international organization and which are defined as an offence under national law. These include:

- attacks upon a person's life which may cause death;

- attacks upon the physical integrity of a person;

- kidnapping or hostage taking;

In order for these acts to constitute terrorist acts, they must be carried out with the aim of seriously intimidating a population, or unduly compelling a Government or an international organization to perform or abstain from performing any act, or seriously destabilizing or destroying the fundamental political, constitutional, economic or social structures of a country or an international organization.

President Kagame has been using all these brutal methods against his potential challengers or those perceived to be, he has gone beyond his borders and killed his political dissents or kidnapped them like Lt. Joe Mutabazi from Uganda. In light of Rwanda's direct and indirect promotion of terrorism against his own people and even beyond like Congo and elsewhere, Rwanda obviously qualifies as a "state sponsor of terrorism" and, after formally being declared as such, must be immediately subjected to the sanctions of the United States and European Union which are legally bound to impose on state sponsors of terrorism.

## 2.7 Asiel Kabera was a humanistic man

Asiel Kabera was an adviser to President Bizimungu and after Bizimungu's resignation he remained as an adviser to the then new President Paul Kagame but also tried to stay loyal to his former boss Pasteur Bizimungu. However, during those days Paul Kagame had lost confidence in him because of his close relationship also with the former Speaker of Parliament Sebarenzi Kabuye who had left the country in exile.

Asiel Kabera was easy to reach in any circumstance, I remember before mobile telephones became popular in Rwanda I used to attend his offices in order to communicate with my family. In those days, we used to work 24/7 due to the responsibility and paranoia of believing that someone is out there to kill Kagame. I remember Asiel Kabera sending his secretary to call me when one of my family members had called to check on me. Asiel was a real man with humanistic behaviour and he was well educated. In addition to that, he was among the few Rwandese men who had managed to keep his culture alongside civilisation, but he was another comrade we lost in minutes and was killed by Kagame's thugs.

After Asiel Kabera's death, a lot was said either by his friends, family and even colleagues. Some people even explained his death but in different versions with some conflicting information for their best interest. It was disappointing because just after his assassination the Rwandan national radio announced that every citizen who was in possession of a weapon should report it to the nearest Gendarmerie post now known as Police station. That is all the government had to do, in regards to the loss of a great man who was a presidential advisor.

The only honest ex-service man who spoke out about the death of Asiel Kabera was Lt Ruyenzi who claimed that a slain politician was shot by a combined force of the Republican Guard and Special Intelligence Services of the police force led by Col. Gacinya Rugumya, in 2000. However, he remained reserved in explaining about what really happened on the day of the innocent man's death, today I Noble Marara will put down a little of what I was able to understand on what happened on the day when the Innocent advisor to the high-profile politician Paul Kagame died.

On the day of his death I had driven the wife of President Kagame to visit her mother, and while I was sat in the car waiting for the first lady Janet Kagame who was still in her mother's house to come out, I heard the bullets. Asiel's house was near the Village Urugwiro, which was where he was shot. The sound came from the area of the presidential palace and the president was in residence at Village Urugwiro. I called on the radio to alert my colleagues and to find out where the sound of bullets originated, also to discern the reason why it was near the president's residence.

One of our intelligence staff S/SGT Melchior Hakizimana, AKA Ndadaye, intervened in the conversation and informed me that the situation was under control and reassured me that we should continue with the journey to bring the First Lady home as the road was safe. On my arrival, I went straight to Melchior and asked him what was going on, he said that Asiel Kabera had been sorted, as in the military terms, due to being one of the enemies. Those days it was normal for us to discuss about things. Before I became an enemy as some people call me these days, and so he went on to tell me that it was Lt Joseph Balinda, who is now a Major with Lt Mupenzi Aloys who later became a Captain and later demobilized, that executed Mr Asiel Kabera.

S/SGT Melchior Hakizimana confirmed that he was alongside these men when the mission was undertaken. He presented as confident and behaved like someone who was giving me some good news or sounding like it was saving the whole nation. Yet, I was not convinced but continued nodding to avoid signs of disbelief. However, I immediately recalled that Asiel Kabera was from Kibuye and most Guys from there were being mistreated or killed due to Sebarenzi Kabuye, the man who was a speaker of parliament, who was energetic, empathetic and talented but could not work with the Kagame's. I was disappointed by the actions of our forces but also our leaders who, for the first time, I realised they could kill anyone.

## 2.8 Brig. Gen Dan Gapfizi died a similar way he used to killafande Late Adam Waswa

Brig Gen Dan Gapfizi the commandant of the Reserve Force in the Southern Region passed away in a road accident that took place Tuesday the 25/06/13. The development was confirmed by the Spokesperson of the Rwanda Defense Force, Brig. Gen. Joseph Nzabamwita.

"The RDF is saddened by the news of the death of General Gapfizi, it is tragic, he was a gallant officer," said Nzabamwita in a brief phone interview with The New Times.

According to Nzabamwita, the accident happened along the Kagitumba-Kayonza road. Nzabamwita did not go in detail on how this accident happened however he explained that more information will follow. Hopefully an autopsy will be done to explain to the nation the death of this Gen who holds a long strange history.

Brig Gen Dan Gapfizi was a military transport officer back in Uganda while still in the National resistance army (NRA) Uganda, served as a driver in

Presidential Protection Unit at some point. Dan Gapfizi was later promoted to the rank of 2lt just before attacking Rwanda, Dan Gapfizi was very close to Major Kabura a Ugandan young senior officer who was well known for stubborn behaviour. Brig Gen Dan Gapfizi like many Rwandans who were serving in the Ugandan forces was among the men and women who waged war to Rwanda on 1/10/1990. Prior to that Dan Gapfizi had worked as a youth carder for the Obote regime who reportedly harassed a lot of people including his brothers and sisters from the Rwandese tribe, this was during the time prior to him joining NRA spying for the ruling party Uganda People's Congress of Milton Obote.

Obote's intelligence knew that the Rwandese men and women were joining Museveni's forces and so believed that tracking down the Rwandese community was away of weakening Museveni. Any way Dan Gapfizi was saved and saw the route to join his brothers and sisters in the NRA, distanced himself from criminal gangs of UPC youth group, and Gen Fred Rwigema gave him counselling therapy sessions due to the guilty he was experiencing.

Back around 1991, it was reported that, Dan Gapfizi travelled with Col Joseph Karemera who was the head of medical in RPA to Uganda with the late Adam Waswa. Dr. Joseph Karemera pretending to be travelling to Uganda for work related issues, knew very well that together with Dan Gapfizi will look for any possible opportunity to eliminate Afande Adam Waswa, Dr Joseph Karemera had tried to inject a poison to Late Adam Waswa but it was clearly explained that he was going to Uganda get treated by his specialists, the now late Dan Gapfizi reported that he was going to Uganda to seek medical help. They boarded the Late Adam's car that was travelling to Mbuya military Hospital.

Late Adam Waswa was the head of the army after Gen Fred Rwigyema death, and Kagame was still hanging around as (PC) political coordinator a position given to him by Museveni to link politics and army duties and then report back to Uganda, through Museveni's brother Gen Salim Saleh. Paul Kagame was not satisfied he wanted to become the overall commander of the army, he never wanted any one higher than him in ranks, and so even though Lt Col Adam Waswa's position was much similar to what Col Ndugute was doing after Adam Waswa death but was not known as the army commander like Adam Waswa, Ndugute was known as operation commander who reported to Kagame. This gave Kagame the opportunity to become the army commander.

While Late Adam Waswa was driving back from Mbuya it was reported that their car was involved in an accident and Adam Waswa died on the sport however his body guard known as Kalimba nicknamed Kalema who was later killed on his arrival in Rwanda. Reported to the colleagues, that his boss Adam Waswa had not died on scene but was strangled by Dan Gapfizi, while him and Dr Karemera pretending to offer first aid check after the accident, the young soldier explained that they were immediately pulled a side pretending to offer help to their boss.

Lt Col Adam had travelled with two body guards and the second his whereabouts are not known till to day even though before his disappearance, he was regularly seen crying repeatedly but unable to explain the reason why. Lt Col Adam Waswa the young charismatic senior officer was gone as well in a way that was not explained, like his predecessor.

Brig Gen Dan Gapfizi is the man who was a driver and later (MTO) military transport officer to become the head of a division, he was used by Paul Kagame to eliminate many commanders and so the likelihood of having been killed in the same way is high. It may take long to be verified but one way or another we will find out, and if it was a real accident then afande Rest in Peace whichever way we will remember you in one way or another, my condolescence goes to his family and the Rwanda Defense Forces who are experiencing what the families of late Adam Waswa and Charles Ngonga had to keep up with.

Brig Gen Dan Gapfizi who was rarely seen in public also had served the country in many different positions and among them were 7th battalion, 101 battalion, 301 Brigade, 204 Brigade, 2nd Division, 1rst Division. Dan Gapfizi however was demoted together with Kiiza to the rank of 2$^{nd}$ lieutenant even though they were seniors to many commanders, Dan Gapfizi who was so hungry to get rich all his life had developed the habits of stealing from the civilian population wherever the RPA forces captured which resulted in his demotion together with Kiiza but was later Promoted to Major after kneeling down a number of times in front of Paul Kagame begging for forgiveness.

Unfortunately, Kiiza was left to die as 2lt even though they had committed the same crime; simply because he did not accept to beg for forgiveness, he died after the war and died of poisonous injection from Kanombe military hospital. Dan Gapfizi is the same man who was used by Kagame to eliminate Colonel Charles Ngoga. He was assassinated because he competed with the commercial milk market of Major General Paul Kagame. More than six times, the milk of Colonel Charles Ngoga's cows was poured right in the middle of the road by President Kagame's body guards. Col Ngoga asked whether the strong man of Kigali Paul Kagame really believed he had fought for Rwanda's freedom alone. These sour words constitute, from now on, an imminent danger, more so as he was shown to have plotted with those who were preparing a coup. Finally, he was killed with a violent poison poured into his drink by Colonel Dan Gapfizi.

Brig Gen Dan Gapfizi, like many of Kagame's butchers, participated in a number of a necessary killings, which resulted in putting him at risk because after all the secrets he has been holding and having retired to settle in inkeragutabara or reserve force was now being seen as a threat especially now that the country is developing enemies on a daily basis, inside the reserve force and outside the country. The whole nation needs a good explanation of how this man died, who should have been spared to face justice at some point.

# 3 Chap III: Kagame simply a dictator

## 3.1 Similarities between former president Idi Amini and Kagame

I wish to point out a few issues that make President Paul Kagame a replica of Idi Amin of this millennium. When I was growing up as a young man in Uganda, I was told many stories about the greatest dictator President General Idi Amin Dada until his fall in 1979 by Tanzanian forces. I was too young to experience his atrocities but my family like other citizens surely had live under his terror for numerous years.

A few years after his collapse in the early 1980's, I remember the kind of fear my Uncle who had served in Amin's forces lived with all the time due to the atrocities of the guy he served. Idi Amin was named "Kijambia", Luganda language meaning "Mr. Machete" due to his brutality and extermination of Ugandan elite, the Press and any potential critic. Un-like me and my age at that time, it is evident that President Paul Kagame who was a teenager, in high school during Amin's regime might have envied Idi Amin's rule of tyranny in order to oppress whoever he deems a critic. That leaves me wonder if history really repeats itself'.

*Here I wish to point out a few issues that make President Paul Kagame a replica of Idi Amin of this millennium:*

Idi Amin encouraged his cabinet and the Ugandan population to "Love their Country", love their leaders, whereas this a noble deed, the actual meaning from a dictator's point of view is to be loyal to the main man himself. We continuously hear Kagame talking about "Kwihesha Agaciro,

Gukunda igihugu".

Conflicting with the Western world mostly when they point a finger on their deeds, here it is worth mentioning that once he had a misunderstanding with his colonial master; Amin evicted the entire Asian community from Uganda. We have seen in the past Kagame expelling different ambassadors of western countries for simple un-diplomatic issues.

Amin talked about empowering women in his cabinet and other managerial posts, although he only managed to appoint Princess Bagaya of Tooro. We see Kagame appointing women to every known position that he creates. I am not against gender equality but this actual act is done by a dictator just to show off to the world and most of all to have a much lesser opposing voice against him.

For the dual, it is on record that Idi Amin invaded Congo and stole plentiful amounts of minerals, which he kept to himself. Kagame has continued to do the same with the guise of different factions in the Kivu province of Eastern Congo.

Idi Amin invaded neighbouring Tanzania, Kagame invaded Congo although one lost the battle and the other dictator won.

Self-pity; When one watches Amin's documentary of his real interviews, while given the chance to talk about his early life, Amin spends vast amount of time talking the hardship he passed through as a child. He talks about the journeys he used to walk to go for his 2 years primary education, the way he was taken "by force" to join the Kings Rifle Army and so on. In numerous speeches given by Kagame since the time he became the President, he seems to lag on the fact and time he spent as a refugee in Uganda, he however forgets 90 percent of Rwandans have experienced refuge life either outside their country or as internally displaced people since the de-militarised zone of 1992 between the RPA and FAR.

Depression; It is reported that at some point Amin suffered enormous mental depression, paranoia and anxiety. It is the same phases that Kagame is experiencing, he loses touch of reality, starts paying un-solicited visits to the districts measuring how much support and respects he still commands and lack of trust to even his inner circle.

Idi Amin killed doctors, ministers, religious leaders, professors, rich businesspersons, opposition candidates and intellectuals. Kagame has done the same but worse more he also exterminates their family members unlike Amin.

Gen Idi Amin ordered the Manager of the National Bank to print out money and make the capital city of Uganda Kampala look like Mecca. He ordered Gen Maliyamungu his then army commander to invade Congo and bring as much minerals as possible in order to get money and build roads and nice houses, hotels, hospitals, army barracks and bought jet fighters in preparation for the alleged enemy. He ended up falling out with Gen Maliyamungu and actually planned for his life, but was tipped-off by his junior subordinates and survived the plot. Kagame like Gen Amin did invade the Congo looted the minerals; build only the capital Kigali a few roads although no hospital, he bought fighter jets and heavy weaponry in preparation for the alleged enemies like Amin. Kagame not only used his loot but also used donor money he acquired as sympathy for the Tutsi genocide to buy the fighter jets and his personal jets. He also has attempted the life of his Army commander like Amin.

General Amin started killing his comrades by shooting them using his State

Research, but ended up hacking the rest with machetes in damping them in places like Mabira Forest, river Nile and another hidden place. Kagame has done more or worse the same. He started assassinating the likes of Lt Col. Wilson Rutayisire, Alex Ruzindana, Col Rizinde and the like with guns and ended up hacking individuals like Kagwa Rwisereka with machetes.

When Idi Amin forcefully took power from President Obote, he was a Colonel, in less than eight years; Amin had promoted himself to the highest rank in the military doctrine. He was obsessed with titles including being the king of Scotland, and acquired an honorary doctorate from South Korea. It is just a matter of the era between the two dictators but we see a trend of similar incidents. Kagame would spare no stone unturned to search for medals and awards like Idi Amin. He has travelled across the globe to be awarded the smallest award possible. He has recently been awarded an honorary doctorate thanks to Turkey.

Suppresses freedom of speech and raising one's media house; Idi Amin is well known for this, he opened up his own media house including a TV and radio stations that he hoped would feed Ugandans with his own propaganda. Kagame is another guy who is on loggerheads with the media be it local or international. Like his prophet Idi Amin, he has opened up his own media house but also a chain of his own online newsletters or blogs thanks to the new millennium.

In recent months, Kagame has advised his henchman Jack Nziza to start up an online newspaper to suppress his much-feared "gang of four" as he termed them (Kayumba, Karegeya, Gahima and Rudasingwa). It is important to mention that as a person who spent most of my youth with Kagame as his body guard and driver, have noticed a wide change of behaviour since he lost these four individuals. I all along knew Kagame's slyness and callousness just after a few incidents with him, which involved loss of our comrades while on duty to protect his life. On reading one General Jack Nziza and Kagame's new online website (http://www.theexposer.net), I had to recall the same sort of words Kagame used on any individual he did not feel comfortable with. This so-called exposer or voice of Kagame is so callous that leaves you wonder if we Rwandans really deserve to be ruled by such a wild man. This all reminds me of General Idi Amin Dada, the dictator of our lives and for sure "History could be repeating itself".

## 3.2 President Kagame told citizens of Rwanda to tolerate and remain silent

The Rwandan authoritarian regime run by President Kagame has forced the citizens of Rwanda into tolerating and remaining silent about any harassment instigated by either Kagame himself or his security operatives. The population has been reduced to strict "big-brother-like" security surveillance where it is reported that one out of six members of society is reporting on others. A few individuals, who dared to say anything contrary to the government has been either incarcerated, savagely murdered or fled the country in fear for their lives.

The government has passed a bill that allows the secret security operatives to aggressively monitor people's telephones. The internet is heavily censured where websites and controversial blogs are restricted and hacked on a daily basis. Individuals who dare question the government activities get slaughtered like lambs. Individuals are harshly taxed on their limited income. Civil servants, government employees and business owners of all sizes are forced to give away a big chunk of their monthly earnings to the government. Kagame has forced the whole country to pay tax for his ruling RPF, Armed forces tax and Security tax.

These harsh taxes have been helped by the cutting of western donor aid due to Kagame's continued destabilisation of the Congo.

President Kagame is determined to rule the country with an iron-fist disregarding anybody's view as long as he stays in power. He talks about his buildings and a clean Kigali city but many Rwandans do not benefit from a clean city at all, maintaining hygiene is a human nature which should not be part of a manifesto for a president.

President Kagame has been attacking at the western leaders and activists just because he was afraid of his poor human rights record. It's so amazing that Mr President Kagame has never had a chance to learn from his former boss His excellence Yoweri Kaguta Museveni of Uganda.

When the National Resistance Army liberated Uganda in 1986 the first thing Museveni did was to give necessary support to the orphans and widows of his fallen comrades. It is in this manner that I got a chance to access formal education. "God bless you President Museveni."

It was not only me but many more orphans received free educations, implemented by Museveni in Uganda. The next thing Museveni did was to allow King Ronald Muwenda Mutebi to return from exile where he had been incarcerated for many years by preceding regimes. This was an important move fulfilling his promise. Museveni guaranteed to the Baganda that he would repatriate their king and he did it.

Museveni further promised the Rwandan refugees that fought alongside him that he would help them return to their motherland, and he did. President Museveni implemented the pension system to support the orphans of fallen comrades as well as widows; this all has become a challenge to President Kagame who has proven to be a very dangerous man to the entire region.

Kagame has failed to repatriate the beloved King Kigeli v Ndahindurwa of Rwanda, who was exiled from his kingdom by the colonial masters while he tried to fight for his people's independence.

HRH Kigeli has since maintained good contact with his people, and has supported refugees around the globe. He has in the past helped refugees including then young Kagame and his family when he was still a boy on the streets of Kampala.

One of the founding objectives of the RPF the present Rwandan ruling party was to abolish all refugees and causes of unrest that dominate our society even today.

Although many of the 1960's Tutsi refugees managed to repatriate after the RPF victory, our beloved king was never given a chance of return.

President Kagame destroyed all the main plans and has instead become a self-centered dictator with no morals. He has destroyed the idea of having political parties contrarily to Uganda where Gen Mugisha Muntu the former Army Commander presently leads the opposition party FDC arguing his point against the NRM the ruling party.

Freedom of speech has become paramount in Uganda where media and other organs can speak freely for those who cannot speak for themselves. When the RNC (Rwanda National Congress) was born couple of years ago no one thought that it would have such an impact on the current government, but it's evident that Kagame's plans have slightly changed and his powers have since been shaken. This has led to more people being jailed and many more have fled the country. The western world that had been Kagame's patron for a long time has since lost confidence in him.

During the last few weeks Kagame has been seen getting closer to the citizens of Rwanda by intensifying his community visits. This could be seen as a positive gesture but on the other hand he has been heard lobbying for a third term while on these visits. It has been noticed that Kagame has in the last few weeks hinted on planning to amend the constitution and have no presidential term limits to levy way for him to rule indefinitely.

This leaves some of us wonder how this ruthless dictator will be stopped from his endless ruthless deeds. Are any of the opposition groups ready to step into a role of transitional government with a solid plan in place to avoid any further bloodshed that seems to cyclically occur when a leader in Rwanda begins to slide into the dustbin of history? If there is such a group they must be forthright with their plan for Rwanda and aggressive in presenting it to Rwandan citizens around the world. Many of the residents of Rwanda have known no other leader other than President Kagame and with the clear history of violence following leadership change these groups must have such a peaceful plan in place that is realistic and non-violent to the people of Rwanda.

## 3.3 According to Paul Kagame all Hutus are convicts of genocide

My Good friend asked me why I was listening to President Kagame when he was addressing over 800 Rwandan youth at the closing of the Youth Connect Dialogue which took place on 30/06/13 at the Serena Kigali Hotel under the theme: (WHAT IS THE THEME?)

For some reason, most people believe that I should not be listening to Paul Kagame's speeches however I love them. It is so excellent for me to listen to these speeches because they give me an opportunity to visit the interior of Kagame's head as well as highlighting a proper picture of what is next in President Kagame's poor plans. Like one philosopher said, the man of knowledge must be able not only to love his enemies but also to hate his friends. Friends waste our time but enemies inform us their weaknesses without realising.

In this address to the youth, President Kagame expressed his anger to the young generation, even sounding breathless at some point during his speech. The President started his speech in a calm manner but went on to a stage where he could not control his words. What surprised me was when he spoke of genocide and even stated that genocide was committed by all Hutus! I was astonished! Yes, we all know that there was genocide in Rwanda but how could one million people be slaughtered by seven million people? Because, I presume, there was around that figure in 1994.

Logically, looking into President Kagame's comments, I really do not think that this man understands pain, trauma or the divisions he is causing in our society, inside the country and outside. However, the president did not remember that after genocide he was the one who was giving donations to the Hutu families who actually saved or hid some survivors in their houses, some Hutu families were even slaughtered because of hiding the Tutsis.

Then the president went on to threaten his neighbours. He sounded as if the message was meant for Tanzania's Kikwete and Obama as he mentioned that he would not speak to FDLR instead he will fight, to even those who speaks on their behalf." I will wait and hit them in the right time,

time will tell" he said. At the same time, he was telling the young generation that the older generation of Rwandans committed crimes of which the young people have nothing to answer, but then the president was adamant that he will never speak to the FDLR which is actually made of young people who left the country as young as six to ten years of age.

At one point the president used racial language when he was explaining about the Europeans and their involvement in African matters; he said that the Europeans left Africa 900 years ago when they were still black before they acquired lighter skin though evolution. What a president's comment! It was not so much the science of the comment but the tone and spirit in which a statement like this was made. Can one imagine President Obama commenting on the same topic?

Going back to the involvement of the west in African affairs, Mr Kagame did not seem to remember that the western countries give aid to Africa, and an enormous amount to Rwanda specifically, to promote good governance and democracy, and so reviewing and following on how African countries are doing would be part of it and written in small prints on the paper work he always signs.

When President Kagame was explaining how genocide affected people including those who were saved by his forces he narrated a story of one survivor who was rescued by the then rebels of Rwanda Patriotic Forces. He narrated that the young man met him in Murambi and thanked him for the rescue when he was dumped in the middle of dead bodies by the enemy thinking that he was dead. President Kagame said that he asked the boy how he was managing to live, according to the president he meant psychological well-being but the man answered that he was alive because the president tells them to live.

Now what did this young man mean? The president narrated that the young man also told him that he was not happy that the killers of his family and the ones that attempted to kill him had been released from jail. Instead the president told him that he takes the blame for releasing genocide convicts. It appears that to Kagame a genocide offender is the one who is in any opposition group. The president then narrated that he saw a lot of people laying in dead bodies, and some of them he believed that were saved however others it was too late, he noted that he told Gen James Kabarebe to stop showing or informing him about those incidents because there was a hard job waiting for him ahead, and that he was trying to avoid making irrational decisions based on what was happening at that time. This message from him means that he had ambitions of becoming a president from day one of creating this rebellion and that is why he eliminated most of our commanders, and mistreated our beloved President Pasteur Bizimungu.

Kagame is experiencing political isolation from the west, as evidenced by President Obama embarking on a tour of a few African countries without any stops in Rwanda, Uganda or DRC. This move sends a message that President Obama is looking for a new leader in the Central African region and further it states that Museveni of Uganda is not key, Kabila in DRC has too much to deal with while showing little to no leadership and that finally President Kagame is losing his hold and grip of being a darling of the West. Kagame has taken a severe blow to his image over the last year with the continued publications of the United Nations Group of Experts reports detailing Rwandan's continued involvement in destabilization of Eastern DR Congo which resulted in large amounts of aid cuts to Rwanda.

President Kagame is now motivating the youth to stick with him when hard times come, this is one of the tactics used by the former Libyan leader which is also written in the Green Book which is a short book setting out the political philosophy of the former Libyan leader, A Muammar Gaddafi. The book was first published in 1975.

President Kagame used to read this book all the time until he finished it in 1999. He called on the youth of Rwanda to fulfil their responsibilities with diligence and commitment in order to make a difference in their lives and their country because they are the strength and the future of Rwanda. He said that We must think carefully about what we invest in our youth because a seed that is not well nurtured will not blossom. "You must look beyond your individual interest because you are not just individuals, you are the nation. You must look beyond education and ensure that each of you uses your knowledge to build, not destroy your nation. Genocide was not committed by only the uneducated. The educated also used their knowledge to kill"

Advising the youth not to hold anything back in their pursuit of a better future for themselves and the nation, President Kagame pointed out that the young people should not have to carry the baggage of their elders and therefore have the opportunity to depart from the past and shape a new and better future: "you stand up against evil as some of you did today, do not do it halfway but with your all. Demand respect for your right to be who you choose to be, stand firm and proud of whom you are. Do not waste any opportunity; we need each and every one of you".

## 3.4 Paul Kagame, Edouard Bamporiki encouraging Hutus to apologise, even those who never committed a crime

Edouard Bamporiki, actual member of Parliament, has been in the news repeatedly since he introduced the idea of encouraging all Hutu to apologise even for those who never committed a crime during the 1994 genocide, or those who had not even been born in 1994. He took an initiative to apologise for the crimes he never committed even though he was only 10 years old during genocide. Immediately after that, his idea was supported by His Excellency Paul Kagame and Prime Minister Pierre Habumuremyi who also apologised in the same way as Edouard Bamporiki who was later heard on news being endorsed as one of the next coming candidates of the ruling party RPF in Parliament.

For God sake, what is going on with our politics! This child was never an interahamwe and also never served the army neither ex-FAR or RPA. If our current government is going to support the idea of apologising for the crimes they never committed what about the reconciliation we have been working on for the last 20 years? What about the stigma experienced by those born after the war? How about Kagame and his soldiers who have butchered refugees in DRC for almost 20 years? Will they apologise to the Hutus? Will Major Karangwa, Major Akili, Col Dan Munyuza, Gen Jack Nziza, Gen Fred Ibingira, Gen Patrick Nyamvumba, Brig Gen Kazora apologise? Will Brig Gen Gumisiriza and his team explain and apologise to the priests and bishops on what happened in Gakurazo? Will they speak to the mother of Nshaija the innocent little boy killed on that day? Will all other Tutsi come out to apologise on Kagame and his Tutsi military men behalf who committed crimes against the innocent Hutu victims who were massacred in Murambi, Byumba, Kagera, Nasho, Gahini, Nyabweshongweizi and Kibeho, plus DRC and etc.?

Like Bazivamo Christopher or Rucagu Boniface both Hutu, Bamporiki believes that the RPF government is doing well when it comes to truth and reconciliation, I believe that Bamporiki is a new Rucagu who will save or sink our nation when time comes, in the opposite way. Yes, Bamporiki may have experienced trauma like many children of that time of horror, however his idea of making the society stigmatised is totally wrong and should be opposed immediately by all of us.

This idea will divide the whole nation, it is corrupting and I urge all my fellow brothers and sisters to think more before acting, like the Ibuka boss said those who committed crimes are welcome to apologise to those affected by what they did and not to be encouraged but when they feel that it is time to ask for forgiveness.

This idea is meant to benefit Paul Kagame and the ruling party who are aiming to stigmatise the Hutu children. He wants to make them believe that they still survive because of Kagame's king's gesture, then make Tutsi believe that they have protection and Kagame have managed to make Hutu kneel down for them. This is not right at all. We should all have the same rights no matter what: the people who participated in genocide most of them died others were released by Kagame from prisons as a way of promoting himself prior to elections. The rest are still serving in prisons and participating in hard labour all over the country, those still on the run are hunted.

Bamporiki like many young men and women from the Hutu tribe have been recruited by the first lady Janet Kagame, she is aiming to capture as many supporters as possible, the project which was discussed between the President Paul Kagame and Gen Jack Nziza is believed to increase the RPF support especially when the time comes, if they have to make a transition between Kagame and his wife. This project is dangerous for the whole nation because it will not benefit the Rwandan citizens instead the individuals. I believe that Bamporiki may have experienced trauma due to his age at the time of genocide and what he went through. He received no support to help him with the trauma when he desperately needed it, and instead turned to poems. When he was accepted by the Tutsi government he had to do everything to impress them.

### *Edouard Bamporiki personal story during the 1994 Genocide against the Tutsi?*

Edouard Bamporiki –I got to know that I was m Hutu when I was nine years old. It was a kind of homework from our teacher who told us to ask our parents about our ethnicity. When I got home, I asked my mother, she said I was Hutu, at that time, my father had already passed on. When I got back to school because we were all required to loudly give our answers, we realised we only had six Tutsi children in my class, we remained friends until the Genocide.

During the Genocide, we were in holidays and I had been admitted to Kibogora Hospital (in then Cyangugu Prefecture) and all of a sudden, I heard people being killed. When I asked my mother, she said Hutus were killing Tutsis.

I was too naive at the time that I remember stepping out and seeing the body of my teacher who had been killed, then ran and told my mother that they were not only killing Tutsis but they were also killing teachers because I didn't know teachers belonged to any ethnic group.

When I went back to school, my Tutsi classmates had been killed and this is when I wrote my first poem, had you not killed them, we would be laughing together. After this, I kept writing, until in 2006, when I stood up to tell my story.

To be honest, before 2006, I did not believe a Hutu could stand up during the Genocide commemoration and give testimony and I was happy when my message was accepted, and I was comforted, which gave me courage to go on. Fellow youth started coming, saying the trust I was promoting across the ethnic divide was crucial.

My argument was, for a young Hutu to step out of the shadow of what was done by our parents, we needed to openly discuss these things. To Make things worse Bamporiki recalls that his teacher was also murdered because of being Tutsi, but then he explains that his family told him that teachers were also being killed, and then Bamporiki in his story believed that Teachers had no tribe: At the same time Bamporiki stated that his teacher used to ask them whether they were Hutu or Tutsi as home work. My God What is going on in our society?

After a traumatic experience, it's normal to feel frightened, sad, anxious, and disconnected. But if these feelings do not fade and you feel stuck with a constant sense of danger and painful memories, you may be suffering from post-traumatic stress disorder. It can seem like you'll never get over what happened or feel normal again. But by seeking treatment, reaching out for support, and developing new coping skills, you can overcome PTSD and move on with your life.

Post-traumatic stress disorder can develop following a traumatic event that threatens your safety or makes you feel helpless. Most people associate PTSD with battle-scarred soldiers and military combat is the most common cause in me, but any overwhelming life experience can trigger PTSD, especially if the event feels unpredictable and uncontrollable.

Post-traumatic stress disorder can affect those who personally experience the catastrophe, those who witness it, and those who pick up the pieces afterwards, including emergency workers and law enforcement officers. It can even occur in the friends or family members of those who went through the actual trauma. PTSD develops differently from person to person. While the symptoms of PTSD most commonly develop in the hours or days following the traumatic event, it can sometimes take weeks, months, or even years before they appear.

The traumatic events that lead to post-traumatic stress disorder are usually so overwhelming and frightening that they would upset anyone. Almost everyone experiences at least some of the symptoms of PTSD. When your sense of safety and trust are shattered, it is normal to feel crazy, disconnected, or numb. It is very common to have bad dreams, feel fearful, and find it difficult to stop thinking about what happened. These are normal reactions to abnormal events.

For most people, however, these symptoms are short-lived. They may last for several days or even weeks, but they gradually lift. But if you have post-traumatic stress disorder, the symptoms do not decrease. You don't feel a little better each day. In fact, you may start to feel worse.

Unfortunately, this patient experience was mishandled, neglected and instead is being used as a political tool, by people like President Paul Kagame who is himself a sadist and requires psychological help, and so this is evident that divisions in Rwanda are being caused by the people who require intervention.

## 3.5 The genesis of the grenade attacks on our land

Kagame's history of sabotage and creating conflict to resolve it in the end and call himself a hero. His excellence Paul Kagame worked as a senior Intelligence Officer in the Uganda's NRA prior to the 1990 invasion of Rwanda.

It is in this force that he devised a rather disturbing system of causing unreasonable conflicts not only among his fellow officers and the entire Army but the whole country and then resolve the same conflicts in order to achieve trust to his superior commanders.

After the liberation of Uganda by the NRA the establishing of the new government in 1986, Kagame did not feel at peace with the population that they had fought against or else any opposition parties to the new NRM.

Being a trusted Director of Military Intelligence (DMI) "BASIMA HOUSE", Major Paul Kagame tortured numerous innocent citizens mostly from the rich Buganda Tribe and anyone who he considered an enemy of the Movement, hence acquiring his Notorious Nick name Pilate (Pilato) the Biblical Roman ruler of Judea who supervised the killing of Jesus Christ.

Maj. Kagame in his Basima house office formed a non-existing rebel group and called it a silly name (FOBA) Force Obote Back Again. The name itself was very silly, reason being that not any sober mind rebel group could say that it was forcing the ousted president back again.

Obote on the other side is said to have been a much-learnt person who could not have come up with such a pre-emptive name FOBA. It is this FOBA that Kagame used to suppress most of the individuals that he was suspicious of. He used the guise of this group to kill not only the supporters of the top political parties such as UPC and DP but also people that had fought Obote on different fronts such as FEDEMU and UFM.

After forming FOBA he ordered the arrests of these innocent individuals, took them to Basiima house just behind Lubiri Barracks where they were tortured and killed. They were all questioned about FOBA activities which they never knew about while he himself knew exactly what he was doing. Maj. Kagame was a stubborn character in the NRA, he chose who to report his activities to and most of the time he disregarded all his senior commanders and went straight to President Museveni. "No wonder he got him out America and forced him onto us RPA struggle".

By 1993 when our the RPF political wing was working tirelessly towards the Arusha peace agreement that meant stopping all military activities and get our cause heard without any more bloodshed, Commander Paul Kagame was busy creating a team of clandestine commandos to destabilise Kigali.

The aim of these well-trained commandos was to back up the 600 troops we had sent to the capital to look after our dignitaries in CND, and sabotage the Rwandan government seemed reluctant for the planned peace agreement. It is hence important to mention that Kagame similar to the then ruling party hardliners MRND were not prepared for the Arusha Peace Accord.

These commandos guised as "Technicians" to have a UN pass to Kigali were briefed by Kagame to inflict as much terror to Habyarimana's government as they could. Their primary task was to kill different political figures of mostly parties opposed to the current government. It worth mentioning again that these parties were fighting the same cause Kagame was supposedly fighting

High profile people like Lando Ndasingwa and others were killed by our own Commandos or technicians just because he was a Tutsi and Kagame wanted to show that Habyarimana had killed him instead. Sometimes I just scratch my head when I see Louise Mushikiwabo (Minister of Foreign Affairs) a sister to Lando Ndasingwa (allegedly killed by RPF Army beside being a Tutsi) defending the President Paul Kagame's atrocities, without knowing even why she was appointed to that position.

After taking over the government President Paul Kagame briefed Major Silas Udahemuka the Intelligence Officer of his Presidential Protection Unit to form a clandestine surveillance regiment which was trained by the Korean Commandos to patrol the city of Kigali and other areas of Rwanda. These surveillance commandos attacked and interrupted the meeting of Liberal Party (PL) before Joseph Sebarenzi Kabuye was forced out of the country.

This was followed by surveillance continuing to harass politicians to the extent of throwing stones to the ex-president Pasteur Bizimungu in 2001 in a Kicukiro garage which belonged to a Ugandan man Kamagara. It was the same commandos who attacked Asier Kabera and killed him. This specific group was made of Lt Balinda Joseph who holds the rank of Major at the moment, Lt Mupenzi, S/Sgt Melchior Hakizimana whom we called Ndadaye.

These commandos continued to operate in the Kigali city dressed in civilian clothes armed with hand guns and carrying their walkie-talkies. These operations still go on with the hand of many different security agencies, which are all under NSS only that surveillance is under the Republican guard unit which seems to be commanded by his excellence Paul Kagame himself.

The police force under the leadership of Emmanuel Gasana (Rurayi) an illiterate former Division Intelligence officer is rather useless and cannot stop any operation carried out by the Kagame's Presidential Protection Unit (PPU) special commandos.

They operate on different mandate and they are un-touchable, share no information with any intelligence organ apart from reporting to the sole man who made then Kagame Commander in Chief.

## *Analysis on the Grenade attacks in Rwanda*

Rwanda as a country formed a police force with very strong capabilities though not given the right chance to utilise these potentials. The force is mad of former RPA officers and men most of whom are highly motivated and disciplined.

This Police force has indicated its capacities when it supported, trained and helped much vulnerable countries such as Haiti, Liberia and Sudan mostly the Darfur region and the present-day South Sudan.

I am therefore left to wonder how such a force with this kind of might fails to protect its own citizens from hand grenade attacks in the middle of the capital city. We have seen grenade attacks for quite a number of times, with a number of causalities and some death.

The police reaction to this has always been either: "we arrested two, four or none. But the investigations are ongoing".

In the beginning, we were informed by the government and police spokes persons that these grenades were being thrown by the FDLR, later the blame was shifted to Victoire Ingabire, and later Gen Kayumba Nyamwasa and Col Patrick Karegeya.

It seems at the moment that they have no one to point the finger at, surprisingly the government has no concrete plans to end these grenade attacks and no clear information of what is behind them.

There is no information to advise the citizens on how to maintain their own safety. It has been reported that some of the suspects of these attacks have been sentenced to life imprisonment and others to many years in jail.

Normally the law suggests that before sentencing any suspect the judges require concrete incriminating evidences. This is the job of the prosecution and police to produce. If the police ever managed to obtain these evidences rather than forces or corroded testimonies, they should know exactly where these attackers come from and their motives.

The rest of us the public have not had any chance of knowing exactly who these so-called criminals or terrorist are and which prisons they have been locked at which it is in itself fishy.

Some years ago, staged criminal like these used to be sentenced to life imprisonment only to be seen the next day on Kigali streets. WHAT A PITTY!!

Given the history of President Kagame's creation and resolution of different ill conflicts, it could be fair that the Rwandan citizens be given actual explanations as to who is responsible to the killings and maiming our children, mothers and the entire population indiscriminately in markets and another public place where we ought to enjoy freely.

## 3.6  Rape: The 'friendly fire' of the Rwanda Civil war in 1994

They were supposed to be treated fairly, as our sisters, our friends our nurses. They devoted their adolescence to running alongside us in wartime. These brave women picked up the wounded soldiers, held weapons and fought alongside many strong young men. The war waged an emotional toll on these women. They were shot at and many died, others were injured, and lost limbs. Many soldiers believed that these sisters were nurses even though they were not all trained to be nurses.

They took responsibility for the wounded and those who became ill. It was as if their caring hearts had been inherited from their mothers. Compassion is showing kindness for others who are in need, and that is what our sisters did during the 1990-1994 war in Rwanda.

These brave women, who devoted their lives to helping countless men on the field and trying to save as many lives as possible, found themselves tormented and raped at night by the top commanders. These young women, many as young as 14 years old, were sexually tormented by those they were serving. They were exploited by the top commanders and threatened with execution if they spoke about their treatment.

Most surprisingly, the then army commander, Major Paul Kagame, would explain to the forces that all soldiers are the same and they should respect these women. However, he would be the same man to order a certain woman to be brought to him spend over 8 hours in his room, and no one would be allowed to access where they were. The briefing to the bodyguards would be that if he needs anything he would call.

Major Kagame enjoyed his time exploiting these young girls mainly the carders. I remember a time when he became so angry after finding out that one of the women with whom he was spending nights with had also spent a night with General Karenzi Karake, this resulted in falling out with Karenzi

Karake for some time.

The nurses and young female combatants were being passed around the commanders, Gen Kabarebe James would jump whenever there was a young female recruit he enjoyed using them for sex. The majority of these women remain unemployed and were excluded from service because most of their rapists are in high-ranking positions in the army, government and ministries. They were sidelined because none of the officials wants to revisit their horrific sexual crimes.

These female combatants suffered betrayal from the commanders they trusted. The abuse of our sisters began when we lost the true commanders of our forces at the hands of the enemy and Major Kagame who was getting rid of those who would not have allowed him to rule the nation with his iron fist. His right-hand men enjoyed abusing these young girls at the time, by even swapping them around, one would spend a night in Mulindi and get sent to Mukarage. Then next night they would be ordered to sleep with another Commander.

Surprisingly, they would even call each other and communicate in Swahili by saying" Nime kusukumia ya Msada," meaning that he has sent him a heavy weapon. Most of the girls would be transported around by young soldiers to sleep with the commanders for months and months. Some of the commanders at the helm of the RDF currently, who are saluted for being good peace keepers, spent most of our war time as young soldiers who became familiar and close to the top commanders for being their Pimps. Gen James Kabarebe who enjoyed exploiting women was rewarded the ministry of defense. Once a pimp and a child soldier now a gentleman.

One of the victims of RPA/RPF women stated that, "women were there as numbers", recalling the trauma of rape which resulted in their career failure.

RPF/RPA leaders such as, Gen James Kabarebe, Gen Rutatina, are remembered by their victims as the worst rapists the young girls experienced. They recall while being sexually tormented many would be worrying about the patients back in the barracks. One of the victims still blames herself because she was taken to spend the night with Gen Rutatina by his soldiers, recalling that at the time Gen Rutatina was the head of Rubaya sickbay, but when she came back two of the casualties had died. She still blames herself that if she had stayed then may be those men would be alive.

When the young female combatants complained to Major Kagame, he said that they should stop sleeping around and if any commander forces them into sex, they should report to him. However, he also said that if they do not stop to sleep around he would shoot them in their" anus." These girls questioned how they would reach him when he actually was never there because he spent most of his time in Uganda, and most of the commanders he delegated to be doing the same.

At some point, Major Paul Kagame threatened one of the then RPA commissioners for conceiving a child. She had fallen in love with one of Kagame's bodyguards of which Kagame did not like, and so when it was reported that the commissioner was pregnant she was ordered to be returned back to Uganda. After the war, she was never seen again. This was her punishment because she became pregnant and resisted sleeping around with every Commander simply because she was in love with one man.

During the war of liberating Rwanda, we had many different sacrifices, those who died on frontline, which was expected because at war that is part of the job. There were also those who were murdered by Major Kagame's right hand men, due to his homicidal thoughts.

However, the crime of raping or exploiting our sisters was not part of our liberation strategy. We regret and sympathize with the victims of these dangerous human rights abuses, which caused trauma and infections of HIV to many of the victims. As young soldiers, we should have done more to protect these innocent girls. We should have stopped these sexual crimes. We should have planned for ways these brave women could have been safe from the monsters that tormented then in the night.

We will always remember and respect our sisters who faced nightly demons but in the morning returned to their duties of saving lives as if nothing had happened despite being wounded emotionally, physically, and psychologically. As for the cowardly men who are horrific rapists and still proudly serving under President Paul Kagame, we will not rest until they face the arm of the law.

## 3.7 Reasons why President Kagame will cling power forever

I wrote this article before the referendum to change the constitution in 2015.

President Paul Kagame has launched a process that he believes can finally end the debate on whether or not he will seek a third term. He has tasked three senior members of his Rwandan Patriotic Front (RPF) to come up with a transition formula.

President Kagame used the platform of the party annual National Executive Committee (NEC) on February 8 to task Tito Rutaremara, Joseph Karemera and Antoine Mugesera to come up with a formula that would deliver change, continuity and stability after 2017, when his constitutional term as president expires. Yet, one wonders why he has to channel all the way through his puppets, we Rwandans knows that his Excellency Paul Kagame will never leave power.

- In 1999 when President Paul Kagame realised that it was time for him to overthrow President Pasteur Bizimungu. He created a commission of enquiry team to investigate corruption on just one single person, Pasteur Bizimungu; this was to find out if his lorry had entered in the country without paying tax as it had been reported. The commission of enquiry was made up of Major Rose Kabuye, Tito Rutaremara and Joseph Karemera. One may wonder why Kagame always uses people who should be mature and intelligent enough to make sense but follows him when he is actually wrong. One should wonder why he has forgotten to bring Rose Kabuye to the team which should decide whether he continues as a presidential candidate in 2017 when she is the one who helped to oust Ex-President Bizimungu. President Kagame is surrounded by a number of hungry cowards who do not know what is next. His primary concern is to highlight any person who does not agree with any of his ideas and then have them killed or be ousted and that is why we still have refugees after all these decades when we are liberated. The RPF tries hard to avoid being victims of the truth; the heart of patriotism was buried by President Kagame just after seeing the lights of Kigali in 1994.

- In 1995 when most Rwandans who returned home were sleeping in swamps, mountains and other destitute places in the country, some of them even relying on United Nations plastic tents. The first thing Kagame thought of was to use every penny he had received from donors to build his house. This house was built in ex-president Habyarimana plot and the plan of the house was acquired from the construction company which built Col Muammar Gadhafi armoured house which was a copy to President Kagame's. Even though the State house was originally supposed to be in Kanombe like his predecessors but Mr Kagame refused to live in the state house because he already had built an armoured house before he even became a president. This house was built from 1996-2002 and Kagame moved in later. This armoured house was built before Kagame was even considered to run for the Presidential seat. So why built a presidential house in a private land when you are vice president and minister defense?

- President Kagame eliminated all his senior party members and those whom he believed could be potential candidates when time came for change. These eliminations were done inside the RPF political party as well as opposition parties. Without mentioning all but apart from Ex-President Pasteur Bizimungu, former chairman Col Alex Kanyarengwe, Major Furuma who is among the founders of RPF, the first secretary general of RPF Major Theogene Rudasingwa as well as Seth Sendasonga and others. He even attempted to kill his former army chief Gen Kayumba Nyamwasa. If Kagame was a president who would accept a transition he would not have committed such acts. He has imprisoned a number of opposition leaders and forced others into exile. If Kagame is confident of his record why keep all these innocent people in detention, exile and others in prison?

- President Kagame is worried about what the international community thinks of his record. This record is extensive and includes crimes committed against humanity during his continued killings inside and outside Rwanda, the killings in the DRC of the refugees as well as the Congolese citizens. We are talking about a president who ordered the killing of his predecessor in an act that took the lives of several French citizens as well as the President of Burundi. In an interview where he was questioned about his role in the downing of President Habyarimana plane he explained that he was at war and so anyone could have died and he was saved not to answer the death of a soldier who was against him.

- During the meeting with National Executive Committee (NEC) for the RPF on the 8th/02/13 President Kagame turned up with two hundred letters of which he claimed were from Rwandese citizens who wrote to him requesting that he should stand for the Presidential elections in 2017. He explained that most of these letters were thanking him and a number of them reported that they may leave the country if he steps down. One wonders why he did not bring the letters which advised him to leave power as I am sure they are some because we all write to him advising that he should leave immediately. He is an embarrassment to our nation and is still desperate to hold power. If President Kagame would accept a transition why bring these envelopes? To me he Â was sending a message to the RPF members not dare think of another potential candidate.

- President Kagame talks of RPF and Rwanda in general to have achieved a lot in the last few years, he actually tries to indicate that Rwanda was actually born after his election in 2003. He seems to forget that Rwanda was there before he was born. We have had the foundations of development since our great grandfathers with our beloved strong kingdom which was destroyed by the Belgians. Yes, I agree he has done his part but not just himself, because even those he has killed or ousted played a part in developing that nation. It is not just him, like Tito Rutaremara thinks, that without Kagame Rwanda would not function, Rwanda has many people who may actually drive Rwanda in the right direction without hate, discrimination, divisions or injustice, corruption or revenge.

I was not pleased with Tito Rutaremara words when he said that, those saying Kagame should go just because his term is finished are being lazy. We are responsible people we have to study everything. We must get a formula that shall give us maximum of change, continuity and stability. There is nothing to study because we know President Paul Kagame is another waste of space that we have to keep up with until he leaves power one way or another. The history of Rwanda is dominated by betraying our leaders when actually they drive their citizens or army to that extent. The history of betraying our leaders starts from Mbonyumutwa who was reburied by Kagame in an unknown place, Gregoire Kayibanda who was killed by Gen Habyarimana, who was killed by Gen Kagame plus former President Pasteur Bizimungu who was kept in prison for many years and now is held in his house not allowed to move. This list also includes the King Ndahindurwa Kigeli V, that we all wish would come back home one day. Kagame trusts his cadette officers who are like robots believes in shooting everybody who dares to question any move for RPF.

- The RPF died a long time ago when President Paul Kagame took over. He has spoiled every area of the party and RPF followers are all suffering from anxiety with the whole country in general. He planted hate and dishonesty in RPF executive committee and all with the motive to promote his poor ideas because he is genetically backward man who is vulnerable, and has made the whole nation vulnerable and anxious. So, this so called appointed group of three commissioned to come up with a formula of whether Kagame should stand or not in 2017 is a procedure but Kagame is not going anywhere because these guys Joseph Karemera, Tito Rutaremara, and Antoine Mugesera are all puppets who will always sing yes to him until the regime collapses

- Finally, President Kagame invested his money in RPF accounts; he mixed all his income under the names of RPF Companies. In order to divert the attention of the members of RPF who witnessed most of the transactions, he owns companies under the names of Rwandese Patriotic Front Such The movement investment arm, Crystal Ventures which controls assets worth more than $500m inside the country. The group owns a construction and road-building company, granite and tile factories, a furniture company, a chain of upmarket coffee shops, a real estate development and an agro-processing venture, Inyange. It also retains a stake in MTN, the leading mobile phone operator, Air Rwanda, with a fleet of top range air buses, and many more.

Professor Nshuti Manasseh, chairman of the board of Crystal Ventures, says half the RF1.5bn ($2.4m) cost of RPF campaigning in 2010 elections was met by donations from party members, the other half from company coffers. We came in when contributions fell short, he says. Nshuti Manasseh is an old boy of President Kagame at Old Kampala Secondary School, where they spent time together studying while still in exile in Uganda. Nshuti Mannaseh continued studying when Kagame dropped out and he still believes in him in terms of Business, he is still someone who Kagame believes can manage his business under the names of RPF.

Mannaseh recently gave an interview full of fallacies about the ownership and procedures of Crystal Ventures. General Kayumba Nyamwasa recently stated in reaction to this interview that It is only a fool who can believe that story. Manaseh talks about money saved from the war!! Where was he at that time and how does he know? He was not even in RPF. He is just 'parroting' outdated lies. I was the first board chairman of those companies, not even Kagame can dispute what I said about the formation and funding of those companies. Manaseh should enjoy the loot and keep quiet. Both Manasseh and Musoni transferred this money when they were Ministers of finance respectively. Big question, what do Ministers of finance have to do with transfer of RPF (Tristar) money? (Note: Tristar was "baptized" Crystal Venture!!).

So, for those who think that Kagame will leave power peacefully after 2017 shame on you! One only has to look as far as his recent and frequent trips around Rwanda where large numbers of citizens gather waving small flags and cheering for their President. Do these Rwandans walk around with these flags in hand? Do large numbers of people spontaneously gather without prior organization and mandates? No! These gatherings, which are very similar to his 2010 campaign stops, are organized and photographed for consumption by the international community in order to continue his façade that his people want him to run for President again when he is the one orchestrating the entire rouse.

## 3.8 2017 Kagame to become a Ceremonial President

The committee which was given the task of what the RPF called political home work to draw the master plan of extending the Kagame rule has come out with a plan of changing the current Rwandan Constitution to create a Post of Ceremonial President.

Paul Kagame former NRA intelligence officer then RPF/RPA general, then Vice president and minister of defense and chairman of RPF, then president of the republic of Rwanda will become a ceremonial president to keep power until 2037. By the time he leaves power he will be almost 90 years old.

Kagame's anxiety and desire coupled with fear of what will befall on him after 2017 has created the momentum of searching within the RPF establishment the ways of extending the rule of President Kagame.

One of the architectures of the Kagame Project is Prof. Manasseh Nshuti who argues that Rwanda's political panorama must be viewed from its unique contexts; present and past, however, if anyone could buy this argument in whole sale would instead argue that the Rwanda's past lost sight when its former leaders started thinking that they are the only leaders with vision. Indeed, in the same manner Prof. Manasseh his selling his ideas, our history tells us all, from the Monarchy, the Post Monarchy from Kayibanda who wanted to change the Constitution, later Juvenal Habyarimana who called himself the father of the nation (Umubyeyi).

Prof. Manasseh is basing his argument on Three Pillars namely, Economy, Leadership and Governance, Sustainability and Continuity. Although none is realistic in Rwanda today, Kagame and his admirers have used these demagogues to lobby for Kagame's life presidency. Let's break down each of the above pillars as are presented by Kagame's project spin doctors.

Rwanda received more aid and loans than any other country on the continent after genocide. After genocide, all the loans that it owed to the international money lenders like IM and World Bank were written off as gesture of solidarity and sympathy. Instead of using this money for developmental projects and poverty eradication, RPF and Kagame has used it for invading its neighboring Congo for economic and political reasons or spying and killing its political opponents within the country and abroad. Now Rwanda has gone back to the pre-genocide debit where it cannot even be allowed to borrow anymore.

Kagame and his Spin Doctors came with another plan of auctioning the country in what they now call Bond selling, where the nation is now under auction by private lenders. Does this really mean development? Not at all, all the wealth is now in the hands of the few notably, Kagame and his family, in-laws, and friends. Unfortunately, this is what Prof. Manasseh calls the economic miracle.

Leadership and Governance, if you ask any a person who knows Rwanda, will tell you that Rwanda is the North Korea of Africa, a police State, where no views other than those of RPF or those praising RPF would be tolerated. Kagame has gone another mile in the politics where even his former comrades, cadres, and founders of RPF have no say in the RPF political decisions. The year 2014, has seen most of the RPF senior and historical are either sidelined or incarcerated in the notorious prisons of

Kagame, the notable ones are the following:

Gen Frank Rusagara, who was one of the founders of RPF and who was one of the RPF designers, Col. Tom Byabagamba who was the Kagame's security top officer, Tharcisse Karugarama the former Justice Minister who advised the president to honor his pledges that he will respect the Rwandan Constitution.

He was dropped from the Cabinet and accused of being an obstacle for the Kagame extension project. Unlike in other countries, all the families of the above RPF officials are under constant and consistent surveillance from the Kagame spy masters.

Madam ODA GASINZIGWA the commissioner of RPF in September under the orders of Kagame accused her colleagues Lt Col Rose Kabuye, Mary Baine, Ambassador Joy Kanyange, Anne Gahongayire and Immy Camarade of tarnishing the RPF image and spreading harmful propaganda against the RPF with intention of creating disobedience of the population against the RPF regime.

All these ladies who are not only war heroines they have been also instrumental in designing the RPF and Kagame's rise to where he is now. Unfortunately, they have been sidelined, and Inyenyeri has reliable information that they cannot even go to a super market without a stringent of spies following them.

We have also learnt that Kagame has been crisscrossing the State of Israel to get some lectures on how a ceremonial post would work. According to the Constitution of Israel the President is largely a ceremonial political figure and the executive powers are vested in the Prime Minister The

President of Israel is elected for Seven year term which is un renewable .Unlike in Israel, the new Kagame project which Inyenyeri news has obtained will give him a ceremonial term of Ten years renewable once, this means that if Kagame is elected as the ceremonial ruler come 2017, he will have another Two terms and his rule will end in 2034.

Paradoxically the Prime Minister will be elected for six years term and renewable once, this post will be occupied by the Kagame likes and supporters as it is today, those who only praise the Kagame regime and RPF will be honored to serve with the new King of Rwanda in the uniform of the ceremonial post of President.

This is what Prof. Manasseh Nshuti and his likes call the Sustainability and stability and continuity after 2017. Unfortunately, the Kagame project will breed hesitation, resistance, chaos and more bloodshed in the Rwanda that has been characterized with tension and wars.

# 4 Chap IV: Kagame's Deceptions, betrayal and paranoia in the name of Power.

## 4.1 We paid our Dues

"A resolution to avoid an evil is seldom framed till the evil is so far advanced as to make avoidance impossible" Thomas Hardy (2015). President Paul Kagame's demoniac killing of his own colleagues and men who served him or those he served under has been going on for so long. I remember a couple of years ago the "Behind the Presidential Curtains" joined many others who had on previous occasions reported some of the historical bush killings which were ordered by Kagame. Lt Ruyenzi and Lt Ruzibiza (RIP) narrated Kagame's killings.

At some point these writers and witnesses were called names of being disorderly and many more insults. However, President Kagame did not stop there instead he continued killing innocent civilians and colleagues. Kagame was successful in many ways whenever it came to ordering the killings of especially civilians and civil servants. Let me not mention any names because nowadays, Kagame has come out publicly to explain his perceived 'rationale' for killing and ordering all his servants/subordinates to kill his opponents. I remember some time back President Kagame would try his best to hide the secrets of his killings and at times he sacrificed his men who he believed would open up to the normal people on the secrets of what they would have participated in. The same reason he wanted 'Gen.' Bosco Ntaganda to be killed by Col. Sultan Makenga.

Now President Kagame admits to have ordered some killings and that he will continue to kill anybody who opposes him. No wonder Kagame and his government welcomed the murder of Colonel Patrick Karegeya (RIP). Of course, like I stated there is no room in this article to mention all names of those he has killed as the list is endless. However, we also have to remember that there those being hunted around the globe, in reference to whom, Kagame continues to stress that 'it is a matter of time'. A friend of mine, who is a reliable source, told me that the day when Gen Kayumba Nyamwasa's Johannesburg home was attacked, President Kagame had arranged a party to celebrate that night had the callous mission been successful. Bear in mind this is celebrating the death of his elder son's, Ivan Cyomoro's, Godfather, but also a former colleague who served his country and Kagame for all those years.

Although President Kagame has always shown being brainless and ill-bred, *"uburere buke",* there are a few things he mastered in his life. Kagame believes that once someone is dead, then everything else about that person is all dead and dusted. Boy, the assassination of Colonel Patrick is proving him as he haunts him more in death than he had ever imagined. Also, Kagame started ordering killings in his early twenties. While working as intelligence officer he would order the killings of just suspects and there was no question because he was trusted by Museveni and Gen Rwigyema (RIP). Little did they know that they were nurturing and creating a serial killer.

If there is one thing that the whole world respects are the International Community and the United Nations but that does not apply to Kagame. With Kagame, he believes that he is above any organisation and that they are only there to promote the American interests. He thinks that as long as he maintains his relationship with America, he foolishly believes that there will be no harm for him enforcing his misguided ideas in anyway. President Kagame also heavily relies on the sensitive part of his country's past, the 1994 Genocide, to target anyone opposing him, including the Human right organisations, nongovernmental organisations (NGO's) and any opposition leader, activists or journalists inside his country or outside.

The stigma faced by the International Community of not doing much during Genocide has helped Kagame develop his way of governance, where he kills and cannot be stopped. President Kagame is short sighted when it comes to defining things, he believes that anyone who speaks out negatively about his government is a terrorist, of course none of them is a terrorist and never was terrorism in Rwanda other than the rule of terror by Kagame's regime. Instead there was genocide(s) and killings. President Kagame however 'stage manages' grenade attacks, and then instructs for terrorism charges to be drawn to his innocent and harmless critics. For us who know this game, called ikinamico in Kinyarwanda, better sometimes just laugh.

Having spent some time studying in Fort Leavenworth College Kansas (USA), Kagame came back trying to copy and paste the USA way of killing or executing terrorists. What President Kagame failed to do, is to differentiate terrorism and being in opposition or critical to government failings. In America criticism is a virtue rather than a vice, something that is contrary to what President Kagame's perception of those who criticise his government as being enemies of the state. Criticism of government action is a fundamental democratic value that whoever equates it to terrorism should be condemned to the archaic ages. By terrorising those who exercise their fundamental and constitutional right of expressing their views, whether critical or not, to the state, Kagame has turned into a terrorist himself.

As I write this article Kagame is Isolated with only Uganda and Kenya in the region as the only countries that he can turn to as friendly nations. Rwanda is indebted to the neck, with the ordinary citizens being conned into lending money to the government in the name of "lending government Rwandan Francs 100,000 for a little profit BNR project". The government has borrowed and borrowed through conventional means and the end up in selling bonds to ordinary poor citizens. Kigali is shining but the National bank is empty and heavily indebted. Thank God, the European Union has got something to offer soon. Since DRC became untouchable and Burundi running away from Kagame for their dear life to stand firm with Tanzania, Rwanda's plans to enlarge the marked was affected and so the investors have had to sit and watch first. The RPF flagship 2020 Vision, by Kagame's own submission during the recent so-called 'leaders retreat', has hit the dead end. This is a fact that vindicates some of us who warned of the consequences of the 'cow boyish mafia' adventures that were wasteful and dangerous like hunting around the Globe perceived enemies and sponsoring endless wars in DRC.

Recently President Kagame developed a new strategy of confiscating the citizenships of those who opposes him, he also advised his right-hand men to find a way of changing and applying the Law where necessary to stop anyone who has lived outside Rwanda to advocate for Rwandans. Kagame believes that the best way forward is to stop dual citizenships. However, he does not recall that even foreigners are allowed to advocate for anyone because Activism has no borders.

I remember Kagame's first days when he could not even speak in front of any audience. He lacked confidence during his first days speaking in public. Like Theogene Rudasingwa stated on a recent interview on Radio Itahuka, people like Theogene, Gen. Kayumba Nyamwasa, Patrick Mazimpaka,

Pasteur Bizimungu, Colonel Patrick Karegeya (RIP) and others used to coach him what and how to address audiences. As time went on he developed the coping mechanism of relying on blaming, scapegoating and reassuring in his words. In other words, Kagame believes that he is the only one who has worked hard for Rwanda. Kagame is determined to kill anyone who do not follow his ideologies, something that has caused anxiety especially to those who know him better.

I remember in one of my articles titled "Rwanda is Ruled by a Mad Man", a lot of people stood up and said that I probably had some personal issues with Paul Kagame. I responded by saying that was not possible because he was someone up there and I was so young and in lower ranks, and so would not have had a personal matter with him. However, I had managed to work out that the man required psychological help. Now there are the same people contacting me, surprised on how quick I managed to understand the man.

Lt Ruzibiza (RIP) and Lt Ruyenzi, I salute you for standing up at the right time to expose the monster. Also, others not mentioned for security reasons and those I never had a chance to meet or know about, your activism will always be remembered. This war of seeking change will continue until the last man. The late American President J.F. Kennedy famously stated, "Let us never negotiate out of fear. But let us never fear to negotiate.". Afande Major Bayingana (RIP) said that Major Kagame was physically unfit and mentally sick to lead the force. We now see that he was right. Comrades we have paid our dues but we still have a journey to finish I love you all.

## 4.2 Kagame self-harming by incarcerating his brothers and comrades

The RPF is falling apart divided and hijacked by those who will continue to clap hands and let it go like MRND. More RPF officials are being interrogated and watched, surveyed and recorded when speaking on telephone. Rwanda has become a police state and jail for many who are unable to even travel abroad, anxiety has become a chronic illness to those who served or still serving the RPF Government. Gen Tom Byabagamba appointed to head Kami the notorious prison, where Kagame believes that he will head the torture of his brothers to aid more divisions within the army.

When Paul Kagame became the head of Rwandese Patriotic Army which later became Rwanda Defense Forces, he immediately started eliminating his colleagues especially those who questioned his competency or who suggested contrary ideas. Kagame rose from Major to Major General following the elimination of his colleagues, and it all happened because he was trusted by Museveni of Uganda who helped us through to the last minute. Indeed, Kagame was entrusted as the coordinator of politics in the RPA/RPF due to the fact that he was the only one Museveni believed that Kagame was capable of listening due to have been close to afande Fred Rwigema (RIP).

Kagame was not a command soldier and had no clue on what was happening on frontline, the battlefield was all handled by our brave commanders such Afande Ndugute Kalisoliso, Sam Kaka, Kayitare and others, the list is endless.

Paul Kagame's behaviour grew from being violent and aggressive to presenting the symptoms of sadism and delusions plus being paranoid all the time. Today as we speak Paul Kagame is self-harming, Self-harm or deliberate self-harm, includes self-injury and self-poisoning and is defined as the intentional, direct injuring of body tissue most often done without suicidal intentions.

The reason we have used an example of self-harming is that Paul Kagame is finishing those who brought him to power, without mentioning the thousands of his colleagues he eliminated over the last 27 years, let's focus on the current arrests of Retired Army Captain David Kabuye the husband to Lt Col Rose Kabuye and Brig. Gen. (rtd) Frank Rusagara.

When Kabuye, was picked up, two days after Rusagara's arrest on august 18, 2014, Gen Nzabamwita stressed that more arrests which will include all the RPF officials who questions or criticises the current system were coming which tended out to be the case.

Without giving further details, Nzabamwita said the duo was held in connection with State security offences. "They are both in the hands of criminal investigation agencies," he said, adding that the suspects' families had duly been notified and due process was being observed.

He said investigations were still ongoing and that the two men would be produced before the courts of law in due course.

There is a continuous panic within the RPF circles where many are subjected to continuous big brother cameras and definitely don't know who will be arrested the next day. The detentions of the above Senior RDF Officers have since sparked speculation that the two officers were in touch with subversive elements in the Diaspora.

Brig Nzabamwita said Kabuye and Rusagara are suspected of being "engaged in acts aimed at destabilising the country. That's why they were arrested and are still under investigation." He said the law will take its course irrespective of the officers' ranks and status, adding, the army believes that the suspects are "innocent until proven guilty." Before his detention, Rusagara had just completed his mission as Rwanda's Defense Attaché to the United Kingdom.

Previously, Gen Kayumba Nyamwasa mentioned the word Munyangire, which means that when Kagame hates someone, he wants everyone serving in his government not to speak with that particular person. And to make things worse Paul Kagame and his men will make sure that, that particular person is isolated and his/her property is confiscated including money, houses or land. It's more kunyagwa, as history indicates that long ago the batware used to take away everything of anyone who would have betrayed a king. In other words, Paul Kagame is a king of Rwanda who should not be questioned about anything but instead all he does to be seen as excellent. The connections between Tutsi families indicates that Kagame will continue to scratch his head because, most of the RPF back benchers are all related either through marriages or direct families, for example Dr David Himbara is a brother to former PPU commander Gen Tom Byabagamba whose movement is always under surveillance reported and at times interrogated, he has been appointed to head the notorious prison of Kami where his brother in law Gen Rusagara may be transferred to spend most of his life. His wife Mary Baine also lost her job recently and remains under the big brother watch, the sister of Himbara and Byabagamba is a wife to the detained Gen Rusagara.

So, the arrest of Rusagara means that all the people he has been speaking to will have to be questioned plus his relatives or friends and families. You wonder why people like David Kabuye was being questioned, simply because of Munyangire. Surprisingly when we spoke to the RPF insiders most of them admitted that the whole RPF is worried about the situation. One said that at some point the world will question Jannette Kagame why as a closer person, who is a wife to the president never sought for psychological help as husband struggles with psychosis. Other prominent RPF members such as Bihozagara, Mazimpaka, Rose Kabuye, Gen Sam Kaka and others were being investigated.

A friend of mine was surprised when I read to him the charges that Gen Rusagara is accused of, speaking to renegades who are abroad also who are critics of the current government. The man burst into laughter and asked how that could be bad, he went on to says that actually there was no evidence to prove that Gen Rusagara had communicated with anyone in the opposition. However, as he was a writer, historian and a comrade to those who fell out with the government, it wouldn't be bad communicating to them.

In Gen Rusagara's case there is a lot to actually laugh about because, when Gen Rusagara left the United Kingdom where he worked as a military attaché, contrarily to other Africans who arrive in Rwanda with containers of cars and television screens computers and microwaves, Rusagara turned up with a container full of tones of books, being a writer, he also loves reading books.

General Rusagara is an intellectual, a sensible man who is among the few RPF officers who are knowledgeable and with no blood on their hands. It is also most likely that this current Tsunami might not leave any RPF senior officials unshaken, especially historicals who will see Kagame as crossing a red line.

## 4.3 President Kagame threatens to imprison to save his name

In 2014, the Rwandan Head of State President Kagame presided over what the RPF call the annual performance contact commonly known as (Imihigo) signing ceremony at Parliament, where Ministers and Mayors signed new performance contacts. The Prime Minister also presented the evaluation report of the 2013/2014 District Imihigo performance, and the three best performing Districts were awarded with trophies of recognition.

It is at this function that president Kagame warned his government officials who according to him swindle the government money or taxpayer's money. In his cunning language President Kagame emphasised the need for local leaders to be decisive in their action with the welfare of the people they lead in mind.

"Imihigo is a performance contract between leaders and those you serve. Citizens will continue to hold you accountable. As leaders, you must put your words into action and walk the talk. As leaders, it is your responsibility to solve challenges faced by citizens in an efficient and just manner. We must uphold a culture of accountability. The progress we have made is not an excuse for complacency. We should look ahead and work to accomplish even more with every step that we take."

On the contrary the Rwandan head of state should himself be questioned on all the scandals involving him or his agents like James Musoni and others who have embezzled money from public institutions. For example, the former Electrogaz which the RPF renamed EWASA, has lost billions of Francs robbed by RPF officials and now they are rebranding it almost the same name it had before. This is the work of RPF spin doctors who work around the clock to swindle public money, all these people have never been brought to book or return the money as the Rwandan leader is trying to convince the Rwandans and perhaps the international community.

Who will be accountable for the Rukara Hydro power project which was supposed to produce 9.2 MW capacities, but instead the Dam produced 5 MW. All the money was swindled by Kagame agents and when the Parliament intervened they were threatened, intimidated and later they dropped the report and all of them were told to apologize. The crime for the members of parliament was that they had established the link and chain of RPF mafias who were involved in the Rukara Hydro Dam scandal in which millions of Rwandan Francs were swindled.

Why doesn't the head of state audit those RPF officials if he is serious with corruption? The answer is simple corruption in Rwanda is supervised by Kagame himself, no more no less. I exposed in one of my article in Inyenyeri journal, how the former RSSB Boss Angelique KATENGWA was coerced to release money of the Rwandan pensioners to the RPF real estate investments. This similar to the former RDB Chief Theogene Turatsinze who was coerced to release billions of Francs and was later murdered in Mozambique. The RPF mafias invested in non-profit buildings and now the buildings are empty because the Rwandan society is a small market and they cannot afford the rent.

Take for Instance, the Kigali Market in the Centre of the City is almost closing because the clients cannot afford the rent, yet they used a lot of money from RSSB. Will the RPF and its Auditor General Mr. Obadiah Biraro bring the Kagame himself and his proxies to book? Will they be forced to bring back all the money they have embezzled? Who nominated the leaders of the EWASA they accuse of embezzling billions of Francs? In fact, the 20 billion marks mentioned by the Auditor-General corresponds with the figure the Inyenyeri investigated embezzled by the top Kagame officials excluding the Kagame loot. For example, how much did Kagame buy the two private jets he rents the government for his own interests? Where did they put the 30 billion Francs they conned from the so called Agaciro Fund? Has anyone dared to question the accountability of that money?

We need accountability which is not selective or discriminative, from the top to the bottom, not going for executive secretaries of Umudugudu, Utagari, or Akarere. However, as Kagame is under pressure from his own RPF historical and founders, it's likely that many will be locked up or humiliated on fabricated charges of embezzlement. We all know when the same president was in that same parliament and said that if necessary he will use the hammer to kill a fly, later his former army chief Gen. Kayumba Nyamwasa was shot and miraculously he survived. Kagame's words go with actions and always target something.

It's a high time that all the RPF historicals told their leader that for the good of their country, RPF and Kagame's own good he should learn to tolerate those he does not share the same political ideology. Indeed, we should all courageously say that Mr. President we don't hate you but we hate what you are doing.

## 4.4 Inyumba Aloysia's betrayal

Alosyia Inyumba a former Minister for Gender and Family Promotion became seriously sick and admitted in Holland hospital in 2012, she run out of money and she sought help from her RPF party she had served almost her entire life.

When the first Lady discovered that Inyumba was seriously sick and needed financial help from the institution she served selflessly, revelations come out that the First Lady said that they could not waste the RPF money on somebody who will not heal.

How did she know that Inyumba will not heal? As more revelations come out, Miss Mary Baine the wife of Col. Tom Byabagamba had a conversation with Ambassador Joseph Mutaboba in a posh area in Nyarutarama were they discussed the possibility of the First lady of having a hand in Inyumba's death. If this is true, then Inyumba did not die a natural cause as we thought before.

Why then the RPF and Kagame would have murdered Inyumba? Kagame's instincts always tell him to eliminate those who know him very well like Inyumba. Inyumba is a lady who sacrificed everything for the benefit of RPF, this was even revealed from the horse's mouth himself (Kagame) during the Inyumba's funeral, he said that during the bush days Inyumba could not spend even her own pocket money abroad mission. This was the character of Inyumba who loved RPF and RPF loved her during Bush days.

The power struggle between Jeannette Kagame and her Husband has created a rift in the RPF. For example, because of the loyalty of Inyumba to the RPF, the First lady was jealousy of her as she thought that Inyumba would be chosen as the successor of RPF and possibly the next and first female Rwandan head of state. According to sources from within the RPF who requested to remain anonymous, this prompted the first Lady to use his killing agent Gen. Jack Nziza to poison Inyumba. It is not therefore surprising that the First lady rejected the financial request of Inyumba because they (Kagame) and Jeannette knew what they were doing.

When Inyumba failed to secure financial assistance from RPF, she contacted Gen. James Kabarebe a colleague and a person they shared thick and thin during the Bush days. It's alleged that Gen. James Kabarebe promised some money but did not keep the promise after learning that the first lady had rejected Inyumba's plea for help. It's likely the Gen. Kabarebe being a graduate of Kagame's school of hate would not have taken a risk of dealing with somebody his boss has rejected. It is at this point that Inyumba contacted the late Col. Patrick Karegeya a former colleague who responded affirmatively and quickly with some money.

*Late Col Karegeya who helped Inyumba when the RPF turned against her.*

We have established that when the Late Col. Patrick Karegeya was strangled last year in South Africa his handset phones were taken by his killers and landed in the hands of Kagame. The Rwandan head of state was furious when he discovered that late Inyumba contacted Col. Patrick Karegeya, he then planned how he would eliminate or side line all those according to him are linked to Col. Patrick Karegeya. It is in this context that Dr Richard Masozera the husband of late Inyumba was sacked as the Director of Rwanda Civil Aviation Authority replacing him with a semi-literate Col. Silas Udahemuka. As the chain of hate and intrigue continues so is the chain of RPF disintegration, when Dr. David Himbara the former Kagame advisor fell apart with him, he left his brother Col. Tom Byabagamba in hot water.

Col Byabagamba had been a top security official of Kagame for a long time, but this did not save him from the wrath of anger from his boss. It is alleged that Kagame planned his elimination by sending him to Darfur, but because of the nature of Col. Tom Byabagamba who is very reserved, the Kagame's killers did not get the window of killing him. In fact, this is the same fate the late Col. Willison Rutaysire the former ORINFOR Director who was murdered in Congo in 2000 when he advised Kagame not to fight Ugandans, the RPF spin doctors said he committed suicide. Col Byabagamba survived the assassination and poisoning but he could not survive the handcuffs back home. The late Police Superintendent Camarade Rukabu was poisoned at the Entebbe International Airport when he was returning from Darfur mission in 2012 because according to RPF sources he had criticized the style of Kagame leadership.

## 4.5 Kagame slapped in the face twice in lifetime

In May 2016, president Kagame threatened to eliminate anyone who would dare attack his country, he stated that it would not take even seconds before he arrests or kill anyone who would tamper with the national security. In his threatening language, the President said that he was aching in his hands while referring to being frantic and could not wait for the enemy to attack his country so that he could hit them hard.

Although a few weeks' later armed people attacked the police post of Rubavu in Gisenyi and took a large amount of ammunitions plus killing over 19 of his troops plus an unknown figure of his police officers.

President Kagame responded by pouring hundreds of RDF troops as well as the police who arrested and jailed civilians and killed the rest. Also, his senior commanders have spent weeks in the area threatening innocent civilians, the head of police Gen Emmanuel Gasana aka Rurayi who also spent a couple of days in the area stated that he doubted if the attackers were from the FDLR fighters. "I think we need to wait and see the outcome of investigations, so far, the style used by these insurgents is different from how normally FDLR plans and executes operations".

After that rancorous attack President Kagame called for a crisis meeting which was attended by mainly his intelligence officers as well as army Chiefs, he asked them to share information and analyse who had sent the enemy, Gen James Kabarebe who is also the defense Minister said that the attackers were from the FDLR insurgents. President Kagame interrupted and asked Gen Kabarebe how they had managed to get on Rwandan soil. Without wasting time Kagame ordered the arrest of all the suspects and in minutes the people of Rubavu discovered that even the local leaders have been arrested.

For so many years, President Kagame managed to enjoy assaulting nations and killing his people unchallenged, but the Rubavu scenario might have surprised him and susceptible that it was really possible that enemies could even capture a town like Rubavu.

Looking back on how Kagame hates and allergic to being challenged, in late 1980's while Kagame was the Deputy Head of the Ugandan directorate of military intelligence, a number of the Rwandese young boys who were in the Ugandan forces based at Captain Kaitare's entourage and Gen Rwigema got drunk, among them was now Colonel Happy Ruvusha and others, then Major Kagame ordered their arrest.

Although after a few hours Captain Kaitare who was heading to war zone in Guru northern Uganda stated that he was going with the soldiers who had been arrested by Kagame for drunk and disorderly, he went to the military police and ordered their release. He went with them to the war zone, he said that Kagame was becoming a nuisance, when he came back with his troops after a couple of weeks Major Kagame had not given up and turned at Captain Kaitare's home in Kamwokya demanding as to why he had ignored the law and discharged the soldiers from jail when he knew they had committed crimes.

He threatened Captain Kaitare that he could potentially have broken the law, Captain Kaitare immediately took the gun out and put Kagame on gun point, he told him that he was an incompetent officer who did not deserve to be in the forces, he told him that they had more important issues such as the enemy to fight but not keeping forces in prisons. Captain Kaitare slapped Kagame twice in the face, Kagame who was sitting on the floor pleaded that we are all Rwandans and now we are fighting each other in exile.

*Capt. Vedaste Kaitare next to a Muhabura journalist with Kagame*

Indeed, Captain Kaitare locked Kagame in a room and left him in to rot, Kagame was taken out by other officers after two days and Captain Kaitare had left him in detention as he headed back to the war zone. Gen Rwigema ordered that Captain Kaitare stay in house arrest due to behaving inappropriately and mistreating a senior officer, the matter had to be resolved by President Museveni and Gen Fred Rwigema after a number of weeks.

Even though innocently Commander Captain Kaitare thought that the matter had been resolved, Kagame knew very well that Kaitare did not respect him and Kagame started to work tirelessly to eliminate him, indeed he later successfully managed to achieve it through his close friends. Commander Kaitare was vulnerable because the person he trusted was a double dealer who gave him away, before his death he attended a meeting with Gen Salim Saleh in Uganda with the wife of Gen Fred Rwigema and what was said in that meeting was disclosed to Kagame by one of Kaitare's friends who was also in the meeting.

Looking at Kagame's challenges he has experienced three slaps in the face now, another challenge Kagame faced was when he was withdrawn from the front line because he was a coward who exposed his comrades after he accidentally fired prematurely. Since then Museveni and Gen Rwigema agreed that Kagame should always be left in the headquarters and based in the intelligence service within the forces because he could not conduct operations. The idea of sparing Kagame in war zones kept him safe and because of feeding his gossip to Museveni, he was trusted in the intelligence service but not in combat, he was later made to become the political coordinator of the RPA.

President Museveni who threatened to block the supplies if Kagame is not made the then RPA leader, managed to confuse and convince the commanders of the RPA that Kagame was a changed man to lead them after they became divided fighting for Ranks.

Since the slap in the face of Rubavu Kagame has started wearing a bulletproof jacket whenever he goes in public, he believes that within his people or the public someone may hit him; A friend of mine joked that "what Kagame doesn't know is that if anyone want to shoot him will aim the head not the chest, so he better starts wearing a helmet as well".

## 4.6 (RSSB) Rwanda Social Security Board coffers dry up and Kagame Locks Kantengwa

The former RSSB boss Kantegwa Angelique was picked from her home by Kagame's security officials accusing her of misappropriation of RSSB funds, flouting tender regulations, donating government property or selling them on low prices compared to other markets.

We all knew that these are fabricated charges as more secrets are leaking from the RPF roof on how RSSB funds were robbed by Kagame to fund all these so-called sky scrapers in Kigali and some other parts in Rwanda. I discussed the issue with Radio Itahuka hosted by Serge Ndayizeye about how funds have been misused.

I argued that, some of the RSSB officials were coerced to release money to the RPF officials in what they called investment project of vision 2020. The RPF mafias have drawn all the money of the pensioners from the savings of Kayibanda and Habyarimana governments to fund their own projects. This follows similar circumstances in which the former Rwanda Development Bank (BRD) Mr. Theogene Turatsinze was murdered in Mozambique.

He was brutally murdered in the traditional RPF style KANDOYA hands tied behind his back, and his body was found floating in the waters of Indian Ocean in MAPUTO. Mr. Turatsinze was thought to have "had access to politically sensitive financial information related to certain Rwandan government insiders", relating to the disappearances of funds from the Rwanda Development Bank (BRD).

To add salt to the wound, Miss Kantengwa Angelique is a brother in Law to Capt. Frank who is a brother to Lt. Col. Rose Kabuye who the RPF publicly accused of subversion and engaging in actions which are prejudicial to the Rwandan State Security. It is alleged that Miss Katengwa Angelique paid a visit to Lt.Co. Rose Kabuye after her Husband Capt. David Kabuye was arrested on accusation of possessing a gun contrary to the law.

Dr Tesi sister to Angelique Kantengwa Capt. Frank, Mzee Kayitenkore (father to Kantengwa); and Frank brother to Lt Col Rose Kabuye). Who was forced out of the army by President Paul Kagame due to Munyangire, Capt. Frank the first air force officer of RPA.

There is a tradition in RPF that if one of its own falls apart with their bankrupt ideology, all relatives and friends are barred from visiting or talking to them. In fact, this was revealed by one of the peers of RPF Tito Rutaremara who asked Gen. KAYUMBA Nyamwasa that when the former lost his mother the RPF colleagues and other officials did not attend the funeral, "didn't this cross your mind that we are not happy with your behaviour" Tito asked.

As more RPF officials are related Kagame finds himself with a hanging rope as he would have locked up more even his own security and advisors. For example, Capt. RUKI a close body guard of President Kagame and Major Patrick Karuretwa an advisor on security respectively are relatives to Katengwa Angelique. As the RPF tradition goes these officials were not supposed to visit or talk to Katengwa Angelique or they will disown her.

If Katengwa Angelique committed the alleged offences of flouting the tender regulations, abuse of office, misappropriation of government funds, as the CID Chief Theos Badege said "misuse of property of public interest, appropriation of unlawful favors, illegal award of public tender, giving for free or charging at lower prices the delivery of public or private goods." why now?

Why should a government official give for free a property? Did the same police officer investigate Gen. Kagame who was the Vice-President and Minister of Defense over the misappropriation of the money for the purchase of military helicopters?

The construction of the Hydro Power Dam at Rukara River which was supposed to have a 9. 2 MW capacity, billions of monies were swindled by Kagame through his RPF mafias like James Musoni and more RPF officials. This embezzlement was never investigated and when the parliament started to question it, they were intimidated and many of them apologised.

Kagame's adventure with people's money in real property in a small and poor country like Rwanda was like swimming in an ocean without a life jacket. Many Rwandans cannot afford the rent and all those tall buildings Kagame called Pension Plaza don't have clients and Rwanda is suffering what economists call housing bubble or economic bubble.

This is similar to the United States Housing project. In 2008 alone, the United States government allocated over $900 billion to special loans and rescues related to the U.S. housing bubble, with over half going to Fannie Mae and Freddie Mac. Moreover, US has checks and balances, Rwanda is a one-man country and all the lucrative real estate projects are managed by the RPF companies, like Horizon, Real Contractors, COTRACO, or those affiliated to RPF with a mask of Asian workers.

Convention Centre which has made Rwandans bankrupt with no insurance and no one will have a pension after retirement, this because RSSB (Rwanda social security board) had to be built before 2020, after a long time waiting of money from the donors but unfortunately with no response. Angelique Kantengwa paid the RSSB money out as instructed by president Kagame, but now has ended up in jail with fabricated cases.

It is not therefore surprising, that as the Kinyarwanda proverb goes, *"Abagabo barya imbwa zikishyura"*. Literally meaning that big fish feed on small fish. President Kagame might be kicking his last kick of a dying horse as he is more likely to lock up all his RPF founders as they are related in one way or the other. Indeed, they have been employed in some of the sensitive and financial areas to act as RPF Bridge in stealing and cover up respectively

## 4.7 The infamous Agaciro Fund

Agaciro, is a Kinyarwanda word for worthiness, value or importance. In president Kagame's context however, one would interpret it as "Rwandan self-worthiness."

It is unfortunate that the president seems to lose a plot when tries to instill these empty values in his population. It is evident that the Rwandan population is fond of doing deeds that they don't believe in just to turn a page. This was evident during the genocide days when people were forced to kill their own friends and even family in order to survive themselves. This has lived to haunt whoever did it up to the present day, just because one's mind was not readily convinced for the deed.

Agaciro is an initiative started by Mr. Kagame and his close allies after the cut of foreign aid due to the allegations that Kagame and his government was supporting a rebel faction in Eastern Congo that is causing tremendous sufferings to the local population.

The international community and the whole world have since asked Kagame to stop his support of these Congolese rebels who have continued to inflict death and atrocities to our neighbor's in the Congo. On a personal level however, this is very disturbing due to the fact that President Kagame himself has experienced firsthand hand refugee life after fleeing to Uganda Gahungye refugee camp when he was just under five-year-old. It is sad to see a person with the same history inflicting atrocities to the same background he was born from.

After the stoppage of the foreign aid that President Kagame enjoyed, he has since started a campaign of milking the local communities as well as those that live far from his authoritarian government. Due to his dictatorial rule Kagame has always been critical to his own diaspora mostly the Rwandan population living in Belgium, France and Canada due to their Francophone inclement. He has at some point banned the country's colonial language and replaced it with English.

This decision took the entire population by surprise given the fact that over 80% of Rwandans were francophone inclined. The French language ban was after Kagame developed differences with France, while he hailed support from the Clinton and Bush American administrations.

Rwandans professionals who had spent most of their lives studying and practicing their professions in French language had to enroll on English language programs just to cope with Kagame's Anglophone.

Schools which were built on French language values way back in time had to change their curriculum while struggling to structure the entire institutions in Kagame's Anglophone. Now that Kagame is having a tough time with his new Anglophone and Americanised master, one should not be surprised if Rwanda swapped English language to maybe Swahili if not Luganda or even Mandarin as he now panders to the support of China.

When Kagame was a darling to the west, he visited his diaspora at some meetings challenging and daring them to come home and build their country and be given jobs. He has in the past insulted the Belgo-Rwandan citizens; that they were lazy and only survived on government handouts (CAPAS) as he pronounced it.

This was very damaging not only to the Rwandans who are residents in

Belgium but also to the European host countries that host a portion of his country's citizens who have for the years felt and made it home.

It is the same Kagame who is now frequenting North America and Europe begging the same diaspora he insulted for their hard-earned cash. It is well known that the Rwandan diaspora has in the past boosted the country's economy by the amount of money sent home each year.

There is no way Kagame should talk about Agaciro or self-respect when he does not respect his immediate neighbors, in this case the DR Congo. Kagame held the rank of Major in the Ugandan NRA, he has however waged different wars to the same commanders who made him who he is; Lt Gen Kaguta Museveni. Is that Agaciro?

Kagame has disrespected and neglected his elder's orphans and widows, the prime example being Mrs. Janet Rwigema. Here one would list names of widows and orphans of numerous senior fallen commanders that fought for the country that Kagame is presently messing up.

It's sad when Kagame talks about Agaciro, when traditionally he should have taken his best friend and elder brother's widow with the best Agaciro possible. Mrs. Rwigema was continuously supported by Ugandan authorities (Gen Salim Saleh) to be precise until recently when Kagame forcefully stopped this relationship due to his intrigue. Is this Agaciro?

Apart from the senior and junior RPA foreign heroes Kagame has impoverished all staunch RPA wealthy supporters. The people gave all moral and monetary support in order to fight the war both in Rwanda and outside her.

Those of us who are old enough remember the selfless efforts of individuals like Silas Majyambere, Valens Kajeguhakwa, Gakwaya who was slain in cold blood days after he crossed to the RPA controlled zone, Rujugiro, Kananura, Karimba, etc. I wonder if this is the Agaciro he sings about?

Kagame is not fit to sing Agaciro, since his actions are opposite to what he preaches. On the other hand, one must stop to ponder the reason why Kagame is begging the same communities he has been belittling all along.

Could it be due to the continued stoppage of aid? If so then he ought to stop shouting and crying foul and embark on strategies that see his country get on its feet and walk straight.

Or could he be noble enough to leave the Congolese people alone and work on ways he could trade with his neighbours while he gets his aid back as he prepares to wean his country off the donor list once for all graduating to his 2020 vision.

Kagame's ego and greed has out grown his reach in the last few years, he will intimidate and milk whoever is likely to give him any possible cash, however little it seems, just to nourish his lavish lifestyle. The Agaciro fund therefore is a personal centered deposit designed to serve his own purposes and use.

Kagame is on the other hand an enemy centered individual whose character is to create as many enemies as he can. He is not ashamed of stealing from rich individuals, the poor citizens of Congo or the teachers of Rwanda.

In other words, Kagame deserves Agaciro himself before he preaches it. "Kagame akwiriye kwihesha agaciro…"

## 4.8 Kagame's obsessions with cars and driving

An obsession is a very serious illness that causes a person to be someone other than themselves. Sources in Kigali have reported how our President his Excellency Paul Kagame experienced an accident on his way from Village Urugwiro heading to the state house in Kiyovu. At the time of the accident he was driving himself as he has always done, this has prompted me to think back when I was still one of the people responsible for his security and transport.

Kagame was the sort of person who enjoyed driving and sadly he was a very bad driver. As very important person (VIP) Kagame owns expensive cars and enjoys all the luxury that goes along with it. He has the opportunity of staying still on the road, even when he drives at high speed. During my time among his body guards he was surrounded by a team of very experienced drivers including myself, with the belief that we were building our nation.

However, accidents occurred although we would manage to keep his car safe. I remember the accident I had at Mulindi near Kanombe as we were on our way from Gabiro to demobilize our heroes that he did not need in the army at the time.

Hours before we left Kigali as I was chatting to Captain Silas Udahemuka, who is now a Colonel, a bird passed by and defecated on Silas Udahemuka's head, then he said to me that he did not think that our journey was going to end safely, he said that he believed it was bad luck. As I smiled I was called on the Motorola to let me know that His Excellency was coming out of his room and so we needed to be ready for a move.

In VIP protection, we had the five-minute car known as the lead car; this one opens the road with alarms and red lights just to inform everyone on the road that they should give way.

The next car was the advance car which goes in front of the President; this car is responsible for guiding the principle car which carries the president. And the final one was the rear-guard car which is supposed to protect the president; this car is normally filled with the most trusted soldiers who can die to save the president.

This is the car I was driving, which is also allowed to hit other cars or even shot what may come from left or right whether intentional or unintentional, they must be hit to save the president because the president does not stop. During my time with the Presidential guards, I drove this car for quite a long time was involved in most of the incidents that happened where I had to hit a number of cars, this was intentional believing that it's a way of protecting the President.

A number of injuries occurred and even the death to the poor people who could not even afford insurance covers on their cars. Even though the cars we were using in VIP protection were very expensive and guarded, they never got even a scratch, but most of us we are still haunted, tormented with regrets and disappointment due causing accidents, death and damages to our citizens.

It is my responsibility to take this opportunity to apologise to all of the people who were involved in that sort of dangerous driving while believing that I was doing a good job for our nation.

Most of the accidents were caused by over speeding. An example is the accident I had in Mulindi, His Excellence wanted to arrive in Kigali in a very short timeframe. We drove 140KPH which was very dangerous, unfortunately a TATA lorry which was heavily loaded coming from front failed to stop, and so as a rear-guard driver I had to overtake the principle car in order to push the lorry off the road.

This was very dangerous and scary but had to do it to save our president as that is what I believed at the time, we never had time to think on the consequences of what we were doing.

I managed to push the lorry off the road, but lost control and my car rolled three times in the farm. However, I thank God there was no death this time. It was the first time when Kagame indicated that he appreciated my actions because he came out of his car and said to me that the lorry was going to hit his car if I had not overtaken him and told him to stay behind. God knows where the lorry driver is today.

On another Presidential transport, we were travelling from Gisenyi, His Excellency Paul Kagame was on the wheel and he was over speeding, as usual. As we were approaching Kigali one of our drivers lost control, he ended up in the nearest swamp and two soldiers died on the spot including 19-year-old Pt. Mushaija, and I wonder what his next of kin think happened to him.

Obviously, like many Rwandans believe, he died to save his country. This occurred on the lead car which was just in front of Kagame's principle car. The lead car was driven by Cliopa Rutonesha, my comrade; poor Cliopa had experienced another accident before while guiding the first lady. The accident occurred at Hotel Meridian where 23-year-old Bugingo Davis lost his leg. Emmanuel Rutagengwa injured both his legs, 29-year-old Aimable ended up in a wheel chair, and Cliopa's back was broken but he recovered.

On the day of the Gisenyi route accident, Kagame was flashing the head lights to the lead car driver signaling him to increase his speed. These drivers were very afraid of Kagame because whenever anyone took the blame for slowing down his speed he would stop the car and punch them. It was a problem because Rwanda is the country of a thousand hills and so the roads were built at an expense and are made of sharp corners at every mile.

President Kagame saw the lead car roll over into the swamp and he never stopped. The driver was in hospital for months and later was imprisoned after being accused of sleeping on the wheel. However even if he had fallen asleep while driving it would have not been surprising because we were always on standby to the President 24/7.

Whether Kagame is asleep or awake we never had a minute to rest, we were over worked and only paid peanuts. It was after the death Desire's Kabila's that Kagame realized the dangers of a hungry body guard because he realized that having managed to pay off for Desire Kabila's death somebody else may pay a hungry one among us for his head too.

Most of the accidents we experienced were man made accidents and mainly by Kagame, a man who was born to Rutagambwa, who was also a driver, this may have been the source of Kagame's obsession with cars. He started with the cars we used to take from civilians as we fought along, until when he obtained the opportunity to lead the country and gain the access on funds to buy every car he desired. He even ended up buying planes and heavy weapons that nations like Rwanda do not need.

But, why and what caused his obsession? Obsessions come about when one fails to get something that interests them or is tempted to get something out of their reach. Once this occurs, the satisfaction is never fulfilled, meaning one is in a constant state of torture. Obsessions can also arise from having something and becoming too attached and controlling to the extent of maniacal proportions like in the case of spouses, children or friends.

An obsession is a very serious illness that causes a person to be someone other than themselves. It can also be caused by a person thinking someone's life is so much better than theirs or thinking their life would be so much better if they had something else in their life. This is why Kagame travels the world over looking for awards and even begging for qualifications, as we all know that he has obtained honorary degrees just to experience the title of becoming a PHD holder and get to be called a Doctor.

In VIP protection, we were to make sure that the president was safe on the road and if anyone needed to save him in case of an accident or ambush, we could do it in any way possible. No matter the cost human or otherwise.

After his recent accident in Kimihurura as he had a press conference, he lost his tongue and accused the USA of having planned to overthrow the president of DRC Joseph Kabila, before his previous elections. This was out of order, a president accusing another country for planning to over throw a different country's President, what was our president thinking? Congo has become the center of the great lakes region politics; he is out of words the world now understands who really Kagame is from A-Z. very disappointing President who is obsessed with cars and to make things worse these cars are bullet proof, no one else can use them in Rwanda as they are expensive to maintain. They are only driven by Kagame who gets rid of them after a couple of years, they get parked in the Garage and until he finds out of a new car advertised in the western countries.

That is our President, who is being praised for fighting corruption in the tiny nation of Africa Rwanda, accusing his comrades of not being accountable of their actions. President Kagame is and has always been corrupt, greedy, selfish, arrogant and more to come.

## 4.9 The poisoning of Paul Kagame

It was a normal Friday evening and all of us on duty at Presidents House expected a quiet weekend. We expected to see President Paul Kagame wearing his fancy tracksuits and bouncing around in his tennis court, or jumping in one of his expensive fast cars and ourselves speeding behind him trying to catch-up in Toyotas Pickups filled with bodyguards, most times ending up in fatal accidents losing comrade's due to his irresponsible high speed.

We were expected to stay on high alert (standby class1) believing that His Excellence Paul Kagame might pop out in a rush ordering us to drive off anyhow. At the time, many of us believed that Kagame's acts of uncertainty, unpredictability, inability to trust anybody, paranoia and worrying all the time was because of him being a very important and influential person in the country.

It was normal for all of us body guards to stay standby with a thought that we might be leaving in the next minute even when Paul Kagame was in deep asleep. Whoever would be found taking of their boots would be punished by our immediate commanders. I later realised that even the commanders themselves weren't aware of Kagame's program. It's now evident that even Kagame himself didn't have a clue of what he was supposed to do for the day due to his condition.

We would be served food and instructed to eat in no minute thinking that we were leaving any moment even when Kagame had no plans of going anywhere. On this specific day, we continued to wait, we waited Friday, Saturday, Sunday all went without seeing Paul come out of the house. There come Monday he was not seen out of the house, now I started to get concerned if everything was ok! And none of us was supposed to enter his house let a lot asking if he was alright.

I reflected on having seen Dr Emmanuel Ndahiro constantly visiting his house over the weekend and hardly any visitor came, not even family which was very unusual for President Kagame's weekends.

So, as I was still asking myself what could have gone wrong, Captain Willy Rwagasana now a Lt Col asked me to drive two of the kitchen assistants to a safe house. These two kitchen assistants had been part of the close body guards prior to being assigned kitchen duties, and had been trusted enough to become chefs. The two soldiers had enjoyed the luxury of travelling on trips abroad and spending time in luxurious hotels with Kagame.

Deep down in me I was skeptical and I knew it was their turn to be paid back by the guy they had served selflessly like all of us. But then again, I believed that probably they had got involved themselves in money laundering or misusing state house funds.

It was later whispered to me by Willy Rwagasana that the two soldiers were suspected of poisoning HE Paul Kagame, of whom he said that was having diarrhea and vomiting for the last three days therefore confirming his disappearance.

At that moment, I was gobsmacked, I kept quiet for about 15 seconds, then took a deep breath. In me at the time I felt helpless, angry, betrayed and frustrated, I had survived a number of accidents trying to protect the man and now had been poisoned by our own boys?

I started reflecting and remembering many commanders whom we had lost in such mysterious and unexplained death.

But I was totally wrong again, the man was experiencing a condition in which faeces are discharged from the bowels frequently and in a liquid form. A range of symptoms including diarrhoea and vomiting, but due to the paranoia that we all shared Dr Emmanuel Ndahiro had declared that the president was likely to have been poisoned. The main cause of the suspicion was due to the fact that one of the kitchen assistants was a brother to famous Alfred Kalisa (BCDI) a millionaire who was once Kagame's close friend but fallen out due to finance issues.

When the second doctor came to investigate, he ruled out the poisoning however the boys had already been tortured and it was too late to be returned in Kagame's kitchen let alone being of any use to even their own families.

When I raised my concerns with Willy Rwagasana about how the matter had been handled, he said to me that this had nothing to do with us because our job was to maintain Kagame's security and those responsible for investigations was Intelligence Officer Maj. Silas Udahemuka and the Doctors who reported the poison scenario.

I reminded Willy Rwagasana how vomiting and diarrhoea was not a new thing to HE Paul Kagame, with reference to when I had to clean his vomit on our way from Kigali to Butare on the highway. But Willy Rwagasana cautioned me never to mention vomiting incidents which were usually caused by among all his ulcers.

The Butare incident is still traumatic in my mind due to Kagame's brutal sadistic actions on the day. What happed was that while we were in our convoy, Kagame being driven in the car in front of the one I was driving, vomited in the car and we had to stop. I took out my cleaning kit and ran to clean the back seat he had messed up. When I was cleaning the mucous, Kagame pretended to have a short call around the nearest bush but when he returned I had not finished because I was polishing the seats.

Instead of waiting for the car to freshen up Kagame brutally punched me in the head using his elbow, it was abrupt and so painful that my head was swollen for two days. I again jumped in the rear-guard vehicle I was driving seated with our Head of Bodyguards Tom Byabagamba who is now imprisoned. He giggled and asked me why my eyes had turned red. I said to him that I had eaten a lot of hot chili before setting off from the base, then he said that unless Kagame's elbow felt like chili. He never said anymore words, but obviously had been watching through the window when Paul Kagame punched me.

To me this was so sad of Kagame, I had been hit by several times for no specific reason, but I didn't believe he would hit me when I am trying to clean his mess. I expected him to thank me for having been sensible enough and be equipped with cleaning kit among all of us and being able to cater to his bad health.

Looking back after many years, the causes of diarrhoea: Diarrhoea is usually a symptom of gastroenteritis (a bowel infection), which can be caused by: a virus – such as norovirus or rotavirus. Bacteria – such as campylobacter, Clostridium difficile (C. difficile), Escherichia coli (E. coli), salmonella or shigella; these can all cause food poisoning.

Kagame's anger and frustration always led him to hitting those around him, he was always irritable with some signs/symptoms of mental illness such as mood swings, impulsive behaviours, severe difficulties with relationships, devaluing people (often switching back and forth from idealizing them) Disturbance about self-image Paranoid ideation (thinking someone is after him)

# 5 Chap V: The First family Honours, power and selfishness.

## 5.1 President Paul Kagame to receive the NRA medal of honour after 26yeras.

In January 2012, President Kagame was expected for four days visit in Uganda where he will be decorated with a medal for his contribution in the NRA bush war in 1981-1986. According to the sources, President Kagame was invited by his counterpart President YK Museveni on his previous visit where many of President Kagame's former commanders; like General Salim Saleh Akandwanaho, General Fred Rwigyema, General Elly Tumwine, General David Tinyefuza and others have all received this honor before. This honor has been going on since the country was captured in 1986.

Last year General Fred Rwigyema received the freedom fighters medal which was never collected because his wife, who was expected at the function, was unable to attend because her passport had been confiscated by Kagame's agents.

This honor begs the question, why now after 26 years is when President Paul Kagame is remembered for his contribution? Most service men of the Uganda Peoples Defense Forces only remember President Kagame as a young intelligence officer who was a captain in 1986. They also remember him as a killer who actually never investigated a case and instead ordered the killing of any suspect that came across him. He moved freely from unit to unit spying on his colleagues.

It was, therefore, not surprising that when Sam Magara, one of the few Munduli-trained officers in the group reportedly hatched a plan to oust

Museveni, the Commander of High command (CHC) moved faster than them thanks to President Kagame's information. Veterans say that Museveni trusted Kagame more than Tinyefuza who, like Sam Magara, is from the Muhinda clan of the Bahima, Museveni is a Musita.

In his book, The Agony of the Bush War, Brig. Matayo Kyalgonza writes about the emergence of cliques during the bush war and how the CHC ordered that "ethnicity should cease".

At the height of ethnic polarization in the bush, Museveni appeared to trust fighters of Rwandan origin, such as Kagame, more than those who were Ugandan. That is why the late Maj. Gen. Fred Rwigyema remained the head of Museveni's protection unit for a long time.

Although the alleged coup against Museveni had been planned to take place when he was away from the bush (between June -December 1981), the rebel leader got to know about it and was able to suppress it. Veterans say, it is Kagame and others who let Museveni in on the secret.

High ranking bush-war generals remember how Kagame tortured a fellow NRA fighter, Jack Muchunguzi, to extract a confession following the murder of another colleague, Hannington Mugabi.

Brig. Pecos Kutesa describes Mugabi's death as caused by a pistol accident. But Col. Kizza Besigye, the only officer who witnessed the killing, was never asked to give evidence.

Muchunguzi was allegedly killed in order to quash a plot to oust Museveni which had been hatched by Sam Magara. Apparently, Muchunguzi knew about the plot.

It is reported that Magara wanted to break the NRA force and lead some fighters to another rebel force based in the Rwenzori Mountain. The Rwenzori group was reportedly linked to the Gang of Four; Prof. Edward Rugumayo, Prof. Dan Nabudere, Prof. Yash Tandon and late Omwony Ojwok who operated in areas of Nyabushozi.

The plot to destroy the NRA, it is claimed was hatched by Muchunguzi, Magara and Mugabi. Hannington Mugabi was reportedly uncomfortable with the plot especially after the chief planner had been killed in Kampala under unclear circumstances. Muchunguzi it is claimed eliminated Mugabi to destroy evidence. We have been told that Kagame drilled safety pins in Muchunguzi's fingers, squeezed his testicles and burnt him with cigarette butts to force him to confess.

Museveni also dispatched Kagame alongside other fighters to verify the authenticity of another rebel force that reportedly wanted to join the NRA. This was the rebel group of Maj. Roland Kakooza Mutale. Kagame and company found the group genuine and Mutale's fighters were integrated into the NRA.

As it's indicated in Lt Colonel Pecos Kutesa's book, Uganda's Resolution: How I saw it: he explains how Kagame, at some point when they were attacked, opened rapid fire when they were supposed to stay silent because they had planned to conduct an ambush on enemy forces. According to this book, Kagame was anxious and shaking thus requiring the High Commander to decide that Kagame would have to stay in the headquarters and continue his lone intelligence work. That is the freedom fighter that will be decorated on 22/1/12. President Paul Kagame (army number RO161) is a Tanzanian-trained spy, Paul Kagame, now President of Rwanda – was the counter-intelligence chief of rebel NRA leader Yoweri Museveni.

Most of the Luwero bush-war veterans are unanimous in their verdict that Kagame was never one of the celebrated NRA fighters yet he was quite meticulous in his role as a spy. His contribution in intelligence gathering and analysis helped Museveni regain control of a mutinous guerrilla force. Sam Magara (RIP) reportedly plotted a coup against Museveni during the early days of the struggle.

In the line of duty, Kagame reported directly to the Chairman of the High Command (CHC), Yoweri Museveni. He was one of the 27 rebels that launched the war with the attack on Kabamba on Feb. 6, 1981, but his military number was a distant RO 0161.

Kagame who trained in intelligence gathering in Tanzania – went on to become, rebel leader, Yoweri Museveni's most trusted spy. Specialising in counter intelligence, Kagame spied on colleagues to establish mainly who was undermining the struggle from within or undermining the authority of the rebel leader.

Conspiracy appeared to have crept into the NRA guerrilla movement at the very launch of the rebellion and this prompted the rebel leader to engage with some fighters to spy on others. Kagame's work was therefore cut out right from the start when the only Yugoslav-made RPG that the rebels planned to use to storm the armoury of Kabamba barracks went missing.

Only 33 people, including Kagame, who attended the meeting at Mathew Rukikaire's residence on February 3 that planned the first attack, knew about this weapon that would help the rebels gain access to the armoury and get more guns. At that time, the rebels had only 27 guns and needed more. The RPG mysteriously disappeared a day before the February 6, 1981 attack on Kabamba.

Although the rebels went ahead with the planned attack, on Kabamba their mission to break open the underground armoury failed, though they went on to liberate the country after four years, it is the right time for the two leaders to resurrect the relationship and avoid the dangers a head after overstaying in power and the bloodshed, after the two countries fought in the Congo, their relationship has been cold for some time with a number of incidents indicating plans to execute each other. It was restarted by Kagame's wife after President Kagame found out that a number of his soldiers are leaving the country.

According to the sources held 800 soldiers have left Rwanda in the last 6 months, this has disturbed Kagame because they all left with the guns, President Kagame believes that getting closer to President Museveni is a means of blocking any support for his opponents.

## 5.2 President Kagame rising from being a failure in school to addressing Oxford University

On the 18th/May/2013 His Excellency Paul Kagame addressed a regional and international audience on a range of issues as indicated on Said Business School Oxford University website. President Kagame addressed issues including African development, leadership and the potential of ICT as an enabler for Africa socio-economic transformation.

President Paul Kagame is known to Rwandans as an autocratic leader who fails to tolerate the political opposition with a large number of opposition leaders in prison. Members of the local communities are silenced and no one is allowed to speak about politics unless and only if they are praising the ruling party Rwandese Patriotic Front (RPF).

It is so embarrassing when I see some westerners talk about the development of Rwanda. Yes, I agree there is some development like building roads, some new houses in the heart of Kigali, Information Technology invested by Americans and some other but this leaves 80% of the population in poverty. Kagame pockets millions of dollars each and every year but his people cannot even afford to eat three meals per day.

The economy of the country is held within Kagame's hands and a few of his government employees. This is very common in many African countries however the only difference to President Kagame's system is that he managed to face lift the city of Kigali into an unsustainable business center that few can actually afford thus requiring him to solicit high profile individuals from the west who continue to sell his image to the whole world. An example is the ex-prime minister of the United Kingdom Tony Blair who has been serving Kagame more than he even served his own country. President Kagame believes it is more important to convince the west then concentrating on his own citizens because they must accept what he says in his autocratic way.

Sometimes I wonder how Kagame is able to fool his western backers with the realities on the ground in Rwanda for 19 years; I can sort of understand because they do not care about the Rwandese anyway. If their own leader doesn't care, as most of these western leaders only care about investments, trading and plan the future for themselves, like President Kagame said at some point, that even invading DRC was planned together with the west.

After leaving Rwanda to seek asylum in Uganda President Kagame's family moved to the north of Rwanda and settled in the Nshungerezi refugee camp in 1962. Kagame's early years in primary school were spent with other Rwandan refugees in a school near the refugee camp where they learned

English, Mathematics, Civics, History, Geography and Social Studies, he also began to integrate into Ugandan culture. At the age of nine he moved to the respected Rwengoro Primary School, around 16 kilometres (10 miles) away. He subsequently attended Ntare School.

The death of Kagame's father in the early 1970s, and the departure of friend Fred Rwigyema to an unknown location, led to a decline in his academic performance and an increased tendency to fight those who belittled the Rwandan population. He would become paranoid to any comment either negative or positive. He was eventually suspended from Ntare School and completed his studies without distinction at Old Kampala Secondary School. He spent a number of years commuting from Kampala to Nairobi as a money changer, dealing in deals such as changing Kenyan shillings to Uganda shillings as well as western money, this also contributed to poor performance. All of those deals he participated in Nshuti Manasseh, who served a number of years in Kagame's government, was by his side.

After finishing his schooling Kagame made two visits to Rwanda, in 1977 and 1978. He was initially hosted by family members of Rwandan classmates in Uganda, but upon arrival in Kigali he made contact with members of his own family. He kept a low profile on these visits, believing that his status as a well-connected Tutsi exile could lead to arrest. On his second visit, he entered the country through Zaire rather than Uganda to avoid suspicion, in 1980 Kagame visited Fred Rwigema who was part of the soldiers who had captured Uganda and later went to the bush war to liberate Uganda in 1986.

As an intelligence officer who was trusted by both President Museveni and Fred Rwigema, Paul Kagame was sent on a number of intelligence trainings to such places as Cuba, Libya and the USA, where he was sent to train as the rest were at the front line.

When Rwanda was captured in 1994 Paul Kagame immediately enrolled in the Germany College studying Business administration through correspondence. I remember most nights I would drive to collect the bank governor of the time Dr. Rutaysire to assist President Kagame with his homework, and return the bank governor to his house early in the morning. I remember when we travelled to a graduation at the Butare University; President Kagame had no higher qualifications, so one of the students asked him what his standard of education was. Kagame was still a minister of defense and a vice president; he presented a grumpy face but managed to handle the situation by promising that he only needed one year to announce his standard of education. President Kagame has had a long way in every way, and now has got something to present in terms of business at Oxford University very surprising.

While in his entourage I used to be surprised especially with his behaviours; he would come up with advice on everything, something that caused the departure of many ministers from his government because they could not cope with his unknowing arrogance. I remember once he wanted to advise an engineer, after asking how that same task is done. Then he would go to the hospital where Kagame would want to advice the doctors on how care should be delivered. I remember when he visited the Kigali Central Hospital; he ordered that the name of the surgical ward should be changed because the name sounded too harsh in our mother tongue, (INZU YIMBAGWA) Kagame believed that it sounded as if it was a butcher.

After this long time of Kagame educating himself, it's s time for him to address the west like many dictators of Africa of the past. The difference from other dictators of Africa is that Paul Kagame is intolerant and dominant, capable of shedding blood, imprisoning at will, inflicting poison and he is able to convince the west with the help of his mercenaries that he is an educated diplomat. What sensible people in this country Rwanda struggle to understand is the same question, how such a leader is accepted in our society for this wrong? What causes President Kagame to behave this way? Research indicates that some of the symptoms of a Narcissistic personality disorder first proposed by Heinz Kohut in 1968, best suits President Kagame's behavioural problems.

Symptoms of this disorder, as defined by the DSM-IV-TR include.

- Reacting to criticism with anger, A shame, or humiliation.

- Taking advantage of others to reach own goals.

- Exaggerating own importance, achievements, and talents

- Imagining unrealistic fantasies of success, beauty, power, intelligence, or romance.

- Requiring constant attention and positive reinforcement from others.

- Becoming jealous easily.

- Lacking empathy and disregarding the feelings of others.

- Being obsessed with self.

- Pursuing mainly selfish goals.

- Trouble keeping healthy relationships.

- Becoming easily hurt and rejected.

- Setting goals that are unrealistic.

- Wanting "the best" of everything.

- Appearing unemotional.

In addition to these symptoms, the person may also display dominance, arrogance, show superiority, and seek power. The symptoms of narcissistic personality disorder can be similar to the traits of individuals with strong self-esteem and confidence; differentiation occurs when the underlying psychological structures of these traits are considered pathological. Narcissists have such an elevated sense of self-worth that they value themselves as inherently better than others. However, they have a fragile self-esteem and cannot handle criticism, and will often try to compensate for this inner fragility by belittling or disparaging others in an attempt to validate their own self-worth. It is this sadistic tendency that is characteristic of narcissism as opposed to other psychological conditions affecting level of self-worth.

President Kagame is married to Jeanette Nyiramongi, they were blessed with four children, Ivan Cyomoro, Angel Kagame, Ian Kagame and Brian Kagame. Like their father the kids are struggling in school and none of them at the moment is officially qualified or graduated in higher education. One of them Ivan was under investigations for plagiarism which lead to absconding from the military academy. Kagame forced him into Harvard university but again the young man left school and declined to return.

## 5.3 Once a good mother now a killer

Jeannette Nyiramongi who once acted as a role model to children turned into a killer like husband. She encouraged singer Kizito Mihigo to come home and build his nation only to then plan his arrest, get him tortured in a safe house and later charged with terrorism. She did all of this because of a single song to reconcile and heal our hearts as Rwandans

In the early 1990's when I met the First Lady of Rwanda Jeanette Kagame, I believed that she was a mother figure to all Rwandese. She always appeared to care for us and would ask us how we were doing. I remember one day around 1997 she asked me if I had a girlfriend, it was a bit funny because that time I had no girlfriend, for some reason she focused on relationships, outings and clubbing, in most of her conversations with any driver who was on duty. She turned up with some interesting questions whenever we drove her out; I believed that she was so innocent. At that time, she was attending Kigali institute of technology (KIST) we would drive her over for her lectures. Those days she used to experience the insults and abusive language from her husband Paul Kagame like all of us did. Even when Kagame was in a relationship with someone, I do not want to mention today, Mrs Kagame who, we normally called Mama Ivan never found out until late, because she was an oblivious woman who was confused.

At times, we used to feel sorry for her because sometimes she would ask us to drive her to her mother's house in Kimihurura whenever Paul Kagame was in a bad mood, or after beating her up. At times, she used to ask us to take her to Kayumba's home due to a good friendship she had with Rosette Kayumba the wife of Gen Kayumba.

Jeanette Kagame continued to live as a house wife while experiencing domestic violence from her husband Paul Kagame till the end of 2002 when Kagame started falling out with his trusted circles. During these days, Kagame had betrayed so many people that he was left with no one to trust apart from those who believed the same way as him of shedding blood such as Gen Jack Nziza, and other Killing machines.

During these days Jeanette Kagame started investing in projects and in even hijacking other projects from individuals, who started the idea before she thought of it. This was because she had started to understand that she could also do something as a first lady. Mrs Kagame worked tirelessly making sure that the Kayumba's fell out permanently with Kagame's so that she could take all of Rosette Kayumba's shares she had invested in the school they shared.

She became friends with Gen Jack Nziza, who is Kagame's right hand man, and well known for arresting and killing anyone who is believed to not support the current regime. Since then Mrs Kagame has been involved in a number of planned killings of different people together with Kagame's intelligence network.

Mrs Kagame has also involved herself in assisting and helping the victims of genocide, and this was the time when she encouraged a young talented Kizito Mihigo to leave Belgium and come back to build his motherland of Rwanda.

Upon his arrival, Kizito Mihigo continued progressing and singing his lovely music of uniting Rwandans. Although, contrary to Kagame's regime, Kizito Mihigo's songs looked at uniting all Rwandan's even though the Kagame's wanted him to only sing genocide of Tutsis and not including anyone else who died before, during and after genocide.

The song which has caused a lot of problems to Kizito Mihigo, and a number of young men in Rwanda, is Igisobanuro Cy'urupfu, in English (THE DEFINITION OF DEATH) in this song Kizito explains that he remembers those who died not only genocide but even violence, revenge, and any death that happened during the war unexpectedly. He goes on say in his song that Humanism should come first before talking about being Rwandan.

Even though Kizito Mihigo was very close to Mrs Kagame due to the projects he had much role in developing by singing the healing songs for unity and reconciliation it did not stop Mrs Kagame from giving him away and getting him arrested. He was put into safe house where he had been for the last few days before being charged of collaborating with RNC/FDRL.

Prior to Kizito Mihigo's arrest, President Paul Kagame was heard as saying in his speech "I am not a singer to please both sides" this was the time when Kizito Mihigo's song was causing uncertainty in the country due to how all ethnicities welcomed the importance of the meaning of the song and the contribution it meant on reconciliation.

Something the ruling government never appreciated and then the intelligence network connected to Mrs Kagame started arresting anyone connected to Kizito Mihigo, and later Kizito Mihigo himself.

Kizito Mihigo is an organist and composer, was born Saturday, July 25th, 1981 at Kibeho, a sector of Nyaruguru district, in the former Gikongoro province, currently located in the Southern Province. Son of Augustin Buguzi and Ilibagiza Placidia, Kizito grew up in a Catholic Christian educational environment. At the age of 9, he began to compose small songs, and five years later, when he was a secondary school student in the « Petit Seminaire de Butare », he became the most popular liturgical organist composer in the Catholic Church of Rwanda.

In April 1994, when he was almost 13 years old, the young Mihigo survived the genocide against the Tutsis, in which more than eight hundred thousand Tutsis were murdered during including his own father. A few years later, this tragedy inspired the young talent to become the organist-singer-author and composer of the most popular songs in Rwanda.

One year after the genocide, Kizito Mihigo composed hundreds of liturgical compositions which were rapidly exploited in several parishes in Rwanda. In 2000, (when he was 19 years old), Kizito Mihigo were already author and composer of over 200 (two hundred) liturgical songs, sung in all the parishes of Rwanda.

In 2003, noticed by the authorities of the country, he was sent to Europe to follow his music studies. In 2008, he received the postgraduate diploma (DFE) at the "Conservatoire de Musique in Paris". From 2008-2010, after his graduation, he was a music teacher in Belgium. In 2010, he founded the KMP (Kizito Mihigo for Peace) a non-profit foundation with the mission of using Art in PEACEBUILDING. In 2011, Imbuto Foundation, the organization of the First Lady of Rwanda, gives to Kizito Mihigo the price CYRWA (Celebrating Young Rwandan Archivers), in recognition of his artistic activities for Peace and Reconciliation.

## 5.4 The selfish president of the tiny landlocked nation of Africa

Back in the bush war, Kagame would come from Kampala packed with luxury meals to last him the entire weeks he spent with us before going back. He would feast on extravagant packed foods from top Kampala supermarkets while the rest of us his bodyguards and the entire army struggled to have enough Maize corn and beans (IMVUNGURE) for a day. He would also bring with him numerous chickens that fed on our scarcely rationed maize corn until they were slaughtered for him. The rest of the commanders who fought the battles in their respective mobile squadrons were served the same maize and beans like all of us.

Kagame's narcissistic nature as a leader was evident from the very beginning. Around May 1991 after the Ruhengeri offensive, Kagame was served a meal that he did not finish due to his bad appetite. The hungry young soldiers who had served him returned the meal together with some biscuits and started eating the leftovers. When Kagame saw them eating his leftover food he came running took the plate and stamped on the food. AT the time, we did not understand his actions but in retrospect it was obvious of his ruling personality then and now. Kagame cares very little for those who surround him and no one is to have something that he would even throw away.

By as early as 1992 Kagame had managed to scheme himself around the RPA command structure and had made himself the Chairman of the High Command and promoted himself to Major General stationed at Mulindi Tea Estate headquarters.

Here at Mulindi the now self-appointed Maj. Gen Kagame enjoyed the luxury of hot water and electricity and a clear supply route to Kabale for his exotic food supply. After the fall of Kigali, "vice-president" Maj. Gen Kagame's lust for luxury grew at an unimaginable rate. He immediately ordered a fleet of expensive bulletproof vehicles while disregarding the crisis the country. This was a time when the government needed to focus money in order to help the returning refugees as well as those who had just fled the country. Yet instead, Kagame continued enriching himself at any cost possible.

He grabbed land from the innocent citizens of Muhazi and started up his Ranch, which he furnished with over 200 Friesian cows flown in from Switzerland, just to prove a point to sponsors of our struggle. Mr Kagame continued to enrich himself by investing the government money in his dairy business (inyange), supermarkets and many investments under his companies' Venture Capital and Tri-Star later named Crystal Ventures.

As if this was not enough, Kagame introduced the unnecessary tax known as Umusoro w'umutekano or Security Tax around 1996/1997 to his starving citizens directly and to all government and NGO employees. This tax resulted in many people leaving the country due to its tough and unrealistic requirements. In addition, he spent an exorbitant amount of taxpayer's and donor money to build airspace surveillance Radar just because he felt uncomfortable with neighbouring countries due to his involvement in regional wars.

After he collected all the citizens taxes and minerals from the Congo he invested the money in banks such as Bank de Kigali (BK), BCDI and Bank Commercial de Rwanda after he conflicted with the top proprietors of each of the bank. These Banks continue to belong to him under the façade of different shareholders whom he controls.

A few years after Gen Kagame purchased the London building on plot 122 Seymour Place, London, W1H 1NR he then rented the property to the Rwandan High Commission in the UK. Surprisingly, Colina Enterprises, the buildings listed owner, is registered in Panama in the name of two close collaborators to the Rwandan Head of State.

Back in 2003, Kagame's nephew Byusa accompanied by Hatari Sekoko in one of Kagame's two US$50 million Bombardier Jets, travelled to Panama to set Colina Enterprise, which subsequently purchased a building from one Bright Grahame Murray for almost £2 million. This three-storied building in the heart of London now houses the Rwandan High Commission, having moved from Trafalgar Square, where it used to share same premises with the Ugandan Embassy. Naturally, the rent for the new Embassy should be paid from the national treasury or the Ministry of Finance, where his excellence Paul Kagame has yet another strong link for executing his misdeeds.

Sitting in the upper echelons of the Finance Ministry is no other than Pitchette Kampeta Sayinzoga, the wife of Kagame's nephew Byusa and the co-director of Colina Enterprise. She is the permanent Secretary of the Ministry of Finance and Economic Planning and therefore ensures the smooth transactions-and to make the landlord and tenant happy.

Those familiar with the famous Kagame Bombardier Global Express Aircraft will see a similar pattern here, as one should recall, the aircraft are said to be "owned " by Repli Investments 29 (pty) Ltd, a company registered in South Africa under Hatari Sekoko, Jean Paul Nyirubatama, who is a close relative to Jeannette Kagame coincidentally, and Manasseh Nshuti as directors. (More can be read here about his personal jets http://kigalipost.wordpress.com/2010/05/28/s-africa-based-luxury-jets-owned-by-rpf-nshuti/)

Sgt Hatari Sekoko was Kagame's driver in Uganda and kept his job throughout the wartime commuting Kagame to and from Kampala in his Mercedes Benz G Wagon (Cross-Country) until he promoted him to the rank of Captain. Apart from that Sekoko is an illiterate mal-trained soldier who spent most of his time as a mechanic in military transport headquarters and garages where he acquired his nickname 'Kibanda' or Conman.

Manasseh Nshuti, the third director of Kagame's Repli Investments 29 (pty) Ltd is a close relative to the president himself. Manasseh was repatriated from Scotland by Kagame himself appointing him as Minister of Finance and Economic Planning, a post he did not hold for long due to critics from donors for his lack of performance.

In a country, still heavily dependent on foreign aid from western backers, it appears that President Kagame has deep pockets when it suits his own balance sheet. Financial and political corruption have been the modus operandi in Rwanda since the RPF took power in 1994. Yet, what about the areas beyond Kigali? What about the rural population that struggles on a daily basis to feed their families? Their hard work has gone to support the life of luxury that President Kagame has grown quite accustomed.

Foreign Aid backers must start holding Paul Kagame accountable to the use of aid monies or this corruption will continue to serve the selfish desires of Paul Kagame himself. There goes the Kagame brand of good governance and transparency that has become the hallmark in selling his image to Britain and other donor Governments.

## 5.5 Why our King remains in Exile part 1:

This article was written before the Rwandan King Kigeli V Ndahindurwa death. He was still living in exile in United State of America. His Majesty the King Kigeli v Ndahindurwa passed away on the 16th October 2016. He has been buried in Nyanza in a very low-key burial ceremony without the presence of prominent Premiers including president Kagame. May his Soul

Rest in Peace.

When I was growing up in 1980's, I always heard stories from the elderly people in my family conversing about our beloved King, words such as (umwami wu Rwanda Kigeli V Ndahindurwa) who they reported had taken the throne at an early age. My grandmother actually informed me that the King had visited my village (Lwebitakuli, Sembabule, Uganda) in the 1970's. I was disappointed that I never had a chance to see him however my elder sister was able to participate in the cultural dance welcoming the King and she even shook his hand (I wish I was there to take a glimpse). On this occasion, the King was given cows and many other gifts from the people.

The King was busy conducting excellent work trying to unite the refugees around the globe and becoming a voice for them where ever they were. Our King wrote letters and met with leaders of different countries just to make sure that his people were comfortable. Some of the cows he was given on the occasion are still at my uncle's farm, I hope he will turn up for them one day. We kept on hearing only good news about our King who tried to avoid another tragedy happening on our land by communicating with the leaders of the time in order to find a solution contrary to war, he moved around to different countries in Africa and managed to keep the Rwandese people together with a strong culture and belief, solidarity and love that has kept us going until today.

He informed the international community the dangers surrounding ignoring what was going in Rwanda just before genocide. He was the King who visited refugees in Congo just after the Habyarimana government was overthrown and most Hutu refugees left for Congo where the RPF soldiers were slaughtering them like animals. After this visit he made in Lubumbashi around year late 1999 or early 2000, the Kagame government started creating rumours that he has rebels and threatened to fight them, a lot of young people were arrested and others killed, people began to become afraid of mentioning the name of our King in fear of retribution.

Former President Habyarimana was afraid of the King's return because at the time most of people in Rwanda understood the importance of a monarchy in a country like Rwanda experiencing ignorance and belief in tribalism. President Habyarimana thought that the King would make it hard for him to rule the poor nation. He was continuously reminded of the history of Kingdoms only based on 1700 or 1800 Kings who may have mistreated their citizens, but ignored the reform which had been done by Mutara Rudahigwa and King Kigeli V's Manifesto of the 1959. Former President Habyarimana tried to ignore even an important point of that our King was modern and not stuck in history.

He was the King who finalised the search for our independence, (Unfortunately never even celebrated). However, he continued staying in touch with people, even when the leaders in power ignored him and his ideas. Many of the fallen leaders did contact him for advice when in exile on how to survive. Our King has always maintained the King's gesture of remembering his people because he understands the problems his country experienced were mostly was caused by the outsiders (Belgians). Like his name, Ndahindurwa, he remains the same with love for his people and tried to make everyone understands that the divisions inside Rwanda were caused by outsiders.

Our King is still seen as a powerful symbol of hope. The refugees had always maintained contact with the King and so the RPF leaders themselves including their former leader who may actually have made sure that the

King returns home. According to the few who knew General Fred Rwigema, they believed that his goal was to stop these lives of statelessness which dominates our society still, but then came the strong man Paul Kagame, everything is about him not the people. Until today the Rwandese people are hungry to see or listen to their King but Kagame continues to deprive them of that choice they are entitled to. This all remains in a book of history on MRND/RPF page.

## *His Majesty Kigeli V Message on the 16th Commemoration of the Genocide*

Fellow Rwandans,

My greetings to all of you wherever you are inside or outside Rwanda.

I love you and I miss you!

As we commemorate the genocide for the 16th time, and as we remember our loved ones who lost their lives in that tragedy, I take the opportunity to ask you to pray for all our loved ones who perished, and to implore our Creator to grant them an everlasting rest.

The tragedy that befell Rwanda left indelible wounds in our collective memory. The loss of our loved ones will remain with us forever. This reminds us our moral obligation to protect every human life.

I insistently ask every Rwandan to work for peace in Rwanda; to live in peace with one another, especially during the times of the genocide's commemoration; to protect everyone's human rights; and to love one another so that the horror that happened in Rwanda does not repeat anymore.

I offer my sympathy to all widows, orphans, and all the less privileged. Be patient and never lose hope because God is with us.

Fellow Rwandans, I love you and I miss you! And it is time for me to return to my home country so that we can, together, build our country the way we wish it to be.

In my New Year message, I told you we will meet in Rwanda this year 2010 and I particularly ask young people to preserve our cultural values of love, solidarity, tolerance, courage, frankness, and humility. These values are crucial to the reconciliation and lasting peace in Rwanda.

Fellow Rwandans, I will always work for the unity of all Rwandans. This is the pledge I have made to God and to all of you as the Constitutional monarch of Rwanda.

I wish you peace. May our Almighty God protect you wherever you are inside or outside Rwanda

*His Majesty Kigeli V Jean Baptist Ndahindurwa*

*But why does President Paul Kagame continuously keep this King in exile?*

He stated that our King will only return back to his country as a normal citizen and not even a cultural leader. The Rwandan parliament is not allowed to discuss on the King's return, and the people of Rwanda have never had a chance to be consulted on this matter. Surprisingly, our King was overthrown by the Belgians not the Rwandans; Paul Kagame like his predecessors always displayed anxiety for the King's return because he was ousted not overthrown. Paul Kagame cannot stand a normal politician let alone a King in any way. President Paul Kagame lost his tongue in year

2000 when he said on the national radio that if the King has an army he will be shoot at. I laughed because in a normal way all RDF soldiers should be called the King's forces because he has always been there for all Rwandans, and so the army belongs to his majesty not his "so called" excellency Paul Kagame.

It does not matter ex-FAR or RDF, if Kagame was a peaceful president he should even have been proud of being called a King's force because peace and reconciliation will only be achieved from where the instability started, and with the King's involvement Rwanda will heal.

The history of the Royal lineage in Rwanda dates back hundreds of years yet many outsides of Rwandan culture may not know much at all about this history. The current exiled King has worked tirelessly to unify his people and continues to do so even though he is thousands of miles from his homeland.

King Kigeli V lives in exile in Washington D.C., he has always said, since his swearing in as the Constitutional monarch of Rwanda in 1959, that monarchists and republicans could live side by side peacefully in Rwanda if he was given his right to reconcile his beloved people. Over the last few decades he has continued to send a message of hope, peace and reconciliation to his people who are scattered around the world. In this curtain, we will unveil his message of peace and unity in his own words.

## *INTERVIEW: Colette Braeckman, Washington DC:*

*"Under what circumstances did you leave Rwanda?"*

Governor Harroy was relieved from his duties by Colonel Logiest and Colonel Logiest, who was fully empowered, had placed the country in a state of exception, which removed all prerogatives from the King. By presenting Logiest to the King, General Janssens had declared that the all-powerful Colonel could kill, save, and do what he pleased... I then requested authorisation to go to Kinshasa as I intended questioning the Secretary General of the UN, Dag Hammarskjold. After dithering for a long time, Harroy suddenly approved the trip. Beforehand, I had questioned Colonel Logiest asking him why we were arresting people without judging them.

With a complete military franchise, Colonel Logiest replied to me, "I am on a mission from my government who sent me here to remove the Tutsis from power and install the Hutus." He was carrying out orders, it was obvious. I wanted to speak with the UN Secretary General as, with the Belgians, there was no hope. Hammarskjold promised to send me to New York, but the Belgian government, while I was in Kinshasa for a week, made it known that I couldn't return to Rwanda. It is, therefore, incorrect to say that I was chased out of power by the Hutus. The people that sent me into exile were the Belgians, in 1961, a year before independence. I denounced this situation before the UN General Assembly, but the resolutions seeking my return were never applied.

*So, you do not blame the Hutus for your removal?*

Absolutely not. The Hutus, at the time, were not against the King, this is why some of them are today advocating my return. What happened, was the Gitarama coup d'état, where the Belgians, Harroy and Logiest, in collaboration with the white fathers, put Grégoire Kayibanda in power. The attacks against the Tutsis were instigated by the Belgians, but the Hutus were not targeting the monarchy. Quite the opposite, if the Tutsis were attacked or chased, it is because the Hutus were made to believe that some noble Tutsis had poisoned Mutara… The people in the country said that the Belgian administrator had given them the order to burn the huts of Tutsis as the Tutsis were the King's opponents. Everyone can confirm to you that the Hutus were accompanied by Belgian commandos. Therefore, *"It was the Belgians who sent me into exile, not the Hutus."*

*Exiled King Demands Role in Bringing Peace to Rwanda*

"Washington DC, October 11, 1998: — King Kigeli V, the King of Rwanda who had been exiled by Belgian colonial authorities from his country when he left to ask the United Nations to help win independence for Rwanda, has demanded a role in bringing an end to communal violence and genocide in his country, it was announced today in Washington DC.

King Kigeli, who had originally warned the UN and the Organization for African Unity of the impending genocide in Rwanda in 1994, made the call at the International Strategic Studies Association's (ISSA) closed-door conference, Strategy'98: The Global Strategic Forum, in Washington DC this past week.

The King said: "I tonight call on General Kagame and his administration to allow my return to Rwanda as King of my People, so that we may put the question of the fate of Rwanda, and the issue of a new constitution which may protect us all, squarely before the population in internationally-supervised plebiscites. General Kagame, as a Rwandan politician and leader who sees the need for reconciliation between all our peoples, can and must put the interests of the entire Rwandan population ahead of short-term political interests.""

*In a profound statement during this speech the King stated the following:*

"He said: "When the Hutu are in power, the Tutsi *live - or die - in fear*. When the Tutsi are in power, the Hutu *live -or die- in fear*. In this dilemma of equally unacceptable options, we must search for a better path."

"I do not seek my return, or the restoration of the Crown, as an end in itself. My sole goal for Rwanda is peace above all," he said. He also urged the United States and the international community to "stop playing around the edges of the Rwandan problem" and to consult with Rwandan Elders, who know the country best."

On numerous occasions and remembrances of the Genocide of 1994, the King has sent messages to his "children," as he calls them. In such messages, he asks for unity and peace in Rwanda. The following are such examples of these messages:

*In his 2010 New Year's message the King stated the following:*

"It has been more than fifty years since Rwanda has been facing many complex issues. These issues are rooted in interethnic violence, poverty, intolerance endemic diseases, etc. It's regrettable that these problems have worsened over the years and have culminated in the 1994 genocide.

We should however not lose hope. Days ahead are full of promise: the end of inequality, peaceful coexistence in Rwanda, justice, civic involvement, the return of love for one's neighbour and the integrity that has always characterized Rwandans. "

*In this same address, he stated the following in regards to the election that was held that year:*

"The year 2010 coincides with the presidential election. This political event is important for all Rwandans. I therefore ask the government of Rwanda and all Rwandans to make sure this election is free, fair, and transparent. This is best way for Rwanda to have the leaders Rwanda deserves.

Fellow Rwandans, I miss you and love you. The time has come for me to return home to Rwanda in order that we can all see each other this year in Rwanda. I will continue to do whatever I can to help achieve peace and prosperity in Rwanda."

During the time of remembrance of the 1994 Genocide in the 16th year the King made, in part, the following statement to his children:

"The tragedy that befell Rwanda left indelible wounds in our collective memory. The loss of our loved ones will remain with us forever. This reminds us our moral obligation to protect every human life.

I insistently ask every Rwandan to work for peace in Rwanda; to live in peace with one another, especially during the times of the genocide's commemoration; to protect everyone's human rights; and to love one another so that the horror that happened in Rwanda does not repeat anymore. "

In all of the Kings statements, interviews and publications it is quite obvious that the King is a peaceful man and wishes to return to Rwanda under peaceful means as the King of Rwanda. The King had a conversation with President Paul Kagame in 1996 regarding his return to Rwanda but it was obvious the two could not reach a consensus as to the terms of his return.

The King, as well as many others who live in exile, want for nothing more than to return to Rwanda under peaceful and unifying terms. One has to wonder if this will ever happen is a present-day Rwanda under Paul Kagame.

*But who was this King?*

Kigeli V Ndahindurwa was born in the royal family in culture which understood the importance of the Kingdom at the time. Born June 29, 1936 he was the ruling King of Rwanda from 25 Jul 1959 until 28 Jan 1961. He was born in Kamembe, Rwanda. His Christian name is Jean-Baptiste and sir name Ndahindurwa. He was raised as a prince as it's generally well known in our country. He attended his education at Groupe Scolaire d'Astrida in Rwanda, and at Nyangezi College in the modern-day Democratic Republic of the Congo.

After King Mutara Rudahigwa died under mysterious circumstances in 1959, he was replaced on the throne by his younger brother Jean-Baptiste Ndahindurwa as King Kigeli V of Rwanda.

Political instability and tribal conflict grew despite the efforts of King Kigeli Ndahindurwa. He was a young King with no support from the western colonisers. An increasingly resistive Hutu population were encouraged by the Belgian military to not recognize the King thus sparking a revolt in November 1959. In 1961, King Kigeli V was in Kinshasa to meet with Secretary-General of the United Nations Dag Hammarskjöld with Dominique Mbonyumutwa with the support of the Belgian government. This led to a coup d'état that took control of the government. The coup resulted in the 1961 referendum about the fate of the monarchy. The majority voted against the monarchy of King Kigeli V and he was ousted. He initially fled into exile to Tanganyika, where he lived in Dar es Salaam (1961–1962). Then he moved to Nairobi, Kenya (1963–1971). He also lived in Kampala, Uganda (1972–1978) and in Nairobi (1979–1992) and since 1992 he has lived in Washington, D.C., United States.

In June 1992, he was granted political asylum by the United States and continues to live in Washington, D. C. He has travelled internationally speaking on behalf of the Rwandan people and repeatedly calls for peace and harmony between the different ethnic and political groups.

King Kigeli V has continued to remember the victims of the Rwandan Genocide and continues to make every attempt to reconcile between all political, ethnic, and religious parties in Rwanda to use the democratic process to solve any disputes. King Kigeli is a friend of former South African president Nelson Mandela.

King Kigeli V was invited by the Delta Phi Epsilon Alpha chapter at Georgetown University where he gave a speech, "The Rwanda Genocide: The Most Preventable Tragedy of Our Time".

In an August 2007 BBC interview, Kigeli expressed an interest in returning to Rwanda if the Rwandan people are prepared to accept him as their constitutional monarch. He said that he had met President Paul Kagame and that Kagame had told him that he and his family were free to return, but Kigeli said that in order to do so, he needed to know if the people still wanted him to be King. According to Kigeli, Kagame said that he would consult the government about the issue

He currently heads the King Kigeli V Foundation, whose mission is to bring humanitarian initiatives on behalf of Rwandese refugees. King Kigeli V awards the Royal Order of the Intare to individuals.

Awards and non-hereditary orders and titles, held by our beloved King which has never been held by the so called Rwandan leaders, Kagame has been begging for awards all over the world but I bet he will never get any of these, simply because he is not as peaceful as our King.

King Kigeli V was awarded the Gold Star Award from by the International Strategic Studies Association for Outstanding Contributions to Strategic Progress through Humanitarian Achievement for his work for Rwandan refugees in Africa.

*Orders and decorations received by the King:*

- Grand Cross, Order of the Immaculate Conception of Vila Viçosa (House of Braganza)

- Grand Cross, Order of Saint Michael of the Wing (House of Braganza)

- Grand Cross, Order of the Queen of Sheba (Imperial House of Ethiopia)

- Grand Cross, Imperial Order of the Star of Honour of the Ethiopian Empire

- Grand Cross, Imperial Order of Solomon of the Ethiopian Empire

- Grand Collar, Royal Order of Ismail (Royal House of Egypt)

- Grand Collar, Order of the Tunic of Our Lord Jesus (Royal House of Georgia)

- Grand Cross, Cross of São Tomé, Apostolo by Bishop Abilio Rodas De Souza (Catholic decoration, São Tomé)

- Grand Cross, Military and Hospitaller Order of Saint Lazarus of Jerusalem

- Knight, Most Prestigious Brotherhood of the Most Blessed Sacrament of the Noble City of Lisbon (Portugal)

# 6 Chap VI: Kagame Proxy war in Democratic Republic of Congo and His troubled relations with Neighbouring Countries

## 6.1 A hungry President, the truth behind Congo War

After the overthrow of Mobutu of Zaire and naming it Democratic Republic of Congo, Paul Kagame was convinced that his Government will have the biggest access of Congo's wealth and the right to do whatever he wished without any hindrance.

Kagame made Desire Kabila the new president of the DRC, convincing himself that he would use him to control and grab all he laid his hands on in the Congo. At that time Kagame has deployed the DRC with most of his senior trusted officers to control not only the wealthy country but also President Kabila. Kagame's own right-hand man Gen James Kabarebe headed the Congolese army.

President Desire Kabila got a bit skeptical of Kagame's long time goals and sought advice from his senior officers (Congolese). This came following an incident where Kagame had confiscated arms, ammunitions and vehicles Kabila's government had purchased through the Rwanda army. This logistics included artillery pieces such Ballistic Missiles (BM), Heavy and Light Anti-Aircraft pieces, General Purpose Machine Guns (GPMG),48 Nissan Patrol 4x4 Trucks and 80 Land Rovers Jeeps. Kagame decided to only dispatch a half of these logistics to Congo keeping the rest for himself.

This caused a lot of anger, distrust and chaos to Kabila and his government. In return Kabila ordered the Rwandan forces under their most senior Commander General James Kabarebe to leave the country. He was made to leave the country without taking even the car he was travelling in to the airport, something that annoyed the whole army.

On their arrival at Kanombe International Airport, we drove his excellence Paul Kagame to meet with them. This force was immediately ordered to go to Camp GP (Presidential Guard Barracks) and wait for more orders as they remain on standby. He seemed physically angered and disappointed at that time.

After twenty-four hours, we went to Camp GP with Paul Kagame to brief the forces why they should immediately go back to the Congo to fight Kabila, the man they had just installed in power. Surprisingly everyone supported the idea because at that time all soldiers seemed to believe that they would keep their loot on return from the DRC. These included gems and American Dollars the currency Congo used.

Desire Kabila on the other hand had solicited for troops from Zimbabwe and Angola to take over deployments after the departure of the Rwandese forces. When Kagame's forces attacked Congo this second time, they could not believe how massively Kabila had deployed.

Our forces sustained big losses and casualties this time around. The first Congo war was a bit easier because Kagame negotiated with President Chiluba of Zambia to offer our troops the quickest route to Kinshasa.

When Kagame attempted to ask for the second attack route to oust Kabila on this second time, President Chiluba declined, reminding Kagame that: "I thought Mobutu was a bad man and a dictator what about Kabila you came with to visit me, why fight him now".

This Second Congo War (also known as the Great War of Africa) began in August 1998 in the DRC, and officially ended in July 2003 when the transitional government took power. The deadliest war in modern African history, it directly involved eight African nations, as well as about 25 armed groups. Surprisingly President Paul Kagame created more than 8 armed groups to destabilise the region for his own interests.

By 2008, the war had claimed lives of over 5.4 million people, mostly from diseases and starvation, making the Second Congo War the deadliest conflict worldwide since the world war. Millions more were displaced from their homes or sought refuge in neighbouring countries. This was all caused by Kagame's idea of wanting to make himself the richest man on the globe.

Despite a formal end to the war in July 2003 and an agreement by the former belligerents to create a government of national unity, 1,000 people died daily in 2004 from easily preventable cases of malnutrition and disease. The war and the conflicts afterwards were driven by, among other things, the trade in minerals.

The first Congo war began in 1996 as Rwanda grew increasingly concerned about members of Interahamwe militias and former Rwanda Government Forces who were carrying out cross-border raids from Zaire (currently known as the Democratic Republic of Congo) and thought to be planning an invasion. The militias, mostly Hutu, were entrenched in refugee camps in eastern Zaire, where many had fled to escape the Tutsi-dominated RPF in the aftermath of the Rwanda Genocide.

Kagame's government of Rwanda protested this violation of their territorial integrity and began to give arms to the ethnically Tutsi Banyamulenge of eastern Zaire. It was evident that the insurgents were so weak to attack a country like Rwanda, they had fled to the forests of Congo to try and find a living for their families.

Most of them however had joined Kagame's forces but he kept on lying to the world that he was fighting the Hutu militia when they had actually joined his own army after what he calls voluntary repatriation. When Kabila finally gained control over the capital in May 1997, he faced substantial obstacles to governing the country, which he renamed 'the Democratic Republic of Congo' (DRC). Beyond political jostling among various groups to gain power and an enormous external debt, his foreign backers proved unwilling to leave when asked. The conspicuous Rwandan presence in the capital also ranked many Congolese, who were beginning to see Kabila as a pawn of foreign powers.

Tensions reached new heights on 14 July 1998, when Kabila dismissed his Rwandan chief of staff James Kabarebe and replaced him with a native Congolese, Celestin Kifwa. Although the move chilled what was already a troubled relationship with Rwanda, he softened the blow by making Kabarebe the military advisor to his successor.

Two weeks later, Kabila abandoned such diplomatic steps. He thanked Rwanda for its help and ordered all Rwandan and Ugandan military forces to leave the country. Within 24 hours Rwandan military advisors living in Kinshasa were unceremoniously flown out. The people most alarmed by this order were the Banyamulenge of eastern Congo. Their tensions with neighbouring ethnic groups had been a contributing factor in the genesis of the first Congo war and they were also used by Rwanda to affect events across the border in the DRC.

This was all triggered by Kagame's long arm of theft of Minerals, Ammunitions, Money and Vehicles. Not only civilians and younger soldiers died but also the commanders such as General Massa, Colonel Wilson Rutayisire, Major Ikondere and in the end Desire Kabila himself, Laurent

Nkunda in Prison and others. According to his excellency Paul Kagame our aim was to fight the Hutu militias who were threatening to come back and kill the innocent civilians, however we crossed the border and headed to Kinshasha, but the so-called militias were hiding in the forests of Katanga region and equatorial. After the international community pressure, the Rwandese soldiers withdrew and we haven't seen any militias attack Rwanda, so what else do we need to question the cause of the war that swiped a million of lives?

## 6.2 Kagame's next tactic in order to govern DRC

During the past twenty years, millions of people have died this included the refugees who run away from their native Rwanda and the citizens of Congo, Soldiers from different countries fighting with the Congolese army and many rebel groups. They are fighting to control the land in order to manage the natural resources and reap the financial benefits. Since 1996, 25 rebel groups have been created in DRC and 16 out of the 25 were all created by Dr. Kagame. Much of the fighting has taken place in the mineral rich regions of north-eastern and eastern Congo where gold; diamonds, tin, and coltan can be found which are all used in manufacturing electronics.

The instability in Central Africa has always been caused by Doctor Kagame and a few of his commanders. After Dr. Kagame realised that his tactics had been detected by the United Nations followed by a number of warnings issued to Dr. Kagame from the western countries, he decided to change his logistical tactics.

President Kagame ordered his intelligence officers to relocate the demobilised soldiers to the Democratic Republic Congo in order to play a part in the local voting systems, hoping that these ex-service men would become local leaders and assist his regime in changing the eastern region to obey his system. He also ordered his intelligence staff that they need to use the RPF former carders, who are currently unemployed, to settle in the eastern region of Congo. He repeatedly urged his intelligence officers to work hand in hand with the Congolese authorities, most of the people are Banyamurenge's who are Tutsi's and speak Kinyarwanda.

These Banyamurenge's supported Gen Laurent Nkunda who is being held in Kigali on questionable war crimes charges. Gen Laurent Nkunda was consulted by Kagame and agreed to the idea of seeking the independence for the eastern Congo but through working from the local communities. They reached a conclusion of resettling the ex-service men as mentioned above, to work hand in hand with the Kigali network. Among the plans also were to advice some of the Rwandan investors to invest in Eastern Congo, this however went surprisingly wrong as one of the business men who was approached by Gen Rutatina immediately agreed strait away and promised commissions with the condition of allowing him to form farms on miles of land in one specific area. Something that Col Dan Munyuza first thought that was going to cause some conflict having to have to ask the local citizens to move for this investor to settle.

However, Gen Rutatina, a known unethical medical Doctor (instead of saving lives he destroys lives), insisted that the investor will have to settle wherever he wants, and then also was a condition of allowing him to take 76 workers who were to be working on his farms to build houses. The silly move turned out to become a source of imprisonment for most of them when General Ibingira travelled with this investor to the Eastern Congo with a motorcade of 8 vehicles. President Kagame learned of this plan after a Congolese newspaper published the images of Gen Ibingira and other RDF officers trespassing in the Congo with the investors.

President Kagame, spoke to Gen Jack Nziza who immediately investigated and asked the officers if they remembered what the agreed plan was? He highlighted how the plan was not followed as first agreed upon; he stated that in the beginning the plan was that they will resettle the ex-service men before anyone else, then cadres before investors. The main purpose was to change the locals in order to fight for independence and join Rwanda as they speak the same language with the same clans.

This was the main cause of the "arrests" of Kagame's senior army officers who were directed to be charged with implementing the settlement plan; however, the plan was designed by Kagame himself. Gen Rutatina, a brain child who is actually an Innocent Doctor who failed to know what he is putting himself into because he does not know exactly who Kagame is, if he did he would have walked out a long time ago before even being imprisoned. Gen Rutatina agreed that his role was to make sure that the ex-service men get resettled in the region. This involved knowing the right people to be resettled, who will keep this plan a secret and who will make sure that they will stick on the instructions given from the Rwandan government.

Col Dan Munyuza, an external intelligence director, his role was to choose who to send and settle, what they need in order to function and reporting back to Rwanda. He was also to liaise with the investors as well as the ministry which was to give funds for those who needed references before Kagame's Banks can release funds.

Gen Ibingira, the commanding officer of the reserve force, his role was full clearance on who goes, he was to work hand in hand with the national security service (NSS) on looking at the background of the ex-service men and come up with the right person for the right post and area when they finish resettling them. Remember the Eastern Congo region is full of minerals and so they were looking for people who can be trusted, who would not turn against the Rwandese government on arrival.

Gen Gumisiriza's role was to oversee as he is the division commander of the neighbouring area, he deploys inside Rwanda and on the Congo side. He was blamed for allowing the convoy entering in day light.

This was all supposed to be highly sensitive and he blamed his officers for allowing the mission to be known. He had agreed with his officers to only resettle the ex-service men first who would easily accept orders as they had served in the forces before.

After Kagame received the full report from Gen Jack Nziza, his only trusted General, it became apparent that they had involved "un-veted" business men! he then called an urgent meeting and accused his officers of favouring the rich due to corruption and asked them for more answers. General Ibingira explained that he did not know exactly what was going on as he is uneducated officer. According to the sources held Gen Ibingira cried and knelt down to apologise to his Excellency, he pleaded that he is only good at the front line and executing orders but not the political and intelligence stuff. He was immediately forgiven and the rest were held waiting to be called to court for more charges.

This grandeur clandestine plan, to settle demobilised soldiers of Rwanda into the Eastern Congo, is still under the plans of president Kagame. This is driven by the expansion mentality of dictators that has been manifested in many regions where dictators have existed. It is also driven by the fact that the International Community is just watching and passively awarding the perpetrator with non-sensible award after award. Germany's Hitler and Dr

Idi Amini Dada both used the expansion mentality. Dr. Idi Amini Dada wanted to extend Uganda into Tanzania (the Akagera region of Tanzania).

The difference from these cases is that the whole world reacted and stopped these plans. They condemned the actions of these dictators and even decisively fought them. In the case of the Eastern Congo the International Community has stood by while the dictator continues to unleash havoc in the region unabated, dismantling communities, families and innocent children. The world must stand up again and protect the innocent people who are suffering in the Congo on a daily basis.

## 6.3 A summon to my good old comrades: M23 Saga

With the on-going continued cut of President Kagame's Foreign aid by his long time Western sponsors for the last week or so due to his continued cruelty to our Congolese brethren I feel compelled to speak on this subject. Kagame has done this by directly supporting the M23 rebel group which was on the brink of capturing the city of Goma among others in the Kivu Province of the DRC and with a plan of creating a new Republic of Kivu autonomous from the great Congo. Unfortunately, this maneuver disregards the suffering of innocent women and children involved in this saga.

This has kept me awake for days thinking about the inhumane acts of our President, His Excellency Paul Kagame, who is a product of civil unrest himself. Kagame, like my old brothers, sought safety in Uganda as a child refugee due to the unrest in Rwanda in the 1950/60s.

He was only 3year old when his mother carried him on her back carrying her belongings on her head and moved to Uganda for protection. President

Kagame grew to become a Major in a foreign army. For sure, a person with such a recurring history should not fuel it in any part of the world let alone his neighbouring Congo no matter what the price or gain.

As I was writing this article I received information from anonymous veterans which indicates that the M23 rebels backed by the RDF continued to advance to the city of Goma. This information made me wonder if the cuts in foreign aid would have any impact on Kagame's plans or else stop his intentions.

Of course, the impacts of these cuts still lie in Kagame's investments but not on normal citizens in the village who earns nothing and struggle each day to feed their family. It stays the same because when you have nothing then you have nothing to lose. With President Kagame on the other hand, so long as the M23 continued to advance, capture towns and mineral rich mines, he will continue to benefit from DRC resources and thus compensate for the loss Western aid.

It so embarrassing for a sovereign country like the DRC with such resources and a so-called government to ignore its citizens and let them die in cross fires and under foreign invaders like the Rwanda Defense Forces and the M23.

President Joseph Kabila came out and stated that the presence of Rwandan military forces in the east of the Democratic Republic of Congo is "an open secret." To some of us this statement was troubling on its own, we were left to wonder why a president of the Republic of Congo waited for all this time when people are dying on a daily basis when he knew very well that he was put in power by the same man for the same interest that he is looking for from the M23!

His excellence, Paul Kagame, is the man to answer for the death of Laurent Desire Kabila who is the father of the young Joseph Kabila, the current President of the DRC. President Kabila knows what it means to follow up on his father's death but he chooses to ignore this fact and keep it in his own archives. How can we expect such a President to question the death of a normal citizen let alone his own father?

President Kabila's DRC is 905,355sq. miles (2,344,858 km²) the population of 73,599,190 million; but cannot even maintain its own security despite of all the resources it possesses.

In a rare public press conference last Saturday, President Kabila said that he had also questioned Uganda over its alleged support for the rebel M23 movement operating in the region, yet, Kampala has denied any involvement.

Was it urgent to investigate Uganda, even though it was not mentioned in the United Nations Group of Experts report? However, this was the same man who was shook hands with the devil Paul Kagame few weeks before his announcement, where they intended to make what they called a *"joint force to wipe out the insurgents in region."*

President Kabila knew very well that his excellence Paul Kagame is the master-mind of all that has been going on since 1995 in the then Zaire and now DRC. It is "an open secret" that Kabila knows very well what happened to all his predecessors. He is the president of a country that owns the mineral resources that the whole world wants a piece of, not just Kagame. For over a decade Kagame has recruited and created rebels after rebels including Joseph Kabila himself together with his fallen father just to be able to rule the eastern region of Congo and gain control of any mineral he could get his hands on.

"As for Rwanda's presence, that is an open secret," Kabila said in his first comments on the issue. "Can diplomacy be the answer? In any case there are three roads to a solution: military, political and diplomatic, or all three at the same time."

However, His excellence Joseph Kabila knows very well that he is very weak militarily, and that is why the M23 continued to advance towards different towns of North Kivu province.

The M23 was predominantly a Tutsi rebels group made up of the Rwanda-backed National Congress for the Defense of the People (CNDP). The information gathered from anonymous veterans indicates that the M23 group is made up of the active Rwandese Defense Forces and its demobilised combat hardened former RPA combatants.

It is not easy to differentiate them only and usually only possible if you are a Rwandese yourself. They share the appearance, drill, discipline, language and trained together by the same motherly force of the RDF.

Rwanda has persistently denied reports that it is backing the M23, formed in the DR Congo's eastern Nord-Kivu province in April. When President Paul Kagame was being interviewed on Hard Talk he repeatedly denied supporting the M23 and at the same time he was pointing to himself as a solution. Further, he contradicted himself by saying that the ammunitions that the M23 used are from the government of DRC. That raises the questions of how a foreign president has the knowledge of where rebels from another nation obtain their ammunitions to terrorise the same government.

The report by the UN Group of Experts published in late June said that the

M23 has been receiving direct aid from top Rwandan officials, including weapons, ammunition and recruits. This prompted many western countries to cut or suspend aid which they have been giving to Rwanda for the last eighteen years. Yet, it also raises the questions of 'why now' when it was not the first report released by the experts regarding Rwanda's human rights violations.

President Paul Kagame has been autocratic for nearly two decades, killing innocent people from inside and outside his country. He has ordered the killings of journalists, government opposition leaders, his own soldiers who attempted to advise him on issues that he was not agreeing with and numerous innocent individuals.

It is at this opportunity that I wish to thank the many Human Right activists and media groups around the globe who have not sat back to just watch what is going on in our motherland, but instead they tirelessly have raised their voice to save our people who have no voice. For example, journalist Jennifer Fierberg who is threatened consistently but has worked day and night on her publications www.africaglobalvillage.com and www.salemnews.com in order to expose the regime for what it is as well as the journalists at www.umuvugizi.com. The majority of Rwandese people appreciate the incredible job you are doing which is of more value to us than I can express.

Chief Editor, Charles Ingabire, may he rest in peace, of www.inyenyerinew.org paid with his life in order to bring for the truth of the despotic regime in Rwanda. I also wish to thank the many others who have dedicated their lives and worsened their security for the sake of saving the innocent people around the world. What you have been doing for the last few years has started to indicate the direction of a dictator.

I can guarantee that President Kagame will go one day. As Socrates once said, "where the truth lies it can always win." My message to you all is that our prayers should be for blessings in general, for God knows best what is good for all of us.

I would like to show my sincere appreciation to the opposition parties and political organisations who work around the clock to expose this monster who displays no sympathy toward the women and children who are suffering inside Rwanda and outside. The international community should have done more sooner to heed these messages than to wait for more innocent lives to be needlessly taken in vain.

It is our utmost responsibility. the people of Rwanda, to work together and avoid divisions created by President Kagame who most of us spent our lifetime working for, without understanding exactly what our country needed at the time.

We all need to come together get rid of Paul Kagame's leadership, we served the forces to bring peace not insecurity to our own citizens. I call upon all comrades, those in active service, to learn from the anonymous comrades who have realised the right direction to create sustainable peace for our nation.

President Kagame is presently an isolated island and we need to let him walk alone to his long-awaited destiny, which is either the ICC or Hell to those who believe in the holy books. We should avoid President Kagame's denials and finger pointing. I now believe that the Rwanda Defense Forces understands that President Kagame is a parasite not the leader we needed all along. Our region needs proper young educated skilled and energetic individuals to stabilise the whole region with empathy and sympathy and not the greedy old grumpy coward he is. Thank god M23 was dismantled by the United Nations troops including South Africa, Tanzania and Malawi.

## 6.4 Kagame planning to terrorise Burundi

As I was writing this article, reliable sources from Kigali indicated that President Kagame has already sent a battalion of underground military Special Forces operating in the shadows of different business entities.

Kagame is a man of his words, when he fell out with President Kikwete of the United Republic of Tanzania, he promised him a pay at a time of his choosing. "Those people [Tanzanian President Jakaya Kikwete] you just heard siding with Interahamwe and FDLR and urging negotiations… negotiations? Me, I do not even discuss this topic, because I will just wait for you [Tanzanian President Jakaya Kikwete] at the right place and I will hit you! He [Tanzanian President Jakaya Kikwete] did not deserve my answer. I did not waste my time answering him…It is well known. There is a line you cannot cross; there is a line, a line that you should never cross. It is impossible…" "

According to the revelations from our reliable sources, Burundi will be used as a springboard to attack Tanzania after the fall of President Pierre Nkurunziza, President Kagame will install his puppet that will be working on the remote control from Kigali. The crime for President Pierre Nkurunziza is disloyalty and is perceived to be pro – president Kikwete perceived to be an enemy of Kagame.

The arrest of suspected armed groups in Burundi including a Rwandan was a vindication that President Kagame will never rest in peace until his prophesy come true. The Voice of America confirmed the presence of armed groupings with intention of terrorizing Burundi according to the Burundi government official who talked to VOA.

Kagame has started infiltrating the Burundi territory with his military special forces to destabilize the Burundi government. Intelligence sources say he will order the massacre of the Tutsi in Burundi or opposition prominent figures to discredit the Burundi government to appear as if the Burundi President is the one killing his own people.

This tactic is not a new weapon in the RPF armory, for those who remember the aftermath of signing the Arusha peace accord in 1993. The RPF was only authorized 600 hundred soldiers and with light weapons but the RPF smuggled more soldiers and weapons including the missile that hit the Presidential jet of the Rwandan President Habyarimana. It is estimated that by the time of the genocide, RPF had over 30000 thousand military in CND now Rwanda Parliament.

Unfortunately, the UN under the umbrella of UNAMIR knew or out to have known all these developments. The commander of the UNAMIR forces at the time Gen. Romeo Dallier informed the United Nations Keeping Force docket of the United Nations but they did nothing to stop the RPF from smuggling weapons or keep the weapons under the hands of the UN.

Therefore, the Kagame regime is under international pressure after the defeat of the armed proxy in Congo M23, and the recent BBC Documentary which exposed the lies of Kagame and his culpability in the genocide that cost Many Tutsis and Hutus. The international big eye is on Kagame and he doesn't want this, he is therefore trying now to export his brutality to Burundi so that he can get a break of the international attention.

Similarly, the dead bodies we witnessed in Lake Rweru was another thorn in the Kagame throat, its unfinished business, both governments have failed to cooperate to establish the origin of these people who were brutally murdered in cold blood. Although all investigations pointed the finger to the Kigali government, Kagame through his mouth piece the Minister of Foreign Affairs denied that these people are Rwandan Citizens.

However, the Minister's denials did not add up, because many Rwandan have disappeared and continue to disappear, yet their families have not been informed of the whereabouts of their loved ones. Why then the Minister of Foreign Affairs recklessly fails to grasp the consequences of conspiracy to commit crimes.

We have therefore established, that president Kagame is planning to kill Burundians both Tutsis and Prominent Oppositions figures in Burundi under his undercover special forces so that it appears that even the previous dead bodies in Lake Rweru have connection with Burundi. We therefore warn the Burundi government to be vigilant and take extra mile in identifying all these deadly traps of Kagame.

Relations between Burundi President and Rwandan leader have soured in the last months. The reason is that President Kagame wants to be the only Bull in the East Africa. While he wanted to settle old scores with President Kikwete using President Pierre Nkurunziza, the latter refused to cooperate. We know how on several occasions Rwandan leaders called the Tanzanian President "a genocide and terrorist sympathizer", "ignorant", "arrogant", and "mediocre leader". The relations deteriorated following the recommendation by President Jakaya Kikwete of open negotiations between Rwandan, Ugandan and Congolese leaders and their respective armed opposition in order to bring durable peace and security in the African Great

President Kagame while attending the African Investment Summit in London was warned in private by the UK government not tampers with Constitution to extend his rule. This did not go well in the stomach of President Kagame, he immediately closed the BBC Local Program despite the fact that the Documentary that exposed his lies and crimes was in English. He has now ordered his Justice machinery to setup and inquiry in the BBC headed by his former Prosecutor General Martin Ngoga.

It is therefore not surprising that President Kagame is meddling in Burundi affairs so that the international community could shift its cameras from him to the other conflicts in the region, and Kagame may present himself as the best man do mediate.

The latest Burundi instability in Burundi should be fully investigated and not left for natural cause and President Nkurunziza should continue to seek diplomatic, political and if necessary ready for military to defend his country from Kagame aggression who is trying to drag the region back into conflict.

The Tanzanian President should not also be complacent as he is preparing to step down. According to sources in Kigali, General Kagame has also been frustrated by the attention Tanzanian President has been receiving from World powers. Until a few years ago, Rwanda and its dictator was the darling of the West. The attention from the West has since dwindled, and president Kagame is very allergic to this.

## 6.5 Kagame misses the opportunity to Kill Nkurunziza

Reliable sources informed us that President Kagame with his partners in doing their evil activities had planned to down President Nkurunziza's official jet if he had attended the swearing ceremony of the Tanzanian President John Magufuli

President Nkurunziza who has very close relations with neighboring Tanzania did not turn up to the swearing ceremony for his incoming counterpart John Magufuli. Kagame shaking hands with Magufuli Tanzania's new president, Dictators Mugabe of Zimbabwe and Museveni of Uganda looking on.

Indeed, the US officials had warned that the great lakes region will be set on fire in the same way the Rwanda Presidential jet was brought down almost 2 decades ago. President Kagame while attending an official function to recognize the people who saved Tutsi during genocide, he publicly attacked his Burundian counterpart of whom he accused of hiding. According to Kagame, President Nkurunziza has gone into hiding in his own country since he failed to attend the swearing ceremony of President John Magufuli of Tanzania.

However, as I have mentioned above, Kagame is not only frustrated of getting his plan wrong but also his intelligence was outsmarted by President Nkurunziza. The big question now remains what will president Kagame do next? Ironically President Nkurunziza knows from the bottom of his heart that he is hunted by not only his neighbor but also the most powerful nations such as US and Europe know that a terrorist plan against him and his country never the less, they have kept silent.

The news received from the USA regional observer, is a warning that the international community is allowing president Kagame liberty to commit evil, will not only affect the region but might spill over the entire continent and beyond.

President Paul Kagame has not only threatened Nkurunziza but previously had warned Tanzania's president Jakaya Kikwete. It imperative that we advise all regional politicians such John Magufuli, Pierre Nkurunziza and anyone who do not support Kagame's ideologies to be very vigilant.

## 6.6 The suspected Rwandan Killing hand in Burundi

Barely a few days after Pierre Nkurunziza has been declared the winner of the controversial elections in the tiny Central African nation of Burundi, a top Burundian general and close aide to President Pierre Nkurunziza was killed in car ambush in capital Bujumbura. General Adolphe Nshimirimana, was widely seen as the Burundi's de facto internal security chief and even considered the regime's number-two.

*Who was behind the assassination of Gen. Adolphe Nshimirimana?*

Our sources learned that the Rwandan ruler Kagame has been planning different assassinations of targeted Burundi Security officials including Pierre Nkurunziza himself. We further learnt that the hit list included:

- Agathon Rwasa: the Burundi prominent opposition who has now joined the Burundi Parliament.

- Pontian Gaciyubwenge: the former Burundi defense Minister

- General Prime Niyongabo.

- Will Nyamitwe: Senior Advisor in charge of Media, Information and Communication at Office of the President of Burundi - Office of the President of Burundi

President Kagame accuses the above officers for interfering with his coup plans and reneging on the plans of ousting President Nkurunziza in the aborted Coup which had been put in action by Gen Niyombare who is currently in Kigali. In the chain of events, Kagame accused President Nkurunziza of refusing him entry to President Kikwete of Tanzania when he declared him enemy number one he advised him to talk to his enemies. President Kagame said that he did not want to talk too much on the Kikwete comments but according to Kagame, he will wait for Kikwete at the right time and place and hit him.

There were speculations that Kagame approached Nkurunziza for killing Kikwete and Nkurunziza declined and from this day that Nkurunziza became the next target for assassination either politically or physically. Indeed, Rwanda is now harbouring several generals and senior Burundi officials who are fighting the Burundi government. The escape of the former CNDD/FDD Secretary General Hussein Rajab from Prison was planned and executed in Kigali and Hussein Rajab is housed along other Burundi senior officials in Kigali on Rwandan Tax payer.

Kagame accused his Burundian counterpart of not delivering and according to Kagame, Nkurunziza should go "If your own citizens tell you, we don't want you to lead us, how do you say I am staying whether you want me or not," Rwanda's President.

What does Kagame has to do with Burundi deliverance? Why is he more interested in interfering in the neighbouring nation for the Third term or deliverance when he is seeking the same in his Country?

The sudden death of the Uganda former Spy Chief Gen. Noble Mayombo was also coordinated by Kagame who accused him of conspiring with Col. Patrick Karegeya to protect Kabuga Felicien who is wanted for Genocide in Rwanda in 1994. Although President Museveni did not mention the people who put those Ugandan Security forces on the hit list, he mentioned some enemies in the region, who are those enemies in the region?

President Yoweri Museveni revealed. "Our security services have been looking at criminally-minded characters in the region, who have been saying that by eliminating NRM cadres, they would finish the NRM. Mayombo's name was high on that list, and of course also Museveni's, as the head," the President said at the burial of Gen. Noble Mayombo and former permanent secretary in the defense ministry in Kijura, Kabarole District.

Similarly, Kagame has been publicly saying that he regrets for not having borders with South Africa, for those who know the character of Kagame, we know he meant crossing there to destabilize the South African Nation, the way he has done to Congo and now Burundi. Kagame's fear is South African and Tanzanian armies that are in Burundi or on the borders with Rwanda. We have also learnt that Kagame was spiting venom to his Security officers in the meeting he chaired himself recently reminding them that, Gen. Kayumba is under South African Protection. What interest does the South African Nation have in Gen. Kayumba? Kagame asked.

Therefore, the leaders in the region, need to handle Kagame with strong gloves, he is not a man to do business with and as usual because he is a despot guilty of even bloodier slaughter.

## 6.7 Kagame an honest man

He was called a liar, a killer, and once a psychotic patient. However, a while ago he proved the whole world wrong when he turned to be an honest man. Why do we rate him an honest man? I remember sometime back, President Paul Kagame would sacrifice anything to protect a secret; these ideas of keeping every mission or plan secret left all Rwandans moaning, because a large number of service men and women became victims of just knowing a lot! The honest man we are talking about today has forgotten the whole idea as to why he killed our brothers who knew a lot and could not keep secret.

Whilst addressing residents of the Northern and Western provinces in Nyabihu, President Paul Kagame said those who compromise the security of Rwanda will be dealt with decisively. Those who choose to minimise the importance of the lives lost embolden the terrorists and hence is a demonstration of double standards.

The killing of Rwandans has been normalised by most people, and for the foreigners, they even ignore us when we talk of being killed or a head of state threatening to kill innocent people. This is because death or killing is normal in Rwanda. We heard the honest man his excellence Paul Kagame threatening opponents that he will start shooting at them in broad day light and Rwandans either clap hands or stay quiet. You wonder how someone claps hands when a head of state threatens to kill fellow countrymen or countrywomen!

We are living in a tiny place like Rwanda, smaller than Buganda kingdom, or Wales, full ghosts and criminals such as President Paul Kagame and his right-hand men, plus a population of 11 million who are incapable of consenting to anything. Ruled by a weapon, a bunch of right hand men to the President, are getting richer whilst the rest are being guarded, and stressed at all times.

So, let's first see what is normal? Because Mr. Paul Kagame may be right when suggesting killing his opponents, by normalising it:

The word normal is frequently used to describe all sorts of things including behaviour, personality and even appearance. But is there such a thing as 'normal' and if there is, how do we know what is 'normal'? Professor Gordon Brown and principal teaching fellow Martin Skinner from the Department of Psychology explore this issue. Professor Gordon Brown states "People's ideas today about 'what is normal' are very different to beliefs in the past, and also differ between cultures. However, even within a culture and at a given time, people's idea of what is normal can be changed and can alter people's behaviour. For example, telling high energy consumers that neighbours consume less energy can cause the high consumers to reduce the amount of energy they use, and telling hotel guests that most previous occupants of their room recycle their towels can increase recycling. These are examples of 'nudging' people's behaviour in a desirable direction by telling them what is normal. Nudges often apply when people don't really know (until they are told) what 'normal' behaviour is".

Even though these psychologists define normal in a neutral way, by promoting culture as an engine to drive normality, logically, 'normal' is defined as conforming to a standard; usual, typical, or expected. This is where we Rwandans are stuck by believing that we have got to do what the leaders want, not the other way around in a democratic way where leaders should listen to the voters as the majority.

When I heard the speech of our President Paul Kagame threatening to kill his countrymen, I recalled all the people he has killed and declined to admit to. This time though he became an honest man, simply because he managed to speak out, something he failed for so long. He threatened to kill a lot of people recently, what left me surprised though is that Kagame has changed his way of working:

## Kagame wants them all dead

From secretive to talkative and abrupt in words, threatening fellow regional leaders and actually killing people in foreign countries. Paul Kagame was once a popular leader who was trying to build his profile around peace, is now known as a killer. He has threatened to kill Jakaya Kikwete the president of the republic of Tanzania simply because they disagreed on how peace can be achieved in the Greatlakes region. President Kagame sought help from President Nkurunziza of Burundi, the idea was to use the Burundian intelligence network and track down Kikwete's movement and get him killed. Poor Kagame went on national TV and announced how he was going to kill Kikwete, and so Nkurunziza realised that the man was not fit enough to keep a secret, and immediately he reported to Kikwete. The Tanzanian government announced that all Rwandans on their land be returned to Rwanda in order to strengthen security at home.

## President Desire Kabila killed by Kagame

Up to now, Kagame is planning to eliminate Nkurunziza as well, just because he walked out of the deal. Kagame has tried everything to destabilise South Africa and failed. He is the same man who killed President Desire Kabila Senior, just because they fell out due to DRC's natural resources that Kagame had turned a source of income. He went on to make three attempts to kill the younger Joseph Kabila who was protected by mercenaries from Angola and Namibia for some time.

You wonder what the world sees in Kagame if not trading with him and keep a blind eye. He managed to get in power after downing a plane carrying two presidents; he also made five attempts to kill president Museveni of Uganda, when they disagreed on DRC matters. President

Museveni had to give up as Kagame had started to divide his army and arming them on side. Museveni in his words said that "Kagame is a mad dog"! If we are not careful it will bite us, he then decided to follow him until today. He knows very well that Kagame is totally out of order however to save his skin he has to keep following. President Kagame's crimes can go on and on however nobody cares. He has attacked individuals in countries such as South Africa, Mozambique and threatened people in Western Countries.

## 6.8 Kagame and Museveni troubled relationship

For many years Paul Kagame failed to cement the historical bond created by his two senior commanders and or brothers' president Yoweri Kaguta Museveni and Gen Fred Rwigema. It had been agreed between the then Commander Fred Rwigema and Commander Yoweri Museveni way back in Tanzania that after liberating Uganda, they would carry on and help Fred liberate his own country (Rwanda) the country his parents had fled when he was only a toddler. A few years after liberating Uganda from Idi Amin Dada they continued to fight against President Milton Obote's autocratic regime.

On this second liberation 5 years NRA struggle, Paul Kagame was introduced to Yoweri Museveni by commander Fred Rwigema who had both fought liberation wars way from Mozambique and making Paul Kagame the 27th founding members of NRA.

Most young Rwandan refugees in Uganda participated in this liberation war because it was the only way to find a safer living due to their oppression by the Obote regime or as the only way to get arms and hence return to their mother land on liberation of Uganda.

Like most people know, Museveni is a man who keeps his promises the only promise he failed to keep is the term limit issue, though I will not go any further on this issue. He therefore kept his promise not only until when we evaded Rwanda but supported the war all the way through until the stopping of the Genocide.

After the liberation and stopping of the genocide, president Museveni paid his first state visit to Rwanda where he was welcomed by President Pasteur Bizimungu and vice president Paul Kagame. The relationship between Uganda and Rwanda was like a child and parent relationship. I remember we had to make people stand on the Kigali – Gatuna road from Nyakyonga to Amahoro National Stadium just to show how welcoming and appreciating RPA were.

In his words president Museveni talked about how (Moto) fire started in Mozambique to liberate the Africans and that they will continue. He continuously mentioned General Fred Rwigema as the best freedom fighter of all times in his speech along with other African freedom fighters he had worked with all the way along, including Julius Nyerere who he addresses as Mzee (elder in Swahili).

He went on to say that he was pleased to see that Paul Kagame who was a young man had grown up to develop into a leader, something (Kagame did not like). He also mentioned names of a few of our fallen and living commanders as his boys this did not sound good in Paul Kagame's ears at all.

Although Paul Kagame was angered by his visitor's speech and the fact that he did not praise him but instead his fallen comrade, he could not react in his usual silly manner due to the fact that Rwanda was still reliant on Uganda in many ways especially the defense. Museveni thought that

Rwanda could be home to all Ugandans and Uganda to all Rwandans, during that time one could cross the borders of the two countries with no passport. This was President Museveni's big ideas which he had extended to the creation of the East African block of countries.

However, Kagame had negative feelings about the entire idea since he viewed it as being dominated by his former boss and the fact that though he was the Vice President, he saw himself as the president instead.

After helping Desire Kabila liberate Zaire, both Uganda and Rwanda continued to engage in the wars in the DRC which later saw both countries fight two times. These endless wars have created loads of instability in the entire great lakes region. Apart from the Congolese citizens these wars fueled hash relationships between the two presidents. Uganda on its own lost two Companies of well-trained young special force Hima boys in Kisangani by the much combat experienced Rwandan troops.

Most of the commanders and troops on both sides were opposed to the actual war due to the fact that the people of Uganda and Rwanda were more or less like brothers, and actually the Rwandan army had been born off the Ugandan National Resistance Army with their commanders and comrades still serving on the other side having trained together. With such incidents and situations, we lost many comrades who were opposed to the fact that they couldn't stand the fact of fighting fellow comrades. Lt Col Rutayisire Shaban was one of the officers who opposed the battles between the two armies. He mentioned this to President Kagame and being the man, he was (the first RPA spokesman) and an intellectual, Kagame didn't like the idea so he ordered his execution by a fellow senior officer. Gen Kayumba was among a few of the officers in Rwanda who couldn't cope with the idea of fighting comrades.

Gen JJ Odong the then army commander of Uganda was instructed by his commander-in-chief to meet his Rwandan counterpart. I remember him meeting Gen Nyamwasa who was the army commander of Rwanda then, however on their return to their respective command headquarters, Kagame ordered his troops to carry on with the battle in Kisangani. I remember we made several visits in Uganda to meet Museveni in order to calm down the situation which had gone out of hands.

When the Congolese war finally ended, what followed was Paul Kagame's intelligence network helping Lt Col Kyakabare and Lt Col Monday to escape the Makindye Military Prison, these two officers had been detained with serious charges however Kagame's boys took them to Rwanda and they soon after declared war against Museveni's government. Uganda was continuously used as a gateway for Rwandan dissidents who sought refuge in different parts of the world from their oppressive ruler Paul Kagame.

During that time Uganda, also was holding numerous Rwandan dissidents who planned attacks on Rwanda, while the Rwanda government continuously planned to form armed groups that would destabilise Uganda and welcomed Colonel Muzora who had fell out with the Ugandan government.

Col Muzora was to only be found dead and dumped outside his front door after so many years in exile. However, what is more disturbing is that the Ugandan intelligence service indicated that Rwanda knew about his death, and hence the relationship between the two countries depended on the two leaders (Kagame and Museveni).

A few years ago, Gen Kayumba Nyamwasa escaped Rwanda to South Africa through Uganda. On his escape, Rwandan officials contacted

Ugandan officials asking them to detain him and stop him from fleeing any further, the Ugandan officials refused to arrest him and instead assisted as they believed he had a genuine cause to flee.

After Paul Kagame failed to get Kayumba back he made a phone call to Museveni and threatened that "he Museveni should bear the consequences of not arresting criminals like Kayumba and letting them pass through his country to foreign countries". On another occasion, again Paul Kagame cautioned while making his parabolic speech that "once you live in a grass thatched hut/ house you deserve not to play with fire since it might be used to burn yourself".

A few days after these two speeches, the Buganda Royal tombs were burnt down just to show Museveni what damage he can cause on his soil. At one-point Kagame rang Museveni and mentioned to him that he knows every move of his life from what he eats to how he sleeps. This was very stressful to Museveni who in actual sense is getting aged.

It should be remembered that Kagame was the head of intelligence in Uganda for a number of years and so he knows the sensitive part of Ugandans and mostly the Buganda kingdom. This took Museveni time to convince the Ugandans on what really happened; he had to use King Ronald Muwenda Mutebi in order to calm the Baganda tribe down due to the fact that they had lost part of their ancestral history for just some ill minded politician.

Prior to that but just after Kagame's first warnings we saw the fall of Colonel Noble Mayombo a young energetic, well learnt jubilant uprising senior officer who held various posts during his time. This distinctive officer had urged Museveni to overthrow Kagame and insert somebody else who would maintain security in the region instead of destabilising it. He was the man who planned on how Kagame's jet can be downed, but also, he is alleged to have engaged with Kabuga Felicien who is accused of assisting the interahamwe during genocide.

Col Mayombo a royal to the Tooro kingdom and a close confidant to president Museveni who had fought the Congo war was later poisoned during a meeting through a glass of water, he died of multiple organ failure after being flown to abroad for treatment in Museveni's presidential jet. On his funeral Museveni said that he had been killed by a group of great lakes region spies who did not like peace, but stressed that he had more Mayombo's who would continue to fight for peace in the region.

Museveni had to visit the late Canon Rabwoni, Noble Mayombo's father and the entire Tooro kingdom with very little answers since he was still in shock of what Kagame was capable of doing on his soil from as far as Kigali. It should be however noted that Museveni had never underrated the capabilities of Kagame in Uganda due to his knowledge and influence in the country.

These killings, love hate relationship has been going on all these years. Paul Kagame is at present very uncomfortable and he is trying any possible ways of stopping Uganda from sponsoring any opponent against him. He has at recent used Andrew Mwenda the greedy Ugandan journalist who was paid to publicise Kagame on the globe to revive his relationship with his former boss Museveni forgetting the uncountable Ugandan troop he has ordered for their execution in the jungles of Kisangani and the entire Congo under the command of Gen Kazini a man he personally had hated before he left Uganda in the 1990s.

Kagame has out of desperation used Gen Karenzi Karake who served in

Museveni's protection unit before the Rwandan struggle to try and revive his relationship with Museveni despite of the fact the later was detained without trial for allegedly aiding the escape of his colleague Gen Kayumba. After failing on all fronts, Kagame has recently asked his wife to jet in Uganda and try desperately and revive the long-lost relationship thus carrying her entire family to a brother that he has hurt for such a long time Museveni, to try and attract some sympathy.

I am however left to wonder how long this unfounded relationship will last given the fact of all the preceding incidents that took lives of young men and women of both countries. It is evident how shallow president Kagame thinks his people are and belief that they shall forget and move on but I highly wonder if Ugandans will be able to forget the dark days they faced by Kagame and his forces in the Congo.

Kagame visited Uganda on two occasions since the Kisangani incident. He should have done it 17 years ago and hence avoided the Kisangani incidents saving lives of innocent comrades rather than turning up at this time as if nothing ever happened. This is common to him anyway. He is a type of a person who would sleep on one's door step if he is desperate for any assistance and once he gets it, he would use any possible means to harm the same person that helped him.

President Museveni on the other hand is an ailing dude who is desperate to not cause any conflict to any of his neighbours let alone wild Kagame who he knows so well. To Museveni, Kagame is like a mad dog that you are happy not to annoy because of its bitter bites. Yoweri Museveni and his brother General Salim Saleh Akandwanaho have kept their promises when it comes to helping Rwanda, just for the sake of the agreement they had with General Fred Rwigyema. It has been a hard time for the last couple of years after Kagame stopped Fred's wife Jeannette Rwigyema from travelling and confiscating her passport. This angered Salim Saleh who was very close to the family of Fred, among the reasons why Museveni started engaging with Kagame was to diffuse his anger of mistreating his former commander's wife Fred Rwigyema.

## 6.9 Kagame Concocting Regional Battle

President Paul Kagame believes that neighboring countries such as Tanzania, Burundi are harboring his enemies. On reflection Kagame understands that since he has decided to rule his country against the constitution, any Rwandan could wage war against his government. Kagame is doubtful that his opposition may use all options to get rid of him or his counterfeit leadership.

In Kagame's back lobe he knows that, The Rwandan opposition did everything democratically possible for the last couple of years to make the world understand that Rwanda is ruled by an iron fist ruffian.

"One of the Rwanda Patriotic Front members told me, I quote "the opposition has achieved an important move because they have taken time to highlight Rwanda issues internationally which has made Kagame look incompetent".

A comment made by one of the Rwanda National Congress member, - stated that the opposition had achieved a reputation and foundation for a meaningful change, to those who had interest in listening to the honesty opposition leaders, it is time to walk behind them to the end. There was days Kagame went hunting his critics around the globe, shooting and attacking neighboring countries just to eliminate those who disagrees with his government".

Some western leaders as well as Africa and Asia understand the opposition's cause and are pledging support for a meaningful change. However, the opposition continue to preach for non-violence and avoidance to another bloodshed. unfortunately, Kagame has gone against the opposition's preaching and demands and instead has gone for a third term to remain in the office.

Recently it was announced as expected after a referendum approved constitutional changes to allow him to run for three further terms and could potentially see him stay in power until 2034, When Paul Kagame will be 77 years old. Mr Kagame said Rwandans had made it clear they wanted him to lead the country after 2017, and had no choice but only to accept.

Sources from Kagame's circles indicate preparations for war, Kagame is undisputable that he will be attacked from Burundi at any time, his acumen is very much interested in eliminating the top men of Burundi government especially the army officials. Also, Kagame believes that his outrageous relationship with President Nkurunziza of Burundi may attract his opposition seeking help to invade Rwanda from Burundi.

Another factor surrounding Kagame is the ill connection between Rwanda and Tanzania and instantaneously after ex-president Kikwete's handover to John Magufuli. President Kagame directed his foreign secretary Louise Mushikiwabo to try and resurrect the relationship of the two countries. However, this has not worked out well, the most worrying thing is that President Kagame is holding Nkurunziza's top commanders who attempted a coup previously.

Currently, Kagame believes that President Nkurunziza and his neighbour

Tanzania as well as South Africa are sympathising with the Rwandan opposition around the globe. These worries have forced Kagame to be on his guards. The army has been training hard since the end of 2015, in order to protect Kagame's regime in face of eventual attack.

*Below is Kagame's 2016 New Year's message to Rwanda Defense Forces:*

Officers, men and women of RDF; on behalf of the Government of Rwanda, my family and on my own behalf, I wish you and your loved ones a happy and prosperous new year 2016.

The end of year, is always an important time for reflection and introspection as we take stock of our achievements and challenges with a view to setting ourselves new targets. A new beginning also brings with it fresh aspirations and resolves to improve upon past performance.

In this regard, the RDF can look back on the past year with a sense of pride for numerous achievements made amidst diverse challenges. You should be encouraged by the steady progress registered during the course of the year 2015. In particular, your contribution to the safeguarding of territorial integrity, as well as internal and international peace and security should provide you professional satisfaction.

I wish to commend you all for the continued professionalism, vigilance, integrity, and dedication that have enabled us to maintain the precious peace and safety that all Rwandans, foreign residents and guests have continued to enjoy in our country. I fully expect that you will maintain these positive attributes through 2016 as you discharge your duties with honour, loyalty and diligence. Always remember that your core duty is to preserve the vital safety and security environment within which further socio-economic development can take place for the benefit of Rwanda's present and future generations.

As we celebrate the beginning of a new year, let us all spare a thought for our comrades who paid the ultimate price in the line of duty, so that the rest of our citizens and mankind may live in peace. We honour their memory, we salute their sacrifice, and we pledge continued support to the families left behind; may you all, their living comrades find the strength and resilience to continue with their and your mission.

As always, this new year comes with new challenges and opportunities. We will definitely be confronted with more threats which require conventional and unconventional approaches to overcome them. We therefore need to remain focused and resilient to defend our nation. There is no doubt that working together we shall raise the Rwandan flag higher as we stay the course, on Rwanda's journey of transformation.

May God Bless You All.

*Thoughts for reflection.*

- Now, since when did President Paul Kagame change his words? he is sending New Year messages to the Rwandan defense forces?

- He was able to read the power point slides during new year's message to the nation, without insulting anyone? where he accepted to rule for another three terms, in a humble manner?

- Also in his new year message he mentioned that he was ready to work with his critics? the critics he is still hunting but ready to speak with at the same time?

- For the first time Kagame has not verbally insulted the opposition or the west since his referendum witticism.

## 6.10 MONUSCO/SADC will wipe Rwanda out one day.

When the Rwanda soldiers attack DRC again, President Kagame's government may be wiped out by the MOUSCO/SADC/FIB, and this is because the SADC nations have credible evidences which indicate Rwanda's role in the instability of DRC and other nations in our region.

The recent rebels attack on Burundi with the help of Rwanda was Kagame's desire and intentions to overthrow President Nkurunziza of Burundi simply because he declined to side line with Kagame in isolating Tanzania. Indeed, President Kagame's delusions urged him to believe that FDLR may cross to Burundi if the UN pressure continues; he believed that with FDLR crossing to Burundi, Tanzania may easily help them to attack Rwanda.

Kagame who was holding on to Burundi deserters combined with the M23 who had been hiding in Rwanda, were enforced by a few RDF forces to attack Burundi. With the help of MONUSCO forces, the Rwandan backed attackers were defeated, although 100 dead bodies were reported, I obtained reliable information pointing the finger on RDF death toll of over 300, more soldiers abandoned in the jungle after the MONUSCO/FIB hit them hard until now.

While attending the news conference in village Urugwiro on the 15th/01/2015, President Kagame finally got things right, with regard to FDLR when he answered that journalists have eyes and ears so they should answer for themselves on FDLR issue, Mr President believes that any negativity to his government is a crime and should not be answered by him.

Kagame looked restless with breathlessness, at times could not even respond on time, forgetfulness accompanied with asking the journalists to repeat questions or even blaming the microphones. This is a sign of confusion and disorientation scientifically called "Delirium"

A senior clinical psychologist we approached told us that, he sees this as part of Our President's anxiety, stressing that anxiety cause's shortness of breath.

"Anxiety related breathing issues tend to be a result of hyperventilation. Hyperventilation is also known as "over breathing," and it occurs when your body is receiving too much oxygen and is expelling too much carbon dioxide.

Although the bodies need oxygen, healthy carbon dioxide levels are still important. When you are taking in too much air and letting out too much oxygen, it can cause your body to feel like you're not breathing enough. Anxiety hyperventilation is often caused by one of two issues:

- Breathing too fast, such as during an anxiety attack when your body is in fight/flight mode.

- Thinking about your breathing, which may cause you to take in more air than you need.

The latter is common in people with health anxieties and panic attacks. These individuals are often concerned about their health so they start to control their own breathing, and ultimately try to take in too much air in order to feel their chest expand for a full breath. The body often doesn't need that much air, and shortness of breath occurs.

The senior psychologist argued that his excellence Paul Kagame may benefit in applying anxiety techniques when answering sensitive questions.

Also, the disappointment of not being able to give orders to kill as he does inside Rwanda causes him frustration that the president cannot afford to get hold of FDLR, and the refugees in DRC so he gets them killed, as he labels the young people to be genocide suspects. This has made the president uncomfortable whenever he hears anyone mention about FDLR or any other idea or solution rather than killing, the president's mind set is killing (Killing mode). Research indicates that, people with personality disorder easily become frustrated due to a minor disappointment: '' Does anyone else get racing thoughts after what should be just really minor disappointments?

An example was given when a personality patient volunteered to explain how disappointments can affect them: ''I have noticed that if I'm promised or offered something, no matter how small, like it could just be picking up an item at the store for me, even if I didn't really care until they offered it, and then that person forgets, decides they don't want to, or just seems not to care anymore, I become incredibly frustrated and I can hardly look that person in the eye or talk to them, even if I don't want to make a big deal out of it feels so hurtful. Especially because I am very co-dependent''.

When the President was given a complement of having some Rwandans who see him as a role model, was also asked to mention his role model, unfortunately what made the whole conference and the followers wonder, the president said that his role model is the Rwandan citizens because they listen to him: what remains mystery did the President really understand the question? '' The definition of a role model is someone who others look up to, or someone who has attributes and traits that make him a good person to try to be like". Not the people you lead, who actually sees you as a role model.

His Excellency Paul Kagame also mentioned that he is planning to strengthen the security alongside boarders and continue begging for SADC to kill the refuges for him in DRC in particular and the FDLR rebels in general. Behind the Presidential Curtains advises that the President continues the idea of staying inside his tiny Rwanda because the day his army dares to cross the border, blood will be shed than ever because SADC/FIB will respond the way M23 was wiped. Rwanda as a country will be destroyed and Rwandans in general will be killed once again which will not only affect Rwanda but also the neighbours.

More importantly newspapers including mine we will miss Kagame's absurdity, without enough to write about because there will be peace after Paul Kagame's regime. It will be disappointing for newspapers such as Rwanda Times, Rushyashya and the Exposer plus Igihe.com as there will be no one to pour praises and advocate for. Papers such as Inyenyeri news will have to focus on sport and music which is not followed by many Rwandans. President Kagame's arrogance and ignorance, pretending to know when he really has no clue, discussing international market, human rights and freedom of speech when he is actually the main obstacle for all that.

Free and simple advice for Kagame and his government is to try and sort the mess he started as soon as possible, stay inside Rwanda and do not cross to DRC otherwise you be hit hard.

## 6.11 The Great Lakes Region muddle on Again

In DRC, serious offenders absconded following Prison fire, In Rwanda reports indicate on-going trainings of Burundi rebels, the big brother of Burundi Tanzania Opposed AU forces intervention, Kagame pleaded for military intervention in Burundi but with no Rwanda's role. Pres Nkurunziza of Burundi against AU force intervention blames Rwanda for instability. It looks like the Great lakes regional conflict could be on again

Despite greatly improved security after the surrender of "M23", the protracted conflict in the Democratic Republic of the Congo persisted with other armed groups in the country's east failed to lay down their weapons.

Some time back the UN official warned "We are not at the end game," Martin Kobler, Special Representative of the Secretary-General and Head of the United Nations Organization Stabilization Mission in the Democratic Republic of Congo (MONUSCO), said as he briefed the 15-nation body on recent developments in the strife-torn central African nation.

He stated that, since 2002, more than 11,000 combatants of the Forces démocratiques de libération du Rwanda (FDLR) — an armed group formed by leaders of the genocide in neighbouring Rwanda — had been disarmed, demobilized and reintegrated into Rwandan society, he said. However, an estimated 1,500 combatants of that group were still active and their leaders were stalling implementation of the Congolese Government's six-month voluntary disarmament plan.

Kobler stressed that, "This was a serious signal of non-cooperation. Standing still means we are moving backwards," Mr. Kobler said, stressing that the FDLR's dissolution would be a turning point that would fundamentally alter and improve security in the entire region. He backed the consensus among the Southern African Development Community (SADC) and the International Conference of the Great Lakes Region to use the "military option" against factions unwilling to disarm.

Echoing that concern, Mary Robinson, Special Envoy of the Secretary-General for the Great Lakes Region of Africa, said the FDLR's process had yet to gain sufficient traction to show true credibility, creating a "worrying dynamic" in the region. She underscored the need to preserve the earlier consensus built on armed groups, to remain focused on Security Council resolutions on neutralizing the FDLR and to fully implement the Peace, Security and Cooperation Framework for the Democratic Republic of the Congo and the Region.

Meanwhile: On the 7/01/2016 fourteen people were killed in eastern Democratic Republic of Congo Thursday morning, the army said in a sign of the ethnic tensions that persist in the conflict-torn region. Nine other people were being treated in hospital for injuries. The killings took place in Miriki, around 110km north of Goma, capital of North Kivu province. According to local authorities and the military, the attack was planned by rebels from neighbouring Rwanda. Bokele Joy, administrator of the Lubero area under which Miriki falls blamed the FDLR (Democratic Forces for the Liberation of Rwanda).

A local human rights defender, Souleymane Mokili, supported the army saying he had seen the bodies of the victims, which bore "machete and bullet" wounds. The FDLR rebels have been regularly accused of heinous crimes against civilians in the area. The rebel group was founded by some of the perpetrators of Rwanda's 1994 genocide who fled into neighbouring Congo and is estimated by analysts to have more than 1,000 members.

At the same time, it's reported that, about 1,000 former fighters the M23 which MONUSCO believed had been wiped out, from a Democratic Republic of Congo (DRC) rebel group broke out Tuesday from a camp in

Uganda where they were being held as soldiers were trying to repatriate them, the Ugandan army said.

"A thousand rebels from the M23 (group) have escaped" from the camp in Bihanga, about 300 kilometres southwest of the Ugandan capital Kampala, a spokesman for the Ugandan army said on the official Twitter account. "They said they were worried about their safety if they were sent back to the Democratic Republic of Congo."

Several of the ex-rebels were wounded by gunshots after those in the camp refused to board army trucks sent in before dawn to take them to the airport, according to M23 chief Bertrand Bisimwa.

A Ugandan officer speaking to AFP on condition of anonymity admitted the operation had encountered "resistance" and confirmed that several in the camp were wounded by bullets.

The Ugandan army said the camp had been holding 1,373 former M23 fighters. An AFP reporter at Entebbe airport saw 120 of them board a plane bound for the DRC.

The Ugandan army spokesman, Lieutenant-Colonel Paddy Ankunda, said via Twitter that troops were now searching for the 1,000 "who escaped the repatriation". He insisted that "no member of M23 was forced to be repatriated towards the DRC."

But in Kampala, where he lives, Bisimwa disputed that. He said the attempt to return the M23 former fighters to the DRC was "a violation of international law" and of a peace deal reached a year ago between the DRC and the group.

The rebels' 18-month war, during which they briefly seized the key DRC town of Goma, capital of mineral-rich North Kivu province, was brought to an end in 2013 by government troops and UN peacekeepers. The fighters fled into neighbouring Uganda and Rwanda.

They signed papers in May vowing not to fight again in return for a possible amnesty. M23 leaders last month warned they would fight again should agreements fail. The defeated rebels told AFP of mounting frustrations among the group's confined-to-camp fighters.

While the M23 was defeated, multiple armed groups still operate in a region that has been in conflict for the best part of two decades. Much of the rebel activity consists of abuses against civilians and illegal exploitation of natural resources such as metals, ivory or timber.

At the same time, it's reported that in BUKAVU: Fifty prisoners including convicted murderers and rapists have escaped from a prison in the east of Democratic Republic of Congo after a fire, a local administrator said on Friday.

Fifty prisoners including convicted murderers and rapists have escaped from a prison in the east of Democratic Republic of Congo after a fire. The inmates broke out of jail at Kamituga, 170km southwest of Bukavu, the capital of the strife-prone South Kivu province, "taking advantage of a fire," Desire Kubuya Masumbuko said.

Kamituga is the gold-rich economic capital of the Mwenga territory overseen by Kubuya, where security forces have trouble dealing with several armed groups. Just one prisoner remained in the jail after the others took to their heels late on Wednesday and by Friday morning, none of them had been recaptured, Kubuya said.

Those on the run include "20 convicted men, two for murder and 18 for rape," Kubuya added, expressing fears that the jailbreak would lead to "a settling of scores."

Rape and killings are endemic to the eastern Kivu provinces of the DRC, which have been wracked by warfare, ethnic strife, and armed conflicts over land and control of mineral resources for more than 20 years.

Congolese authorities say that North and South Kivu are the two provinces in the vast central African nation most seriously affected by "sexual violence related to conflict." Mass jailbreaks occur frequently in the DRC for lack of sufficient funds for the penal administration and the dilapidated state of old prisons in the former Belgian colony. National and global human rights organisations regularly criticise detention conditions in these institutions.

BUKAVU: Fifty prisoners including convicted murderers and rapists have escaped from a prison in the east of Democratic Republic of Congo after a fire, a local administrator said on Friday.

On the other side, Burundian refugees in Rwanda are being recruited into rebel groups, a charity said in a report. US-based advocacy group Refugees International said that men and boys in Rwanda's Mahama camp, run by the United Nations and Rwandan authorities, were being recruited into "non-state armed groups" and faced threats if they refused. The charity added that the Burundian recruits are trained in Rwanda and efforts are made to send them back to Burundi via neighbouring Democratic Republic of Congo.

"The arming of Burundian refugees in Rwanda would not only represent a grave violation of international law, but also a serious threat to peace in Burundi and the entire region," said Michael Boyce of Refugees International. "In that context, refugees' claims that some Rwandan officials turn a blind eye to recruitment, and possibly even facilitate it, are deeply disturbing," he said.

The report found at least 80 cases of alleged recruitment, with some refugees saying they were, "trained inside Rwanda, transported in Rwandan military vehicles, and trained by Kinyarwanda-speaking individuals wearing military uniforms." Refugees gave conflicting accounts of which groups they were being recruited into, including long-standing National Forces of Liberation (FNL) rebels and a new group named 'Imbogoraburundi', meaning "Those Who Will Bring Burundi Back". The Rwandan government has in the past denied allegations of involvement in recruiting rebels.

Refugees International said "the civilian and humanitarian character of asylum has been and continues to be undermined in Rwanda, in violation of international law," and called for recruitment to stop and for those responsible to be punished.

Burundi's crisis began in April when President Pierre Nkurunziza announced his intention to run for a controversial third term, which he went on to win in July. More than 200,000 people have fled the country in the last eight months, according to the UN. Burundi has repeatedly accused Rwanda of backing rebel's intent on overthrowing the government in Bujumbura, allegations Rwanda had denied.

Surprisingly when the African Union suggested to send AU troops in Burundi was against the idea. TANZANIA opposed an African Union plan to deploy as many as 5,000 peacekeepers to stem violence in neighbouring

Burundi and backed a political solution to the East African nation's eight-month crisis.

Tanzania's Foreign Affairs Minister Augustine Mahiga stated that was going to try and convince the AU to reconsider its proposal and give a chance the regionally backed negotiations, which restart in Uganda on Dec. 28. 2015 but with no clear direction.

The African Union on Dec. 18th 2015 went on and approved troops for Burundi, where violence spurred by Nkurunziza's bid for a third presidential term. The AU also suggested it would send in a force even if the Burundi government is opposed it, saying another genocide would not happen on its watch. Burundian officials, given four days to agree, have rejected the plan, saying it would violate the country's sovereignty.

The Rwandan Government advised military intervention before any other nation, Rwanda's President Paul Kagame said the eight-month crisis in Burundi may need armed intervention to quell the violence, while ruling out sending Rwandan troops. At the same time President Nkurunziza of Burundi accused Rwanda of destabilising his nation, even went on to say that the AU forces should be sent to Rwanda because it's the source of his country's instability.

Rwandan Kagame said that, "The crisis in Burundi is political, not military, but it may require some level of military to quiet down the guns," Kagame said. "We are appealing to Burundians to sort out their problems." However, Kagame said Rwanda would not be directly in any such effort.

Tanzania has historically played big brother to Burundi, and expects its view of events on Burundi to be taken seriously. It also tries as much as it can not to be at odds with Bujumbura. It is currently hosting more than 120,000 refugees from Burundi, according to Mahiga. On a personal note, Mahiga must be approaching the Burundi crisis with a mild sense of dèja vu.

Burundian officials, were given four days to agree, AU forces intervention but have rejected the plan, saying it would be a violation of the East African nation's sovereignty. Burundi President Pierre Nkurunziza says he will consider any deployment of African Union peacekeepers in his troubled nation and attack against which he will retaliate militarily.

"Everyone has to respect Burundi's borders. In case they violate those principles, they will have attacked the country and every Burundian will stand up and fight against them," Nkurunziza announced in a national address on Wednesday that sent shockwaves through the international community and left many wondering how the continental union of nations will respond. "The country will have been attacked and it will respond," he said.

Kagame rejected the "childish allegation" that Rwanda had stoked instability in Burundi and said his country's troops would play no part in any intervention. Nkurunziza's opponents say he violated a two-term limit set out in accords that ended a civil war in 2005.

Nkurunziza faces increasing opposition from the AU and the international community over his unpopular quest to extend his tenure as president of the tiny central African nation. He weathered a May coup attempt and won a disputed election in July, though violence has continued.

According to South Africa-based security analyst Stephanie Wolters, Nkurunziza's brio comes as no surprise, as Burundi's top elected official has been building up to the statement with increasingly strong rhetoric since first proposing constitutional changes allowing him to seek a third presidential term.

Wolters, who heads the Conflict Prevention and Risk Analysis program at the Pretoria-based Institute for Security Studies, says Nkurunziza's direct challenge to the AU, which only recently began flexing its muscles in terms of continental peace and security issues, bodes poorly for continuing peace talks in Uganda.

"I think the fact that Nkurunziza has said he will attack African Union troops, it's not a blow to the AU," she told VOA. "It makes his government look entirely irresponsible; it makes the government look like a government that doesn't want to resolve a crisis. The African Union now, of course, is going to have to figure out how tough it wants to be in response to that."

While the AU has legal backing to send in troops anyway, that move might only escalate the conflict, thereby defeating the primary purpose of a peacekeeping force. Rather than overruling the president, Wolters suggests AU officials should instead put peacekeeping plans on pause and strike a deal to round out its complement of neutral military and civilian observers in Burundi.

She also says Nkurunziza's threat could backfire: In recent years, Burundi has been an active contributor to AU peacekeeping missions, which means Burundian soldiers may find themselves face to face with their former battle buddies.

"Nkurunziza may well say, 'we're going to combat AU forces,' but there's really no guarantee that the army is going to do that," she said. "In fact, this is a key point here. The army has been less than willing to participate in Nkurunziza's crackdowns on civilians, and so his threat may very well be very hollow. This may very well be the point at which the army says, 'that's it, we've had enough of this guy, we're not going to go combating African Union troops, who, sometimes, we fight alongside.'"

Nkurunziza's comments were issued as the specter of regional conflict, messy regional politics and ethnic violence loom: Burundi and neighboring Rwanda have long been politically at odds, with Burundi frequently accusing Rwanda of meddling in its affairs. Most recently, Bujumbura alleged that Kigali recruited Burundian refugees to overthrow Nkurunziza's government.

Complicating things further, the presidents of the two nations are from the two rival ethnic groups that clashed in Rwanda's 1994 genocide. Both tiny nations are dwarfed by the giant, messy Democratic Republic of Congo, who's social and political troubles often spill over borders, wreaking havoc throughout the region. This saga Nkurunziza Vs Kagame has been ongoing since 2015 and no one knows how it will end up as President Kagame has been elected for another 7 years term up to 2024.

# 7 Chap VII: Kagame love hate relationship with West

## 7.1 The panel Vs Greening and Kagame

In 2008 President Paul Kagame visited David Cameroon in the UK who was the head of the opposition party the conservatives. Among all, he met Andrew Mitchell who was the main contact and among the conservative party donors. Andrew Mitchell was and is still a very close friend of David Cameroon. Mr. Mitchell is a successful business man who had supported the conservative party in the UK all long. This meeting was an important one mainly for Paul Kagame who had an opportunity to meet David Cameroon who was a contender and possible next leader of Britain at the time.

When President Kagame became very close to Andrew Mitchell and Cameroon he then benefited from what was known as generosity of sympathy from what had happened in Rwanda in 1994. President Kagame began receiving regular visits from Andrew Mitchell and his Umubano organisation which helped in building schools in Rwanda; according to the reliable sources we are holding these men exchanged letters and envelopes of unknown presents.

The depth of the relationship between Andrew Mitchell and Rwanda's hardline leader was revealed as the senior Tory had visited the African state many times in the past.

Mr Mitchell was criticised by human rights groups for lifting a freeze on £16million of British aid to President Paul Kagame's regime on his final day as International Development Secretary in September of 2012.

Documents released by the Department for International Development suggest Mr Mitchell had promised Kagame he would continue pumping in aid money despite concerns about the regime's dire human rights record.

Most of the visits related to Project Umubano, the voluntary project set up by Mr Mitchell and David Cameron in 2007 to help 'detoxify' their party's uncaring image.

These revelations answer the focus and the attention on the unlikely friendship between Mr Mitchell and President Kagame, whose regime is accused of repression against political opponents at home and arming a murderous rebellion in the neighbouring Democratic Republic of the Congo.

Internal DFID documents, released under the Freedom of Information Act, show that in a phone call in February 2011 the men discussed Mr Mitchell's decision to increase aid to Rwanda from £60million a year to £90million, much of it poured into the Kagame regime's coffers as 'budget support'.

Two months earlier Mr Mitchell had flown to Rwanda to see Kagame for a '90-minute tête-à-tête followed by lunch' in which they had 'friendly but robust' exchanges. That meeting followed Kagame's controversial re-election with 93 per cent of the vote.

Mr Mitchell reluctantly froze the £16million aid payment to Rwanda after a devastating UN report on the regime's support for the bloody rebellion in the Democratic Republic of Congo.

Other major donors, including the US and Germany, have continued their aid bans. But, in his final act as International Development Secretary, Mr Mitchell released the money.

A senior Foreign Office source called the decision a 'mistake'. The British government continues to struggle in making a decision of whether the aid will be stopped or not, the panel interviewed Justine Greening the international development secretary on the 13th/11/12 in regards to the Rwandan aid. During the evidence session where Justine Greening testified she appeared nervous and could not seem right provide adequate answers to most questions. Yet still, early signs indicate that her main focus is to release the aid. The evidence session ended with no proper result and it was only the panel allowed to ask questions.

Justine Greening was asked what the decision will be in regards to taking action on Rwanda aid, either releasing it or stopping it completely. She appeared to struggle to come up with a convincing response to the panel; however, she indicated that she would like the aid to be reinstated because of the visible development in Rwanda.

I wish she knew what really goes on inside our communities where no one can afford a dose of paracetamol and the aid money goes straight to the RPF ruling party and gets whisked to foreign banks as well as other investments. This caused a lot of questions from the panel many of them asking Ms. Greening if the violence in DRC had ended while others asked her if the issue of human rights violations had been assessed further. She was also asked about Kagame's luxurious expenses of spending $10,000 on hotel room in New York. Ms. Greening then indicated her future plans and tried to distance herself from such questions and Andrew Mitchell by explaining her plans for when she took over the position from Mr. Mitchell and the development in Rwanda.

She further spoke about meeting the nongovernmental organisations as well as the Rwandan Government, also she explained that she is waiting for the United Nations to discuss with other donor countries to see where they stand even though many countries already have closed the aid chapter for Rwanda. She promised the final decision to be announced next month.

But what is all this about? Let's look at the reports that have come up with the same result on Rwanda vs the DRC issue.

- Human rights watch
- Amnesty international
- GoE group of expert's reports
- United nations report

The countries that stopped aid without even needing to review their decision include a number of European countries, and are as follows:

- Germany
- Belgium
- Sweden
- Holland
- Denmark

The United States of America opened the act stopping $20 million which prompted most of the countries mentioned above. But why is Britain struggled to make a decision on this matter?

Rwanda joined the Common Wealth Countries a couple of years ago; this is being used as a shield to confuse the whole Nation. Rwanda switched from speaking French to speaking English this also can be used as shield for the government to convince its citizens that some investments are on about.

The main problem that we as Rwandans are having today is the reality of Rwanda being led as a dictatorship. The western leaders have proven many times that they cannot work out who is a dictator and who is not. They cannot do it simply because they do not care, because if they did Justine Greening wouldn't be discussing about releasing the Rwanda aid at the time.

In Africa, we have no proper democratic leaders, exclude South Africa and Ghana please, the rest are just as confused as their donors who use aid as investment. Justine Greening is one of the conservative members who participated in the Umubano in 2008 in Rwanda, like many others she was misled and left for Rwanda to participate in charitable work. The other UK officials who travelled to Rwanda are as follows: (in the positions they held at the time 2008)

- Geoffrey Clifton-Brown – Shadow Minister for International Trade and Development

- Tobias Ellwood – Shadow Minister for Tourism

- Justine Greening – Shadow Minister for the Treasury

- Jeremy Hunt – Shadow Secretary of State for Culture, Media and Sport

- Mark Lancaster – Shadow Minister for International Development

- Francis Maude – Shadow Minister for the Cabinet Office and Shadow Chancellor of the Duchy of Lancaster

- Andrew Mitchell – Shadow Secretary of State for International Development

- David Mundell – Shadow Secretary of State for Scotland

- Brooks Newmark – Assistant Chief Whip

- Desmond Swayne – Parliamentary Private Secretary to the Leader of the Opposition

The PPCs participating in Project Umubano are:

- Harriett Baldwin – West Worcestershire

- John Bell – Clwyd South

- Ron Bell – Blackpool South

- Rob Halfon – Harlow

- Damian Hinds – East Hampshire

- Chris Kelly – Dudley South

- Pauline Latham – Mid Derbyshire

- Wendy Morton – Tynemouth

- Hazel Noonan – Coventry North-east

- Mark Pawsey – Rugby

- Maggie Throup – Solihull

This trip was and still continues be repeatedly criticised by the opposition party Labour which was in power at the time. On the 08th/11/12 when Andrew Mitchell appeared in front of the panel he made it clear that not only did David Cameron know that he was going to release the aid but everyone did and it had been discussed and agreed to for the aid to be released.

Justine Greening, at the panel, pointed out that due to development patterns in Rwanda she would agree for the aid to be reinstated. Many interested parties are questioning if there is something else behind this potential decision because we are talking of a head of state that use the aid to do the following:

- Kagame's RPF party is worth $500 million, the aid is injected in the party's business to keep it going.

- Why should Britain give $ 83 million when there is clear violation of human rights in DRC and in Rwanda? The DRC refugee's camps, their children are being forced to join the M23 rebels, look at the political prisoners in Rwanda.

- The money given by Britain subsidizes government budget which is diverted to bank roll wars and entrench a one-party dictatorship.

- The big chunk of Aid is stolen and/or invested in private business such as Tristar and the government Ministers of finance banking foreign currency in Mauritius.

- Why should Tristar invest in foreign currency while it is earning in local currency? This is money laundering and capital freight. Hard currency earned from donors is quickly siphoned out.

- Kagame spends £10,000 a night hotel room when his citizens cannot afford the basics, the eastern DRC has been destabilized with war crimes for a decade because of this same man.

Whether the aid is released or not Kagame will continue to destabilize the region. He still needs to invest in the Congo as well as steal the minerals for his personal and professional gain. The Congo is the leading producer of Gold and Diamond and Rwanda itself does not own or claim to have an investible amount of geo-strategic minerals for consumption on the global market.

In 1996 the reason why we attacked Congo has rapidly shifted and no Rwandan leader including Kagame himself remembers why we invaded in the first place.

## 7.2 Anxious wait of the UK government decision on Aid provision to Rwanda (2012)

As I sat on the sofa watching the American elections, Barack Obama and Mitt Romney waving flags for the same cause but just with different ideas on how to move their country forward. Obama promising to strengthen the economy with Romney promising to fix it, Romney explaining Obama's failures and explaining how he can achieve a better change while Obama focusing on change and reminding the voters of his achievements.

It went on and on for a while with the western media explaining very clear in detail, it was so interesting for me as someone who was born in Uganda during Idi Amin's regime, then grew up in Dr Milton Obote's autocratic government then ended up joining the Rwandese Patriotic Front which later President Kagame became the leader.

I then immediately recalled what is going on back home with Madame Ingabire Umuhoza who is imprisoned for just daring to form a political party, the FDU-Inkingi, to run against Paul Kagame. Generals who saved our nation when they were desperately needed are now in exile. Normal citizens were forced to vote in Kagame's favour with the members of parliaments appointed, not elected, what a nation? Not only President Kagame and his unconvincing politics but most countries in Africa are experiencing the same scenario, West African countries are even going through coup d'état what Africa??

Now that President Obama is re-elected we all hope he may focus on foreign policy, like his predecessors on their last term they looked on that particular policy towards the end of their second term.

President Paul Kagame who is typically praised for stopping the 1994 genocide is now regarded as one of the master minders of everything that happened in Rwanda during the genocide as noted in the Mapping Report (2010).

As indicated in the current UN report as well as the Human rights watch report, the region has been unsettled due to Kagame's wars in the Congo. The M23 is one of the rebel groups that has made Kagame benefit from the man made humanitarian crisis but also scratch his head. This particular rebel group which still threatens the region has led to many questions being asked in western countries. Aid has been stopped by many countries due to Kagame's influence in the Congo and on the 13th/11/2012 the British government will discuss whether to discontinue or approve their large amount of aid to Rwanda. Many are eager to learn the findings and how the decision will be made after exchanging and abundance of evidence. This will be a big challenge for the members of parliament, as Kagame has immediately and abruptly sentenced Mrs. Victorie Ingabire Umuhoza's to an eight-year sentence.

According to the Rwandan laws once someone is sentenced you can argue with the punishment not the reason for the sentence. So, the western countries remain with many questions on whether the Rwandan government is maintaining justice in regards to political prisoners however it should not only be about Ingabire, it should be about every political prisoner being held in Rwanda.

Kagame is now anxious about the outcome of the 13th/11/12 parliament hearing on Rwandan aid. The International Development Committee will examine the decision by the Department for International Development to withhold, and subsequently disburse, budget support to the Government of Rwanda following allegations about the Rwandan Government's role in the conflict in eastern DRC, and the decision of other donors who withdrew budget support not to reinstate it. The first evidence session will be on the 13th/11/12 and the average Rwandan citizen is struggling to afford their basic needs. The ruling party, Rwandese Patriotic Front (RPF), and Kagame its chairman himself are pumping every nation's penny in business making certain that his companies are functioning well while begging for the donors to continue sending aid, and making the average Rwandan pay more while earning less or even nothing.

The movement's investment arm, Crystal Ventures, controls assets worth more than $500m inside the country, according to Financial time (September 24, 2012). The group owns a construction and road-building company, granite and tile factories, a furniture company, a chain of upmarket coffee shops (in Kigali, Boston, London, Washington and New York), a real estate developer and an agro-processing venture, Inyange. It also retains a stake in MTN, the leading mobile phone operator.

This makes it perhaps the largest quasi-private business venture in the country, and with 7,000 staff, the second-largest employer after the state. It also puts the ruling party in an enviable position when it comes to financing politics. Relative to the size of the country, the RPF is one of the best endowed political movements in the world. In the sub region, only Ethiopia's ruling EPRDF, under Meles Zenawi, the recently deceased prime minister, has built a more formidable business empire.

Professor Nshuti Manasseh, chairman of the board of Crystal Ventures, says half the RF1.5bn ($2.4m) cost of RPF campaigning in 2010 elections was met by donations from party members, the other half from company coffers. "We came in when contributions fell short," he says. "From the beginning, we said we should have our own resources so that we are not indebted either to business people who want favours or foreign people like Gaddafi," says Mr Musoni, referring to the late Libyan leader's penchant for using cash for influence among his African peers.

By necessity, at first, the RPF pioneered new business. Initially, according to Mr Musoni, this involved trading, financing small enterprises, and taking charge of the coffee crop that had been left to rot. But with time, the movement's investment arm became more strategic.

In 1995, it launched Inyange, an agro-processing venture that has grown into one of Rwanda's largest companies producing bottled water, milk and fruit juices. In 1998, it persuaded South Africa's MTN to provide mobile phone services in what looked then like a marginal market. The RPF fronted much of the capital required. Crystal Ventures has since sold down its 49 percent stake twice, earning $110m, according to Prof Manasseh.

It was a shrewd investment. Less so, perhaps, was what happened to the proceeds. The group bought two executive jets, which it then leased to – among others – President Kagame, from a base in South Africa.

Nor has that been the only controversy involving RPF-linked businesses who were accused by UN experts of plundering mineral resources during neighbouring Congo's wars. Another frequent charge is that they have crowded out other investors, and enjoyed favoured status when it comes to government contracts.

Crystal Ventures' Intersec, for example is the only private security outfit authorised to carry arms. "Where there is lucrative business they (RPF) control it. Things are not as open as you think," says a prominent business person in Kigali.

Professor Manasseh however, rejects the charge. "Our objective is not to monopolise. The interest of the party was to run businesses if there were no other investors," he says.

Crystal Ventures is now considering selling Inyange (Kenya's Brookside, owned by the Kenyatta family is interested). It intends to sell off its "Bourbon" coffee shops for franchise, and is debating whether to offload its 20 per cent stake in the Rwandan Investment Group, a $70m venture capital fund. Mr Musoni says the party also plans to list several interests on the Kigali stock exchange.

Kagame and his RPF have turned to selling shares to foreigners; this has always been done by Captain Hatari Sekoko, Kagame's right hand man in business. He has been working closely with the Chinese investors who he used to borrow money from RDB (Rwanda Development Bank), after that they bought the plot which involved Jari Club formerly known as 5th Nyakanga Hotel, they also bought the Muhima police station land and moved the as far as Gitega.

This Chinese investor in the names of Billy used to be a blocker in Hong Kong, has been an influential figure in helping Kagame wire transfer money into safe havens such as Mauritius and some South American countries. He was misled though and was made to sign the paperwork worth 20% shares when he actually owns nothing in this business, the new hotel known as Marriott is being built and will be known as Billy's when its actually owned by Kagame himself. The Chinese Company which built Kagame's house, Kigali Tower, which Kagame forced to move the Bus station just to get that plot, was also given to his son Ivan Cyomoro last month. This comes after some complaints from the construction company CC claiming that until today they are still demanding to get paid for the men used while building this particular house.

With these examples of financial abundance in Kagame's Rwanda one has to wonder why his search for foreign aid is so rabid. With the amount of revenue from Crystal Ventures, the abundance of properties, airplanes and vehicles what exactly is Paul Kagame using the foreign aid for? Has there been any accountability or legitimate reports conducted by outsiders for the use of foreign aid ever been conducted? Who holds the government of Rwanda accountable? The RPF is known for doctoring their own reports and news (read The New Times and Andrew Mwenda) so an outside agency would be required in order for an accountability report to be legitimate. Although, anyone who knows about Rwanda knows they do not look kindly at outsiders investigating them, because the truth always comes out.

In light of the assets Kagame has amassed hopes are high that the UK will continue to hold Kagame accountable by suspending aid until his backing of the rebel groups in Congo cease. Reinstating the aid to Rwanda will only serve to reward Kagame for destabilizing a neighbouring country.

# 8 Chap VIII: oppositions party power struggle, disunity and Weakness

## 8.1 Political parties in Rwanda

*Squabbling, Backbiting and Divisions of Rwanda Political Parties Let Down Rwandans.*

The Price of disunity of Rwanda opposition political parties operating outside the country will not only cost them dearly but will also significantly deny Rwandans a choice of the leadership they cherish and deserve at this critical moment.

Rwanda's democracy movement needs some serious soul-searching if it wants to secure its aims. In all these years, Rwanda Opposition political parties operating outside Rwanda have not lived up to their expectations. It's time to ask what they have achieved in those years, as many will be celebrating almost their Two decades birth day. Are they any nearer now to their goals?

The current turbulence in the coalition of CPC and other opposition political parties cast doubt on whether they really stand firm to guard against any weather from Kagame who is not only a cunning and deceitful president but has a multitude of powerful supporters and lobbying organization that is protected by strong weather guards.

For answers, one only needs to look at the fate of veteran opposition leader Mr. Twagiramungu Faustin who has changed political parties since 1990. It is estimated that more than 20 opposition political parties have mushroomed since then, both within the country and outside. Even in the days of bloodshed during genocide and massacre of many innocent Rwandans opposition political parties failed Rwandans for selfish reasons. And where are they now?

In Rwanda, many politicians who are brave enough to ask RPF and Kagame the direction of where he is steering the country have end up in Prison, among them is Victoire Ingabire whose party has been divided since she was arrested despite the sacrifice she made to go and face the monstrous regime of Kagame.

Mr. Deo Mushayidi of PDP Imanzi is serving life imprisonment yet his party has not moved a stride that befits the price Mr. Deo Mushayidi paid for facing Kagame's brutality. The RNC needs to move another walk to bring on board all its former members who left their party for different reasons. Whereas it is a right for anybody to choose a political party of belonging, it should also be a serious concern for a political party to lose members in unclear circumstances.

As many opposition politicians are rotting in the most notorious jails of President Kagame, so are many people suffering from abject poverty. They are being taxed for even their small land which is as barren as Sahara Desert. Why in the first place should a person pay tax for the land he /she use for subsistence farming?

Why should a person pay tax for his own domestic house? Many Rwandans cannot afford all those taxes especially in the rural areas where agriculture is the survival. Why should you tax a person who operates a business whose capital is not worth 100,000 FWR?

The Gacaca courts left untold suffering of unfair and wrong convictions, yet these courts were closed with a promise of a new law that will give a window of appeal to the affected people. They have never been allowed to make these appeals as the law that closed Gacaca courts stipulates. Because the RPF government as deceitful as always, they convinced the whole world how successful Gacaca Courts were, they then feared not only a flood gate of appeals but also an embarrassment of miscarriage of Justice exhibited by these courts.

Again, the suffocation of the free press, freedom of assembly, the continued incarceration, and killings of innocent people, education has become a luxury rather than a necessity; it's a privilege rather than a right. Indeed, those who cannot afford money for medical insurances, the RPF officials have confiscated their property, yet Kagame deceives the world that medical insurance is free.

Kagame and RPF have doctored the statistics regarding the development index and people in the villages are intimidated or coerced to tell the foreign visitors that everything is well. All the streets of Kigali and other towns are spotless of beggars and other small business of hawkers. The picture of the Rwanda to foreigners is different from the reality of our own people who cannot even get a meal for a single day.

These are the really needs of many Rwandans irrespective of their background whether Hutus, Tutsi or Twas, the common none issues that have pre- occupied our opposition political parties is the real cause Kagame is still in power today. As I have mentioned above, it's almost 20 years under Kagame authoritarian and militarism rule, yet the aim of dislodging Kagame by opposition seems as elusive as ever. But why?

It's no longer a question of the inability or an incapable RPF to run the country or its ruthless repression of its own people. Nor is it a question of the failure by the international community to put sanctions against the Kagame regime. Perhaps counting years is not long enough for fundamental change to occur in a country ruled by a repressive regime, even though it seems like an eternity for dissidents who have devoted their lives to the pursuit of democracy. Many believe it's time for serious soul searching, which could lead to a new impetus.

I think our politicians are naïve and no more than activists, they are even less active than activists. They don't know how to take power and they have no strategic policies. That's why many have failed to work with the veteran politician Mr. Twagiramungu Faustin, for those who could remember the days of 1990s, if he had not been Mr. Twagiramungu, it would have been difficult for the RPF to infiltrate the Habyarimana regime. Yet many political leaders we see today just follow the people, they don't lead the people.

Never in our history did we have such an excellent mobiliser but also controversial political figure, such as Mr. Twagiramungu Faustin, but sadly, those qualities have failed to grab any opportunity for power. Therefore, politicians should learn to see and grab a window of opportunity at the right moment because such windows cannot not stay open for long or forever. President Kagame is at his weakest link, this is an opportunity for all the political parties to put aside their differences and put the interests of Rwandans first.

Unfortunately, many influential politicians have chosen to follow their own path, ignoring unity. If they could unite, I'm sure the story might turn out differently. Unity is the one thing that strikes fear in the heart of any authoritarian government. It is the most effective weapon Rwanda's pro-democracy forces could hope to wield, yet it has never come within their grasp. The lack of unity continues to provide room for the authoritarian, military regime of Kagame.

Rwanda opposition must marry of perish

The political Parties operating outside the Republic of Rwanda are missing an opportunity at this moment in time where Kagame and his RPF are mobilizing to change the Rwandan Constitution. Indeed, this is a rare political opportunity to unite and resist by all means necessary the Kagame constitutional coup. Kagame is determined to confuse the world by pretending that he does not want to stay however willing to hold on power.

The current economic conditions where Rwanda is facing the highest debt in the Rwandan history and the political uncertainty could be the trigger and be used as a good ground to forge an alternative, and bring down the RPF system peacefully. Alas, Diaspora forces are wasting golden chance to unite and bring about the change every Rwandan is yearning for.

They have difficulty trusting one another or group trusting another on power. The dogged problem has always been who should be who first; they did it before the 'animal' was finally killed. The RNC Party, FDU Inkingi, and other political forces operating outside Rwanda have a daunting task now to change the system in Kigali. Unity for the opposition forces is paramount, if the threat of removing the current government in Rwanda is to become real.

By unity they could form a formidable force that would be reckoned with against the long worn out party called the Rwanda Patriotic Front. The RPF fortunately or unfortunately is regrouping, and so long as are left unchallenged, they have the backing of the small but significant opposition that has been bought or intimidated who have forged a partnership to show the international community that Kagame is not only loved by his own people but has no opposition to challenge his political appetite.

Rwandans and the opposition in particular as they known to have short memory, we forget easily our history, just 21 years we have forgotten what caused Genocide and how the opposition was manipulated by the MRND regime to participate in genocide, even some of the opposition parties who had previously prevailed against the late President Habyarimana regime.

They will resume their lives, despite irreparable socio-political damage brought about by ruthless regime in power in Kigali. The Rwandan people have paid the brunt of Kigali brutal policies and it is time the country move away. The clique in power has no intention of leaving power under any circumstances unless the opposition extraordinary to change tactics, strategy and method of work.

Time and again, the world was warned that Kigali bends to shed more blood of innocent human beings in the country, but the powerful nations were indifferent and still like that. Rwandans and the opposition should not sit and think that the world is moving closer, or their voice will be heard, to make this point clear, if the RPF did not resist the late President Habyarimana regime, the Rwandans including Kagame would still be in exile. To put the record straight, let's do it ourselves and let's do it now not tomorrow.

The Rwandan Opposition forces haven't lived up to the expectation of the Rwandan people. Their sectarian orientation goes against new order. It has alienated many, and somewhat work in favor of the dying regime in power. Why don't these people unite or seek genuine intercourses and alliances among themselves.

For RPF to go therefore, the strong opposition parties like RNC and FDU Inkingi forces must make unity attractive to other political forces. There is chance to do just that. Alliance is the way to go! Political marriage for all is overdue, so to squeeze life out of the RPF, also lobbying and planting truth, reconciliation and forming the pillars of the future as it appears the journey for change is at the beginning.

## 8.2 The Genesis of Marara's fallout with Rudasingwa

In summary: We continue to dig deep on how Rudasingwa's self-centered style of leadership caused divisions following a letter dated Sun, 18/09/2011 written by Noble Marara, begging for the building and strengthening of institutions.

*Rudasingwa*

Dear Maj Theogene Rudasingwa and my fellow members of our beloved organisation RNC, I would like to thank you for the work that you have been doing for the last couple of weeks which proved as an impact in terms of exposing Kagame's Government that seems weakened.

I believe that you have been working hard to highlight some of the areas that need strengthening in order to keep up with the demand of strong institutions that our country desperately deserves.

First of all, brothers and sisters, I understand that organisations and political parties work under the umbrella of policies and laws, including being honest between members and being empathetic towards each other. These empathies and honesty between members can only be achieved once we have policies in place.

Allow me as a team member to suggest that, RNC should implement the policies and hold those responsible to account for their actions, most importantly; organisations should provide a means of how to work together and guide every participant in making sure that there are no divisions.

The capacity of parties to discharge these functions effectively should be controlled by the regulatory environment, which is created by the leadership that is not self-centered but with the ideas of all the followers.

This should include both the external and or internal policies and laws that govern the entire organisation.

The question now is the level of effectiveness that the RNC organisation performs. It is obvious that a lot has been done by the member's voluntary efforts however I personally deem it the right necessary time we need to have some governing policies and or statute in place if we are to have a greater impact against Kagame.

There are still significant challenges, especially in countries where RNC face low or eroding grassroots like Rwanda. There are also problematic issues in countries where the RPF is still believed to be a saviour of our nation. We need to ask the question:

- Is this dominating force the right vision for the Rwandese future?

- I believe that there is a challenge of planting more cadres plus recruiting members.

- I believe that we are still weak in terms of finance and we have done less in international relations.

- We have a crisis of public confidence due to the continued imprisonment of opposition members plus the intimidation of those thought to be our followers inside the country. But we are not working together as necessary. This has caused the rise of questions in most of our high-profile supporters in western countries.

There is considerable variation in the role, function, organizational structure, and philosophy of different types, it is evident that RNC has done little to finalise the above-mentioned areas. We need to have an organisational structure between bottom-up 'mass-branch' versus top-down 'caucus-cadre' structures. Members should have the (right) chance to elect those who are able to deliver for the best of the country, party, and organisation. We need to consider the competence of the persons being elected in any position if we are aiming to achieve the quantity and quality of the delivery.

If these have been acquired without my knowledge as a member I will have been left out, and so I kindly request that we get a proper discussion. If those areas are fully covered then we will need our leaders to work hard on informing us about our achievements, strengths and weaknesses.

## 8.3 Is Rudasingwa's arrogance destroying RNC? (Before RNC divorce)

Elitism, Arrogance and Lack of internal Democracy Will Destroy the Rwanda National Congress (RNC). Dr. Rudasingwa Theogene with his former Boss Kagame are co- founders of the "Munyangire" (*Hate the one I hate*) within the RPF. This is a syndrome is not only being exported to the

Rwanda National Congress by Dr. Rudasingwa Theogene, but is slowly and surely eating up the whole party. For example, when Mr. Rudasingwa Theogene left Rwanda for whatever reasons, he never rose against the Kigali regime, it's until the departure of Gen. Kayumba Nyamwasa that he started becoming provocative and with other former RPF senior officials in 2010 they started the Rwanda National Congress.

*Munyangire at heart: President Kagame with Rudasingwa*

According to Dr. Theogene Rudasingwa and many Rwandans believe that the RPF regime is suffocating the fundamental freedoms of Rwandans, like free media, freedom of assembly and violets the human rights. Amazingly, Dr. Theogene Rudasingwa has made it a habit if not a custom by attacking whoever, criticizes the style of his leadership. While many Rwandans are yearning for democracy, freedom of speech, and other human rights, the style of Mr. Rudasingwa does not give hope that something fundamentally will come over the horizon of the Rwanda National Congress that he is slowly turning into a personal enterprise.

As much as many Rwandans need a regime change in Kigali, they need an opposition which is quite strong, democratic, but not changing a gang of bad group and replacing it with another group that is even worse than the one replaced. Therefore, it is my conviction that if there was a true democracy in the RNC, people like Dr. Theogene Rudasingwa would have never seen the light of day. Unfortunately, its otherwise sound constitution of RNC that contains a few fatal flaws, it's now an open secret that some RNC leaders also have a weak devotion to democracy, and indirectly some are actively plotting to overthrow it.

Dr. Theogene Rudasingwa, unfortunately, enjoys an almost unbroken string of luck in coming to power within the RNC ranks. He benefited greatly from the dictatorial atmosphere in Rwanda, humiliation of a section of some Rwandans, lack of confidence within a section of opposition, and lack of interest by some members of the opposition who have just remained silent not because they like Kagame, but because they know very well the attitude and behaviour of Dr. Rudasingwa Theogene.

In fact, the ascendance of Kagame to the throne of RPF after the sudden and mysterious death of its founder and Leader, Gen. Fred Rwigema, is no different to the rise of Dr. Theogene Rudasingwa to the mantle of RNC leadership. Some prominent former RPF members who decided to keep silent, Maj. Alpohonse Fuluma, Maj Mupende, Maj Bizimungu who were among the founders of RPF and the initial members of the First Rwandan parliament after genocide, has not joined RNC. Others like Dr. Polly Murayi, Paul Rusesabagina, Lt. Jeanne Mulisa, Kazungu myself just to mention a few, have failed to work with Dr. Theogene Rudasingwa's Leadership style.

Critics of democracy might claim that Dr. Theogene Rudasingwa was democratically elected to the ranks of RNC. This is untrue. Dr. Theogene Rudasingwa never had the popular votes to become what he is now in the RNC and the only reason he got the job was because the RNC leaders entered into a series of back-room deals. Some claim that Rudasingwa's rise was nonetheless legal under the RNC system. The problem is that what was "legal" under the RNC system would not be considered legal under a truer and better-working democracy.

Dictators' rise to power for many and various reasons, for example, Kagame's political terror and state-run propaganda has inevitably worn him support from Rwanda and in the Diaspora not out love but out fear and survival. Kagame in the last election won more than 90 percent of the vote and through his propaganda is campaigning for the change of the Constitution so that he can stand again after is constitutional, mandate expires in 2017.

It is my belief that accountability is one of the disciplines leaders must foster to improve their effectiveness in a way that lasts. A cycle of cynicism occurs when leaders announce wonderful aspirations (e.g. vision, mission and strategy statements) but fail to deliver.

Over time this cycle breaks down trust and erodes commitment. Leadership sustainability requires leaders to take personal responsibility for making sure that they do what they say. Accountability also increases when leaders expect and accept personal commitments from others and follow up on those commitments.

Over time, leadership is sustainable when the leader's agenda becomes the personal agenda of others. For example, Dr Theogene Rudasingwa is a man who does not only hate advice, but he fights it altogether, when I advised him on the matter of Radio Impala, he first told me to apologise for the allegations, and poor me I apologised for giving him the information that he did not want to hear, I had the arrest warrant of Aloys Manzi from the French Police of which I shared with Theogene Rudasingwa, this arrest warrant clearly showed Aloys Manzi as a wanted man for stealing public money, Rudasingwa told me that everyone has history and this has nothing to do with the RNC. He ignored my advice, yet the truth is that, I had foreseen that Radio Impala was falling in the wrong hands, he has consistently tried to undermine the free criticisms for his leadership and for the shortcomings of the Party in general.

According to Ulrich and Smallwood (2004), leaders build accountability in others, and for themselves, through consistent with your personal values and brand, consistency with a leader's personal values are another way to ensure change is sustainable.

"Value consistency helps leaders to think and act with continuity so that their stance and actions are clear both to themselves and to observers."

To have sustainable impact, though, "a leadership point of view needs to become a personal leader brand". Finally, as much as leader's demand accountability, they should allow accountability on what they do, it's through this lens that the fans of RNC and many Rwandans who are thirsty for the regime change in Rwanda would like to see in Dr. Theogene Rudasingwa and other opposition leaders in Rwanda.

The brute strength of President Kagame's regime has been the weakness of the Rwandan opposition. The Exiled Rwandan Opposition Party (RNC) composed mainly of the former Kagame allies is suffering from intrigues and this has threatened its survival.

## *Kayumba with Rudasingwa*

Kagame as leader of the Rwanda Patriotic Front was Instrumental in stopping the country from degenerating into chaos after genocide. However, some of his colleagues have deserted him accusing him to be a dictator and intolerant to divergent views. Interestingly, the rift between Dr. Theogene Rudasingwa and Gen. Kayumba Nyamwasa is solely on the same path which led them to leave RPF.

The above rift has threatened to tear the party apart and some of their party members have told us that Dr. Theogene Rudasingwa and Gen. Kayumba

Nyamwasa have held several meetings to resolve their differences but all in vain.

According to the reliable information from some of their supporters, the rift between these two founding members of RNC is exacerbated by their close friends who don't want to see Dr. Rudasingwa continuing to lead the RNC. The pending elections within the RNC has been dominated by intrigues and has been postponed several times because of the same reasons, Joseph Ngarambe, Jonathan Musonera, Theogene Rudasingwa and Gerald Gahima are likely to be phased out of the RNC establishment because they are accused of misappropriation of RNC funds and arrogance.

Furthermore, some of their supporters who approached us have accused Gen. Kayumba Nyamwasa of supporting the enthronement of Gervais Condo or Maj. Micombero which is vehemently opposed by Dr. Theogene Rudasingwa who wants another term. According to Dr. Theogene Rudasingwa, Gen. Kayumba Nyamwasa wants to bring a person who will be under his command and will rule under his shadow, a tactic RPF used during its armed struggle in 1990s when it used Col. Alex Kanyarengwe and Pasteur Bizimungu respectively.

"If Gen. Kayumba wants to lead the Party let him do so and he enjoys my personal support and I will vote him, but bringing in a person that he will use to rule under his shadow is unacceptable" Theogene Rudasingwa said.

He further said that his differences with Gen. Kayumba Nyamwasa are based on the way he uses a clique of former RPF soldiers many of them were under his command, this clique of Soldiers organize meetings in the name of RNC which is wrong because some of these meetings might be against our rules. Among the clique of Soldiers mentioned by Dr. Theogene Rudasingwa, include Captain Kaje Alpha in Canada, Maj. Nkubana

Emmanuel, 2lt Rutabana, and Maj.Micombero.

"Some of these soldiers fly to Africa holding meetings in the name of RNC which we don't know; this is not good and must stop." The continued differences between the prominent leaders of RNC have affected the entire leadership were two camps have been created, those supporting Dr. Theogene Rudasingwa and another one for Gen. Kayumba Nyamwasa, therefore this articled should not be interpreted as a message of dividing further the RNC, but we intent to warn them that their differences have serious consequences for the party and Rwandans whom they claim to represent. Indeed, it has already affected the RNC and without doubt has strengthened the RPF regime and Kagame in particular will win the next general elections without any hassle.

## 8.4 General Kayumba save RNC or risks Dr Rudasingwa tearing it apart (Before RNC divorce)

Gen Kayumba: The man that all Rwandans want as a leader Kagame want him dead as mixed reactions continue to trail around the style of leadership of Dr. Theogene Rudasingwa many people are asking why Gen. Kayumba Nyamwasa has continued to keep silent, this will not only weaken the RNC but might see dramatic exit by many supporters from the Rwanda National Congress Party.

### *Dr. Rudasingwa with his wife*

Many members of the Rwanda National Congress have expressed their genuine concern of poor leadership of Dr. Theogene Rudasingwa from the way he handled the Impala Radio which was meant to be the voice of the RNC in particular and the Opposition in general to financial management of the Rwanda National Congress, yet Gen. Kayumba has refused to actively intervene in the party and extinguish the fire before it burns the whole party down.

Rwanda National Congress belongs to all of us, we must not allow it to be destroyed and we must save it from one man show and join hands to make it great. When leaders remain silent or inactive when there is a conflict within party, the followers do not only lose sense of direction but also get worried about their political future. The Rwanda National Congress should come with new settlement which can unite its members and our country.

Therefore Gen. Kayumba Nyamwasa should come up with principles that will define the Rwanda National Congress leadership and how the party will be led in accordance with the wishes of the members the party but not the wishes of Dr. Theogene Rudasingwa

The British Second World War Prime Minister Winston Churchill told the House of Commons and his Cabinet that he has nothing to offer except blood "I have nothing to offer but blood, toil, tears and sweat." Indeed, we have nothing to offer to our country and of course the Rwandan people except blood, toil, tears and sweat.

## 8.5 Rwanda National Congress (opposition party) disunity was predicted.

The split that occurred in heart of RNC in 2016 has been prophesized long before and many people outside and within RNC labeled me a mole for Kigali regime, despite the fact that I had equally exposed the naked side of the Kagame murderous regime.

Rwanda's most prominent opposition politicians under the umbrella of the Rwanda National Congress have failed to agree on the path and the philosophy on which they should run their party; hence a splinter group led by the former coordinator Dr. Theogene Rudasingwa has been formed under a new name of the New Rwanda National Congress.

Accordingly, the opposition entered the 2017 election divided and weakened, rendering the re-election of President Kagame and the Rwanda Patriotic Front without any hassle.

In brief, while President Kagame is known for his brutal rule, the weak and divided opposition will not only legitimize the Kagame sham elections but will undermine the fundamental principle of free and fair elections since there will be no strong challenger come the presidential election in 2017.

The falling apart of the RNC was not only detrimental to their party and supporters but equally to all Rwandans who would have benefited from a strong opposition giving Rwandans a chance and choice of leadership through competitive politics.

Whereas I do recognize the democratic process of the Rwanda National Congress, however, I do find it improper resolving disagreements by splitting the Party which is the only hope for many Rwandans who are yarning for change in Rwanda.

I have personally advocated a free and independent media that doesn't have any influence by anyone, that's why Inyenyeri News has maintained its integrity and professionalism; however, this has come at a cost, because all the members of the Rwanda National Congress and some other opposition parties have labeled our paper as working for Kigali Regime.

Although I have personally been attacked by President Kagame labeling me as a thug, this did not deter many of the Rwanda National Congress officials from mistrusting our paper. Interestingly, as I have already mentioned above, what is happening today, I had prophesied it long time ago and warned them that if you don't unite u will perish one by one. Indeed, they are falling like ripe mangoes, from grace to grass and without gravity to hold them together.

The Rwandans cannot afford more divisions, the death of Col. Karegeya was very painful and a set back to the Rwanda National Congress and was a loss to all of us, but more so to our cause. Therefore, the splitting of Rwanda National Congress at this moment in time is rubbing salt in the wound of many Rwandans.

Why can't Dr. Rudasingwa and Gen. Kayumba Nyamwasa regardless of their differences put the interests of Rwandans first or at least Second? There is no problem for people in an organization to disagree, in fact its healthy, because at least we had started to see a different party from the RPF where Kagame is the RPF and RPF Kagame.

What is however, breaking people's hearts is the way these two pillars of RNC are trying to resolve their differences. We appeal to all concerned people in RNC and in Particular Dr. Theogene Rudasingwa and Gen. Kayumba Nyamwasa that Inyenyeri news will continue to act as your independent platform without fear or favor. Independent media is a powerful force in the struggle to change closed, repressive regimes into open and productive societies. We should avoid bickering and intrigues at this critical moment, RNC needs more than ever Dr. Theogene Rudasingwa and Gen. Kayumba Nyamwasa working together.

## 8.6 Continuously Mourning for Col Karegeya boosts enemy morale

On 1 January 2014, Karegeya was found dead at the Michelangelo Towers, an upmarket hotel in the Johannesburg suburb of Sandton in South Africa. Many observers concluded that he was murdered under Kagame's order for political reasons. Since his death, each year, Col Patrick Karegeya is remembered a by RNC party members, friends and his family.

I am a believer that Col Patrick Karegeya should be remembered through building and focusing on his foundation rather than continuous mourning. The legacy of Col Patrick Karegeya should be used as badge of legitimacy by the opposition. Readers should not get me wrong, we all remember Col Karegeya every day but what is urgently needed is to maintain focus.

His death has triggered continuous mourning in the circles of the Rwandan opposition. While the death of Col. Patrick Karegeya was a big loss to the Rwandan opposition and even those who sympathize with the Kigali regime, but the continuous mourning plays in the hands of the Kagame regime.

For many of us who followed and watched the Untold Story Documentary of the BBC TWO, Kagame and his killing squad said that if you finish off the DUAL (Karegeya and Gen. Kayumba) you finish off the RNC in particular and the whole opposition in general. We need to tell the Kagame and his likes that instead the death and the continued shooting of Gen. Kayumba make our resolve to resist the Kigali dictatorial regime stronger and stronger.

By killing Col. Patrick Karegeya, the Kigali ruling RPF Party orchestrated the fear it has against these Rwandan heroes, emphasizing that by eliminating them, Kagame leadership will live forever or longer. It was a mistake, in the wars that Kagame himself participated in Uganda and the war that brought him to power was not fought by individuals but by the collective determination and the ideology to fight dictatorship and the right of freedom. For example, the first leadership of NRA that brought the President Yoweri Museveni to power lost its first President Prof. Yusuf Kironde Lule, its First Army Commander Sam Magara; however, their death did not deter NRA to continue the struggle and taking the power in 1986. NRA did not get stuck in mourning their fallen heroes.

Indeed, President Kagame knows that the whole of the RPF first commanders died mysteriously, but the war continued because killing the commanders without killing the ideology and the just cause of the war, would be like visiting the deciduous trees in the winter when all the leaves are dry and you think the trees are dead.

The death of Col. Patrick Karegeya should inevitably stir our reflection as the opposition on the current strategy on the move to defeat the Kigali dictatorial regime. His death should not in any way be a platform to show Kagame that we are orphans who cannot continue without him. Col. Karegeya was one of our greatest sons of Rwanda who fought against the injustice not in Rwanda but in the whole of the region. Therefore Col. Karegeya's passing comes at the time RPF government is struggling against public dissatisfaction over corruption and faltering freedom of every Rwandan.

The only way of giving justice to Col. Patrick Karegeya and the meaningful mourning is working hard and uniting all the opposition to remove Kagame from Power. In fact, Rwanda has lost many heroes including Seth

Sendashonga and Col. Theoneste Lizinde who on the sport told Kagame that he is no different from the Habyarimana regime they had fought. Immediately Kagame ordered their elimination, therefore all these Rwandans should be mourned and avenged by working collectively to remove Kagame from power.

The defeat of the elite French forces in the Vietnam war under Gen. Giap was fought by his jungle troops, clad in sandals made of old car tires, they besieged the French army. The French were defeated after 56 days, and the unlikely victory led not only to Vietnam's independence, but hastened the collapse of colonialism across Indochina and beyond.

Even throughout the war against the United States, Giap was defense minister and armed forces commander, but he was slowly pushed aside after Ho Chi Minh's death in 1969. The glory for victory in 1975 didn't go to Giap. Likewise, the death of Gen. Fred Rwigyema and the unexpectedly rise of Major Paul Kagame to the throne of RPF, did not only make Kagame feel complex but also made him insecure because of many RPF commanders who were senior to him.

Gen. Giap stepped down from his last state post, as deputy prime minister, in 1991. But despite losing favor with the government, he became even more beloved by the Vietnamese people. As I have mentioned above, many RPF commanders who knew Paul Kagame like Col. Patrick Karegeya have been sidelined or killed.

Col. Patrick Karegeya a principled man, a lawyer, a soldier, a freedom fighter, many Rwandans love him, we need to strengthen our unity against the Kigali regime. Through his example, he has set the standard for service to country and mankind, whether we are individual or collectively we should continue to call on his legacy by striving to better serve to our fellow human beings and contribute to the betterment of our Rwanda and Rwandans, not continuous mourning, as this would just boost the morale of those who wanted him dead.

## 8.7 A message to our leaders

A general who only fired two bullets all his life is likely to hit us all if we do not reorganize, the opposition is fantasizing to fight Kagame, but at the moment what is required is more than media, mobilising or preaching human rights. Kagame is a dictator who admits it; he outlines the reason and the way to eliminate anyone who questions his criminality. Gen Kagame only used a gun twice in his life but has ordered the death of millions.

Paul Kagame has detained innocent people just to prove that he can hurt his opponents, in Rwanda people are living in anxiety, does not matter whether someone is in RPF, FDU or any other political party. Different people are living different states in a tiny nation full of ghosts.

Strategic planning is urgently needed where we the opposition should be defining its strategy, or direction, and making decisions on allocating its policies to pursue this strategy. It may also extend to control mechanisms for guiding the implementation of this strategy. The opposition should compare itself like a company that is surrounded by other powerful competitive companies; I would suggest here that the formulation of competitive strategy of the opposition includes consideration of the following key elements:

- Opposition strengths and weaknesses;

- Personal values of the key implementers (i.e. opposition decision makers);

- In opportunities and threats;

- Broader societal expectations;

- Work together and value each other's specialties;
- Know the reason why we exist;
- Understand the importance of removing a criminal Defend ourselves from everywhere we get attacked (cooperation of political parties) educating young generations who are scattered around the world) those who fall out with Kagame are they necessarily the saviours or the well-established system in the opposition;

- Positive response where necessary;

- Psychological sabotage;

- Competence leaders.

The weakness and strength and Personal values of the key implementers of the opposition relate to factors internal to the opposition (i.e., the internal environment), while in opportunities and threats and broader societal expectation relate to factors external to the opposition (i.e., the external environment).

Other elements will be considered throughout the strategic political planning process of the opposition:

Work together and value each other's specialities, the opposition has failed to work together, we want opposition of different background to work together, alongside people of other political parties to become agents of change for the Common Good in our country. Together for the Common Good is building a new, broad coalition between different political parties and fellow Rwandans of different communities to re-imagine political life and commitment to the flourishing of all people.

Know the reason why we exist: As Mandela said "Our daily deeds ... must produce an actual ... reality that will reinforce humanity's belief in justice, strengthen its confidence in the nobility of the human soul and sustain all our hopes for a glorious life for all."

We all strive to make our country the best place to live in not only for our generation but for the generation to come, it is the common understanding that we cannot live indifferently to the problems of our country or deal with them individually, because the enemy would want it that way, we should therefore put our togetherness at the heart of our political and economic decision making.

Understand the importance of removing a criminal: The practice of the common good as I mentioned above is the beginning to emerge as a transformative, alternative way to approach our polarized political and cultural life. It is at the heart of a profound political shift that has the potential to strengthen our cohesion and place human dignity at the heart of economic and political decision-making. The Rwandan people have suffered enough under the RPF regime and Kagame in particular; we need a united front to liberate our people from the talons of the vicious prey.

Defend ourselves from everywhere we get attacked: As I said above our young generation that did not see the sacrifice made by their peers are scattered around the global, the opposition has a duty to educate young regenerations and equip them with necessary skills and experience, rather than relying on the old guards as the legitimate saviors.

Positive response where necessary: Deuteronomy 19:21 Show no pity: life for life, eye for eye, tooth for tooth, hand for hand, foot for foot. Kagame's policy as it was described by Major Alphonse Furuma was to kill those he wanted to be killed in what he called political balance of power, he has continued to kill unabated, Rwandans should have the right and a duty to defend themselves by responding positively to the dictator and send him a strong message that enough is enough.

Psychological sabotage: Sabotage is a deliberate action aimed at weakening a polity or corporation through subversion, obstruction, disruption, or destruction. Kagame has killed so many innocent people from Rwanda and even in the neighboring Congo. We need to counter his vicious actions by psychologically weakening politically his interests both internally and externally. The opposition have to create a strong team of both foreign and domestic affairs to de-intoxicate the poison and lies that Kagame has been feeding the international community.

Finally, Competent leaders: The author John Gardner once said, "The society which scorns excellence in plumbing because plumbing is a humble activity and tolerates shoddiness in philosophy because it is an exalted activity will have neither good plumbing nor good philosophy. Neither its pipes nor its theories will hold water."

We all admire leaders who display high degree of competence, whether they are precision craftsmen, world-class athletes, or successful business leaders, political leaders. And most of us want to be seen as competent at our work. For leaders, competence is especially important. It can determine whether followers respect and follow you — or don't. Here are some specific ways to cultivate the quality of competence.

When you think about people who are competent, you're really considering only three types of people:

- Those who can see what needs to happen.

- Those who can make it happen.

- Those who can make things happen when it really counts.

Indeed, at this juncture in our political history Rwanda needs competent leaders, who see what needs to happen, who can make it happen and who can make things happen when it really counts.

In Rwanda, there is only one judge and that is Paul Kagame, the others are stuck in the middle cannot make right decisions, they only have to judge according to what they guess Kagame may like. That is why we have people in jail who may have qualified for bail but denied due to our Judges not being confident enough to challenge a one-man nation.

# 9 Chap IX: My tribute to comrades and my commander

## 9.1 A tribute to Sgt Blackman

He was reliable, responsible and always cared for others, but was harassed to the point he decided to commit suicide. For some reason, he always listened to everyone, younger or older soldiers. As a sergeant, he was in a position to lead young soldiers and work alongside those who were senior to him, men and women, junior and senior officers. He joined the army in the early eighties and as a professional driver he was given an opportunity to become a chauffeur to one of the most important high-ranking officials at the time, our hero, Major General Fred Rwigema. During those days, many Rwandese refugees in Uganda had joined the army and were still serving in the National Resistance Army (NRA), now the Uganda People's Defense Forces (UPDF), led by now President Yoweri Museveni who waged a five-year guerrilla war to the then government of President Apollo Milton Obote, that revolution war ending in 1986.

Major General Fred Rwigema kept him as his chauffeur. He chauffeured Afande Fred in different regions of the country, with high hopes and ambitions for the future. This driver believed that working alongside Maj Gen Fred Rwigema was a gift from God, just because he was in a position to offer his contribution for Rwanda in a way of being part of the transport for the top man. He believed that the time was right and it was a necessity to return the refugees back home to Rwanda in peace or force.

Unfortunately, after Maj Gen Fred Rwigema's death, Sgt Alex Blackman became very depressed, even though he was among the few soldiers transferred from Maj Gen Fred Rwigema's bodyguard group to the high command to be part of the then Major Kagame's guards who had just taken over. Sgt Blackman failed to accept the death of his boss, Maj Gen Fred Rwigema. The first time I met Sgt Blackman, he was very excited to meet me. It was like we knew each other in another life, we would speak to each other and actually as a young soldier he supported me through my role. After the capture of Kigali and installing the new government in 1994, Sgt Blackman was deployed to drive the then President Pasteur Bizimungu.

Sgt Blackman was released from Kagame's group because for some reason he never liked to work alongside Kagame. I had always asked the reason why he never liked to but he always declined to explain the reason. However, it was not only him a lot of young men would always wish to be deployed somewhere else. During that time, the job was a bit harder than it appears now (2013) because we were very few in numbers with a lot of responsibilities, as opposed to now when they are very many in numbers with a good wage. Sgt Blackman was later returned to work with me alongside other drivers for Kagame around 1999. On his arrival, this time he appeared happy and willing to participate in most activities.

All of the commanders in our unit, from senior officers to junior officers, had found Sgt Blackman in the army when they joined. This was a man who had served in the army for nearly twenty years but still a sergeant even though he had held many important responsibilities and missions. When Sgt Blackman came back to work with me, I had been made the head of transport and responsible for Kagame's transport as well as that of the soldiers responsible for Kagame's protection. That meant that I was the one to tell Sgt Blackman what to do, a tough task for me because I had always respected Sgt Blackman who was like a mentor to me.

He had told me stories and had tried to make me revisit the daily activities and life of his former boss and my hero, Maj Gen Fred Rwigema, through conversations. He had explained to me the care, kindness and love exhibited by Afande Fred Rwigema including how he (Afande Fred) had dedicated his life to others. Blackman had become my role model and now it was time for me to tell him what to do. I remember how Sgt Blackman used to buy me sweets when we first captured Kigali, I was eighteen years old and Sgt Blackman was in his late thirties but he still treated me like a young child. One day I asked him to join me in Obekka for lunch, this was a restaurant where we used to go and eat lunch but not all the time, this would be as a treat because we all hated the army food for some reason.

While we were eating I told him that I was very sorry to see that I am now in a position to lead him, when actually he should be among the more senior officers of army at top. I said to him that I was very disappointed to see that all the commanders who knew him had died and those who were serving are instead avoiding him and making young soldiers like me lead and instruct Sgt Blackman how to do the job that he had once actually taught us all. Sgt Blackman smiled and responded, first with a deep breath that was followed by him asking me if I knew the death of our former commanders? In my 'innocent' ignorance I said that of course they died fighting the enemy. Sgt Blackman smiled again and told me to do the job as I am told by my commanders and leave him alone. He told me that since afande Fred Rwigema died he never expected more than what was happening. He then told me to eat food and stop discussing what was going on with our job. Sgt Blackman told me that at some point I will realise that our army and expectations all died the day we lost those commanders, and he described our command structure as shambles. Sgt

Blackman narrated again the failures of our army and concluded by saying that all he wishes is to bring up his children in peace but then summarised by saying that it was a challenge as he was not even allowed enough time to spend with his young children.

At that moment, I thought the best way to help Sgt Blackman was create the opportunities of how he could spend as much time as possible with his children as his wish. So, I always asked him to drive the car escorting Kagame's children because after 17:00 hours he would be free to go home as Kagame's children would not require travelling during night hours. Whenever that happened they usually travelled with parents of which meant that Sgt Blackman would not be required anyway. Instead the principle motorcade would be enough for the whole family. Sgt Blackman was pleased with arrangement.

Unfortunately, after a couple days, I was called by, now, Lt Col Willy Rwagasana, who was Kagame's close body guard, who asked me why I was allowing Sgt Blackman to spend the night out of the Barracks. I told him that he was not required during night hours but instead day time when Kagame's children require a driver and guards. Willy told me that I was not capable of leading soldiers because, no one should spend the night out of barracks. I raised the issue of Sgt Blackman's family responsibilities but Willy was not taking any of my explanations on board and instead warned me that I was risking myself and that I was likely to end up in jail.

I explained all the above to Sgt Blackman who responded by telling me that all those commanders were silly young boys who did not know anything. He told me that he was going to his home to stay with his family and was not coming back to work, adding that he had served his time in the army and had requested to retire but none of them accepted his requests. He referred to an example of how all his promotions to the rank of 2 lieutenant had been blocked by the then Col James Kabarebe several times, because like many commanders had hated him due to the earlier close relationship he had with Maj Gen Fred Rwigema.

After a few days, I was called by Willy Rwagasana who ordered that we should go and bring Sgt Blackman to the cell. He instructed me to go with Lt Ruzibiza Kabasha, a short man with very poor judgement, together with a group of six soldiers. I can recall us heading to Sgt Blackman's house near Kanombe Military Hospital. Prior to our arrival, I told Lt Ruzibiza Kabasha that I thought Sgt Blackman was unwell physically and psychologically and needed enough rest and support together with treatment. Lt Ruzibiza Kabasha told me to "shut up". I explained to him that if we were to arrest him in front of his wife for just spending the night at his home it would look disrespectful and so because I was a good friend to Sgt Blackman I requested to be given time to speak to him in the hope that he may come out peacefully.

This was accepted and I made my way to the house and left the other soldiers together with Lt Ruzibiza Kabasha in the compound. I knocked on the door and Sgt Blackman's wife opened the door. After recognising me she alerted Sgt Blackman, who was lying in bed at the time. She ushered me in the bedroom. We shook hands and I asked him how he was feeling, something he did not respond to despite the fact that I was sat next to him on the bed. He was lying next to his three-year-old daughter. I told that the top men were all after him and accusing him of dissertation, suggesting to him that to avoid detention or imprisonment he needed to come with me so we can explain and convince the officers to allow him an official leave. Sgt Blackman responded with very limited words but very worrying saying, "Marara go and tell them that I am not coming and whoever thinks that can take me out of this house should come and get me. I know you and you know me ok. Go leave in peace I can never harm you and I know you cannot, so tell them to come and get me". At this moment, the wife cried and shouted by saying, "you do not even listen to your friend's ideas, you will end up in jail". Sgt Blackman told his wife to 'shut up' and asked me to leave. While I was heading out of the door, Sgt Blackman called me back and hugged me. We then shook hands to say good bye, but he told me not to come back to his house.

In me I could feel that something may happen and so I started thinking of restraining the situation, when I spoke to Lt Ruzibiza Kabasha he suggested that he wanted to speak to him first. I narrated on how Sgt Blackman said that he wanted someone else to fetch him not me. Lt Ruzibiza insisted that he was going to speak to Sgt Blackman. I walked with Lt Kabasha inside the house hoping that if something bad was about to happen, I may diffuse the situation, due to the degree of trust I had with Sgt Blackman. When Lt Kabasha called Sgt Blackman's name I had a loud bang and it was a bullet through the door which hit Lt Kabasha on the fore head. He fell on the floor and I realised that the small pieces of Lt Kabasha's cranium had flicked in my face. He was bleeding heavily and immediately I called the rest of the soldiers outside to help me transport the casualty to Hospital. After I called for help I heard other rapid bullets in the bedroom. Sgt Blackman had just pulled the trigger in his throat and he died in front of his house as was being transported to Hospital.

Lt Kabasha was admitted to Kanombe Military Hospital, where he was treated but never recovered fully, he leaves with a permanent brain damage. Today as I reflect on what happened, I realise that it has now been thirteen years since he departed from us because of neglect and bad leadership. He died a death caused by the same comrades who should have protected and supported him when he was desperately in need. May his soul and many of our fallen hero's rest in peace. This attribute always makes me reflect on the following:

## *Disappointment:*

Disappointment is a result of having expectations that are not met. Expectations may be too high, irrational or unrealistic. Because it is a common experience, disappointment can be handled effectively. However, continuous exposure to unmet expectations and lack of coping strategies may threaten the emotional and physical wellbeing of a person, resulting in symptoms and effects such as depression, anger, apathy, denial and fear.

## *Depression:*

Depression is a feeling of unhappiness and misery and is characterized by continuously having low moods. Some causes of depression include stress from work or relationships, but chronic depression can result from loss and disappointment. The disappointment that comes from the loss of a loved one or the discouragement of a failed business can lead to depression. Depression from disappointment is perpetuated by negativity and the fear of being disappointed again.

## *Apathy:*

Apathy is a condition in which someone becomes indifferent and passive to life. This is because he feels helpless about a disappointing situation and believes he cannot change it. Signs of apathy include lack of energy, continuing in a bad relationship, tolerating monotony, resigning to an illness and frustration with life. People who suffer constant disappointment seem not to care about making changes to improve their situation.

## *Denial:*

Denial is characterized by outwardly pretending that a disappointing situation does not exist. People who go through multiple disappointments would like to overlook the issue at hand with the hope that it will go away. Denial can also come in the form of giving up on goals, ambitions and passions because the person does not believe any of these are worth pursuing. A person who has been disappointed in a relationship may deny his desire to find his true love, and thus block everyone else out.

## *Anger:*

Anger is a reaction to a situation or a person who has not met your expectations. It is essentially an emotional or behavioural backlash to disappointment. Anger can be an instant outburst or a latent feeling that is experienced every day. It can range from having feelings of rage and resentment toward a person and could result to outright violence. Anger also leads to feelings of negativity, depression and helplessness toward situations.

## *Fear:*

Fear is a reaction that a person has toward a real or imagined situation. Fear results from undergoing unpleasant or disappointing experiences. As a result, a person who has been disappointed is fearful of engaging in similar experiences as a way to protect himself from re-living the past experience. Although fear is a natural reaction, prolonged fear can be numbing and can threaten a person's psychological and emotional wellbeing.

## 9.2 A tribute to Afande Col. Karegeya a principled man

Col. Patrick Karegeya was killed by Unsung Heroes? This word unsung heroes were implemented by Gen Jack Nziza when convincing his killers to continue hunting innocent people.

Years have gone by when Col. Karegeya Patrick considered by even the RPF sympathizers as a principled man that you could not buy even with Gold has been strangled in one of the Posh Hotels in South Africa. The question of who killed the Rwanda former Spy Chief legally remains a mystery, but all the clues even with smallest mathematical measurement or dog police smell leads all the way to Rwanda. Why then has investigations taken a year now without arrest and prosecution of the murders of one of the Rwandan, intellectual, a lawyer, a soldier and a freedom fighter who started his career in the former NRA of President Yoweri Museveni of Uganda?

Behind the Presidential curtains have obtained reliable information that some of the evidence has been either disabled or deleted from their sources. For example, CCTV Cameras in the corridors of the hotel which would have given the prosecution the facts of what happened on that critical day have been deleted.

We know that Karegeya booked the Hotel for the person he called his friend, but the names of that person who booked the hotel cannot be forwarded to the prosecution and the prosecution has not taken the task to interrogate and force the Hotel officials to give them information of all the hotel clients who booked and were there during that fateful day.

Again, we have established that prior to the death of Col. Patrick Karegeya, the notorious Kagame hang man Kanyandekwe and his colleagues in crime were in South Africa in constant contacts with Judah Iscariot known as *Apollo Kiririsi* the one that was paid the Pieces of Gold to finish off his friend.

## *Apollo Kiririsi*

Apollo Kiririsi around 15th May 2013 disappeared from the radar of normal business, this is at the time of the disappearance of Ntabana who was not only a relative of Col. Patrick Karegeya but also a friend who recruited Apollo Kiririsi in the external spy network of Kigali when Col.Patrick was still heading that institution.

Our investigations have established with virtual certainty that Apollo Kiririsi did not only know of the kidnapping and subsequent murder of his friend Ntabana but planned it with accuracy and precision. When Col. Patrick Karegeya asked him why he has not been seen for so long, he responded that he was being harassed by the Kigali regime and the disappearance of his friend Ntabana was a shock and scared him, that's why he was in hiding.

## *Aimé Ntabana*

Little did the Col. Patrick Karegeya know that Apollo Kiririsi was not only guilty of the killing of Ntabana but was also under further intoxication by the RPF killing agents?

Indeed, to claim his innocence and proof to Col. Patrick Karegeya that he was still a good student and loyal to him, whenever he was welcomed to the Col's house, he could leave a cheque of US $5000 dollars and could tell Patrick that this was his contribution for the services and friendship accorded to him by Col. Patrick Karegeya.

Unknown to the Col. the money Apollo Kiririsi was splashing out was not from his own pocket, it was from the coffers of the State under the direct command of President Kagame and the supervision of Gen. James Kabarebe respectively.

After the murder of Col. Patrick Karegeya, Apollo Kiririsi flew to Dubai where he met his accomplice and commanders in the murder of Col. Patrick Karegeya, we have established with precision that the passport he used to fly from South Africa was not the same passport he used to fly from Dubai to Rwanda.

Amazingly, as I mentioned earlier of his disappearances, we have established that it is the same period the daughter of SAM NKUSI was in Kigali. This man is famously known for his arrogance and dogmatic attitude in the spheres of Rwanda influence.

It's believed that this young woman who is also a wife of David Batenga, incidentally David Batenga is also a Nephew to Col. Patrick Karegeya was in Kigali when Apollo Kiririsi was training on how to execute this plan of finishing off Col. Patrick Karegeya, RPF calls it patriotism (Gukunda igihugu).

We all know that Sam Nkusi had fallen off from the grace of the Kagame's inner circles, therefore like any other person who would like to regain that glory of shaking hands with the Head of State and get lucrative contracts and of course the security of his finances he had no choice but use his daughter in this vicious attack.

Sam Nkusi is now back in the kraal and he is the boss of the Rwanda Telecom and the information we have he is back on the milk bottle of the Kagame family. Unfortunately, the blood of innocent person will always haunt those who are responsible, sooner than later all those who participated in the killing of Col. Patrick will pay the same price in the same currency.

The history of the Habyarimana family and Kabuga who were in–laws and made huge sums of money during their eras is still fresh in all the minds of sober mind people, why a man like Nkusi who is not only an intellectual in his own right but a well-established business man has a shallow mind on the Rwandan history in just 20years?

Indeed, David Batenga who is Sam Nkusi's in-law happens to be also a Nephew of Col. Patrick Karegeya who was supposed to join his uncle but on the last minute he did not, and since then he has shown little or no interest in the follow up of his uncle's murders. Information sources that reached us acknowledged that he lives now a luxury life with posh cars like Range Rovers and posh a house despite that fact that he has no known employment or business.

We have called upon in numerous time, all the parties concerned to speed up the investigations in the murder of the Rwandan hero Col. Patrick Karegeya, we urged the family and friends of Col. Patrick Karegeya to join hands and seek justice as soon as possible for Col Patrick Karegeya, we know the suspects of this heinous crime, what remains is the will and courage of the South African legal system to stand up for this challenge of intolerance to impunity.

## 9.3 To my Dear commander, Tom Byabagamba.

We are really sorry to see you on handcuffs afande, especially for no reason, but just because you are related to so and so.

Col Tom Byabagamba a soldier who never betrayed his nation or his excellence but also ended up in jail on fabricated cases. Remember Afande you always lead by example. You usually used these words whenever you were debriefing or briefing us. "A true leader is still a leader even when he takes up servants' duty, provided he maintains a human face and added integrity to his self-retained qualities." "A true leader is a person whose influence inspires people to do what is expected of them to do. You cease to be a leader when you manipulate with your egos instead of convincing by your inspirations."

I see you have returned, my love; and your mood is as dark as ever, like during the time of the struggle. Did your soldiers not adore you to your complete satisfaction? I bet they all did despite the dark mood. This dark time in your history and therefore dark mood won't be the exception.

"Self-leaders are still true leaders even if they have no known followers. True leaders inspire by the influence of their characters and general self-made brands. Leadership is defined by the virtues of one's behaviour."

"Contrary to popular opinion, leadership is not a reserved position for a particular group of people who were elected or appointed, ordained or enthroned. Leadership is self-made, self-retained, self-inculcated and then exposed through a faithful, sincere and exemplary life." This week will forever remain in history as when I saw you on handcuffs. I remember the discipline you gave us, you taught us to always work for our nation and make sure that we fulfill our responsibilities.

As a young boy, before I even joined the army, you had arrived at Afande Bitamazire's entourage and you changed the whole structure of his security. As you mentioned he was so social to an extent that his security was at risk. You immediately ordered that his behaviour was not suitable for a purpose and obviously being a good commander, he agreed that it was inconvenience for him to sit on a table with over 30 body guards and eat. You divided his security into groups in order to maintain a good secure environment, plus the hygiene in the home which was uncontrolled.

He immediately made you one of his close body guards, Afande. After Afande Bitamazire's death you ended up as Afande PC (Kagame)'s body guard. You were whisked to the rank of J02 as a result of your performance, even though you were criticised in the end for aggressive behaviour and sometimes rough punishments. But between me and you we know very well the reasons behind all that.

I remember the times when you advised me that a President is not just a person. He/she is a personality for a nation and we have to maintain their security because he/her is the only symbol of a nation that we could not accept to be hurt. I kept that in my mind and afande that is why I had an accident in Murindi as you remember, and of course it was rewarding because he was left unhurt.

I remember when you said that time has come to stop trusting each other, auditing reporting and evidencing had to come in place, you meant that and we did sir. Afande I know that you have done nothing wrong. You managed to keep your name clean. You have never been corrupting and never was a bad leader. You can never betray your country as many have done. It's just divisions created by those who are under intensive threat of divisions created by personal interests.

I remember our irreplaceable squad that probably remains in the same state of confusion that I am today due to your unnecessary arrest. I call upon all of you who have the knowledge of our commander and comrade Col Tom Byabagamba to denounce all the fabricated charges he is being put into together with our commander and only remaining knowledgeable officer Gen Frank Rusagara.:

As stated by one of your fellow Comrades a senior officer as you two days ago: Those of you who remember our folklore stories could remember about a Good Samaritan and the Hyena's story. This is exactly what is unfolding to the RPF/RPA historical. Kagame turned our cause into his personal business; what had been aimed at struggling for freedom and unity of Rwandan people turned into Kagame and family business.

It's unimaginable to see what Kagame has become to this point. Late us see briefly who is Tom Byabagamba;1. Tom of our Original RPA (before Kagame came in); Col Tom has done almost all his military carrier under Kagame's protection;

Tom served as Late Capt. Bitamazire's Aide de Camp (ADC) in the Akagera region skirmishes where his boss and many other comrades lost their lives in a deadly FAR ambush. Tom survived narrowly and he disappeared in the national park which was now under the control of FAR for several weeks till he reconnected with our remnant. (Tom under Kagame's reign): When Kagame came around early Dec, 1990. Tom took up the closest position of protecting Kagame's life from Dec, 1990 probably 2010/2011. Does Tom who has committed his two decades of protecting Kagame's life really deserve those handcuffs and stinky

Kanombe cells?

Below are some of the comrades who may be experiencing sleepless nights due to unlawful arrest to our beloved Commander:

| | | | |
|---|---|---|---|
| MUNGARURIYE CALLIXTE | NKUBITO JOSEPH | GATARAYIHA | KAZENGA FRANCIS |
| JULIUS RWANDANGA | UHORANINGOGA EUGENE | KARERANGABO | ALOYS RUYENZI |
| RUGANZUROSE | ALOYS NEMEYI | WELLARS | PATRICK |
| REMY | KALIMBA | GATSINZI HERBERT | KIRENGA |
| KABAYIJA | RUTIKANGA | MUGISHA | RUZIBIZA |
| RUTAISIRE | RUTONESHA CLIOPA | DIDIER | MUNANA |
| CHARLES ALINGO | MUSHAIDI | SHEMA | CHARLES MUHIKIRA |
| GISHAIJA JOSEPH | FRED RUGUMYAMIHETO | RUGANZU | MATSIKO ROBERT (RIP) |
| MURANGIRA | MWESIGYE | BUGINGO | RUTAGENG |

|  | DANIEL | DAVIS | WA |
|---|---|---|---|
| RUBAGUMYA | KAGAME ALEX | KATO ALEX | KAMAZI |
| MURAIRE | KABENGERA | MUSONI EVARISTE | SAFARI CLAUDE |
| NKURAIJA | CYUBAHIRO BIENVENUE | NKWAYA | BOSCO |
| INNOCENT | BYUMA | WILLY RWAGASAN | HAPPY RUVUSHA |
| RUZINDAZA | MATUNGO CHARLES | GASANA KIBANDA | GASANA RTD |
| GASASIRA | BUGINGO | YAHYA | NDAHIRO |
| JIHANA RONALD | MUGABO JAMES | NDEGEYA | KARAMA |
| TUMUSIME | RUBAMBA DAVID | MUGUNGA WILLIAM | MULINDAH ABI |
| TOBULENDA SEMPA | KARABAYINGA SENTONGO | | |

The list is endless but Just a few of the soldiers you commanded and gave a good discipline, stay strong and your freedom is ours, justice will prevail, today may not be in Rwanda but our society sees what is going on.

## 9.4  Young Muhirwa saga

Muhirwa was young tall innocent and vulnerable born in Rwanda and always wished that one day all people will live in peace, on the other side I was growing up in another country but we both shared the same goal of seeing all Rwandans live in peace and harmony. He grew up in the eastern side of Rwanda while I was growing up in the southern part of Uganda, my parents had left Rwanda in 1959 but his parents stayed in Rwanda hoping that the newly Hutu government was going to do as promised 'democracy, Peace and Development' contrarily to what the government turned up with of killings forcing people into exile.

Surprisingly this young man Muhirwa decided to join the Rwandese patriotic army with high hopes that the newly movement would help him reach his goals of seeing all people live together in peace and possibly harmony. On the training wing, he was discriminated by the majority of young soldiers who believed that all people born in Rwanda were all extremist Hutu's who supported the ruling government of President Juvenal Habyarimana.

He continuously preached peace to everyone but not all listened, Muhirwa was luckily deployed to become a body guard to my cousin Captain Eddy Rwigema, my cousin was a full combat soldier who shadowed Major Murangira and they both worked closely in order to shell the enemy out of all areas of Rwanda. My cousin captain Eddy Rwigema as well Major Murangira both got killed after the war for the reasons that I am not going to discuss today.

After the death of captain Eddy Rwigema the young Muhirwa was not satisfied, he tried to protect his commander when they got attacked, with his MMG rifle he fought the attackers attempting covering fire to create the escape route for his commander but unfortunately Captain Eddy Rwigema realised that Major Birasa of whom they were travelling together in the car was already dead. Captain Eddy Rwigema had already been shot in the leg, he could not see that his body guard was shooting the attackers to create an escape route for him, he run out of the car and landed under the terrace, while under the terrace he witnessed Major Birasa being burnt in the car that they were travelling in.

In the end, the attackers walked towards the terrace where Captain Eddy was laying, Muhirwa was still aiming to protect his commander but unfortunately Captain Eddy Rwigema decided to shoot himself using a hand gun, Muhirwa said that 'Captain Eddy believed that the enemy was about to take him hostage'. Muhirwa went on to say that he recognized two attackers, he went further to explain that the attackers were from the high command, the soldiers that were responsible to protecting Paul Kagame who was our Commander- in- Chief, this is a unit that I was part of but unaware of the mission of course which eliminated my beloved cousin, Muhirwa explained that the soldiers he had recognised among them was Mugabo who was a W01 and later became a full Lieutenant after that successful mission of killing his colleagues.

Muhirwa approached me and explained how my cousin and Major Birasa had been killed by our own colleagues, I said to him that there was no evidence but he went on to say that he had witnessed the killers and will not leave any stone unturned until the killers have faced justice. As a person who was at the time working in Kagame's entourage, I said to Muhirwa that there was no body to report this matter to and that if the two commanders got killed by our own army then the top commanders knew this and if he doesn't stop talking he will be the next target. He walked away from me, I called him but he said that there was no need talking to me any further, after a couple of hours the widow of my Cousin Captain Eddy Rwigema contacted me, she accused me of knowing the death of my Cousin and never told her. She stated that Muhirwa had been to her house and had explained to her all that occurred and also that I had threatened Muhirwa not to say things with no evidences. The widow said that she was going to report all of us to the head of the army, hours later I was contacted by the chief body guard of the head of the army at the time, who said that I had to show them where Muhirwa was staying, I asked him the reasons behind wanting to see Muhirwa and said that they only wanted to ask him a few questions about what he had reported to the widow of Captain Eddy Rwigema.

He went on to say that Muhirwa required some psychological input, I agreed and they came to see me at Kagame's residence where I was staying, I drove in front of them to the address where Muhirwa was staying, the body guards of the then head of the army said that they were to speak to him but later to return Muhirwa with them, he was never seen again.

The questions remain:

- Who killed Major Birasa and Captain Eddy Rwigema?

- Why was Muhirwa taken to answer few questions and never returned?

- Why were Major Birasa and Captain Eddy Rwigema Killed?

- Why is it that the soldiers participated in this killing were from the high command but the concealing evidences from the head of the army?

- Did Muhirwa who protected my cousin to the last-minute die thinking that I betrayed him?

- Why did the widow decide to contact every high-ranking official in the army spilling the beans?

- Muhirwa's family, do they know exactly what happened to him?

- Did Captain Eddy and Major Birasa know exactly what happened to them and their body guards?

- What did the killers benefit from killing innocent commanders and their body guards?

- The people responsible of executing the two commanders and their body guards, none of them is safe as I write this, either wanted or in exile and others have also been killed by those who used to send them to kill. What do people benefit from shedding blood?

In ending this book, I would like to pay tribute to all the Commanders, Comrades, civilians who have perished, jailed or are in exile as result of Kagame's thirsty of power. We will always remember you forever. Aluta Continua.

# INDEX

Adam Waswa, v, 11, 40, 46, 73, 75, 76

AU, 236, 243, 244, 245, 246

Badege, 140

Bagire, 11

Bayingana, 11, 13, 16, 17, 22, 47, 50, 124

Bunyenyezi, 11, 13, 16, 17, 22

Byaruhanga,, 11, 58, 60

Crystal Ventures, 113, 114, 175, 258, 259, 260, 261, 262

Dodo, 11, 56

Gahima, 83, 277

Genocide, 36, 38, 91, 95, 121, 180, 186, 187, 189, 195, 215, 221, 268

Habyarimana, 16, 21, 22, 23, 26, 48, 51, 57, 62, 100, 109, 110, 112, 116, 139, 179, 209, 266, 268, 269, 285, 304, 311

Hutus, v, 24, 26, 48, 62, 87, 88, 92, 93, 95, 183, 184, 209, 265

Inyumba, v, 132, 133, 134

Jeanette Kagame, 168, 169, 170

Jeannette Nyiramongi. *See* Jeanette Kagame

Kabarebe, 14, 15, 41, 50, 67, 90, 104, 105, 133, 135, 192, 193, 195, 296, 303

Kabura, 11, 74

Karegeya, v, 83, 102, 120, 123, 133, 134, 215, 282, 283, 284, 285, 286, 301, 302, 303, 304, 305

Karemera, 49, 75, 76, 108, 113

Kayibanda, 18, 112, 116, 139, 184

Kayitare, 11, 12, 60, 68, 125

King Mutara Rudahigwa. *See* Rudahigwa

Kizito Mihigo, 169, 171, 172, 173

Kizza, 11, 58, 159

M23, v, 201, 202, 203, 204, 205, 207, 209, 232, 235, 236, 238, 239, 240, 255, 257

Mbonyumutwa, 112, 188

Mihigo. *See* Kizito Mihigo

Mitchell, 248, 249, 250, 251, 253, 254

Muhirwa, v, 310, 311, 312, 313, 314

Mupenzi, 16, 73, 101

Museveni, v, 2, 7, 14, 16, 56, 74, 75, 85, 91, 99, 120, 125, 137, 138, 145, 158, 159, 160, 161, 162, 165, 212, 215, 219, 220, 221, 222, 223, 224, 225, 226, 227, 284, 292, 301

Ndadaye, 72, 101

Ndahindurwa, 85, 112, 177, 178, 180, 182, 188

Ndasingwa, 100

Ndugute, 11, 40, 41, 43, 45, 48, 49, 60, 75, 125

Ngoga, 11, 77, 211

Nkurunziza, v, 208, 210, 211, 212, 213, 214, 215, 219, 229, 232, 236, 242, 243, 244, 245, 246, 247

Nyamwasa, 102, 110, 114, 120, 123, 126, 131, 140, 223, 224, 273, 277, 278, 279, 280, 282

Nzabamwita, 73, 74, 126

Nziza, 35, 46, 48, 49, 52, 55, 67, 83, 93, 94, 133, 170, 198, 200, 301

RNC, v, vi, 39, 40, 86, 171, 264, 268, 269, 270, 271, 272, 273, 274, 276, 277, 278, 279, 280, 281, 282, 283

Rudahigwa, 188

Rudasingwa, v, 83, 110, 123, 269, 270, 272, 273, 274, 275, 276, 277, 278, 279, 280, 282

Rusagara, 117, 125, 126, 127, 128, 307

Ruzibiza, 119, 124, 296, 297, 298

Rwagasana, 3, 27, 154, 155, 296

Rwigema, 2, 6, 7, 8, 9, 10, 11, 12, 16, 17, 18, 22, 60, 74, 125, 136, 137, 138, 145, 165, 180, 220, 221, 274, 292, 293, 294, 295, 296, 311, 312, 313

Rwigyema. *See* Rwigema

Salim Saleh, 7, 13, 16, 75, 137, 145, 158, 227

Sam Kaka, 11, 13, 53, 125, 128

Tutsis, 22, 24, 25, 88, 95, 171, 172, 183, 184, 209, 210

Twahirwa, 11, 56, 68

Victoire Ingabire, 102

# ABOUT THE AUTHOR

I was born in Uganda a place called Mityana in 1975, my father told me that I was born in March but then my mother later told me that I was born around Christmas time meaning December 1975. Like many I have no idea what date exactly or month I was born hopefully the year is as they both said to me.

I was child number five among them three girls and my brother Franco Jihana who died in 1987 had also been serving in the Ugandan army National Resistance Army.

My father had passed away when I was 7 years old in 1982 but fortunately my mother and our grandparents put everything they had into us. Luckily we had a very equipped community and supportive that was also related as extendedly, this waved the path for our education morally culturally.

Attended Lwebitakuli Primary School and later moved to Isenda Primary in Iganga Eastern Uganda.

After words I had to join Pioneer Mechanical institute in 1990 this was due to lack of funding for me to join secondary school, received a diploma in motor mechanical engineering, this was one of the reasons why when I arrived in Rwanda I was whisked to the Kagame's because of the Knowledge I had around Vehicles or repairing.

In late 1991-early1992 I joined the Rwanda Patriotic Army where I served untill 2000, while in the army I was among the trusted ones and had access around Kagame's residence than most people due to my hard working style which led to becoming the head of transport, attended numerous courses in the military such as commando, Very Important People protection intelligence trained by the Germans, demining trained by Americans, logistic management trained by the Indians etc.

2001 August I arrived in France where I stayed for a couple of months before heading to Britain where I settled until now.

2003 Joined Riverside College studied Safety Management

2005 Joined Teeside University to study Forensic Science but I was unable to complete the course due to funding and so I had to switch the course to a government funded course and that is how i ended up in Canterbury Christ Church University. 2009 -2012 Graduated in Canterbury Christ Church as a Generic Psychiatrist Practitioner

2015-2016 Joined Greenwich University for professional Development and Mentorship where I gained more Knowledge of Educating young professionals

I am blessed with two Children girl and a boy both the Marara's who are now teenagers played a large role in supporting me to carry out this work of writing the experience of our nation.

Both children born in England but love their nation and hope that one day they will land in Kigali and see the 1000 hills.

Made in the USA
Middletown, DE
23 March 2018